Gary Larson
and
The Far Side

Great Comics Artists Series

M. Thomas Inge, General Editor

Gary Larson
and
The Far Side

Kerry D. Soper

University Press of Mississippi / Jackson

www.upress.state.ms.us

The University Press of Mississippi is a member of the Association
of University Presses.

First printing 2018
∞

Library of Congress Cataloging-in-Publication Data

Names: Soper, Kerry. author.
Title: Gary Larson and the Far Side / Kerry D. Soper.
Description: Jackson: University Press of Mississippi, [2018] | Series:
Great comics artists series | Includes bibliographical references and
index. |
Identifiers: LCCN 2018006258 (print) | LCCN 2018015984 (ebook) | ISBN
9781496817297 (epub single) | ISBN 9781496817303 (epub institutional) |
ISBN 9781496817310 (pdf single) | ISBN 9781496817327 (pdf institutional)
| ISBN 9781496817280 (cloth: alk. paper) | ISBN 9781496817631 (pbk.:
alk. paper)
Subjects: LCSH: Larson, Gary—Criticism and interpretation. | Larson, Gary.
Far side. | Comic books, strips, etc. | Cartoonists—United States.
Classification: LCC NC1429.L32 (ebook) | LCC NC1429.L32 S67 2018 (print) |
DDC 741.5/6973—dc23
LC record available at https://lccn.loc.gov/2018006258

British Library Cataloging-in-Publication Data available

For Lisa

Contents

Acknowledgments

The completion of this book would not have been possible without the help and support of a number of people and institutions. First of all, I received generous support from the Department of Comparative Arts and Letters and the College of Humanities at BYU. I am also especially grateful to Matt Wickman and the Humanities Center here at my university for a fellowship that provided the time and resources to get this project started. In the writing of this book I benefited from the thoughtful feedback and encouragement of colleagues in the field of comics studies: Jared Gardner, John Lent, Tom Inge, Qianna Whitted, Susan Kirtley, Brian Cremins, Nicole Freim, Terrence Wandtke, Ian Gordon, Charles Hatfield, Jeet Heer, Thomas Andrae, David Kunzle, and many others. I was also fortunate to have a stellar research assistant—Anne Hart; she was a smart and proactive collaborator. Other people who gave me helpful feedback on various drafts included Robert Colson, Matt Ancell, Carl Sederholm, Allen Christenson, Stan Benfell, Haley Ward, Jordan Ward, Stan Soper, Greg Soper, Devin Soper, Taylor Soper, and Emma Soper. Lisa, my incredible spouse, was generous and supportive throughout the whole project. Thanks also go to Raegan Carmona (at Universal Press Syndicate) and Garry Trudeau for their ongoing willingness to let me reprint *Doonesbury* cartoons in a variety of venues; in addition, Pete Kelly has been especially kind in helping me to feature Walt Kelly's work in this book and other publications. I also appreciate the support and guidance of all of the editors at Mississippi; Vijay Shah was especially great in shepherding this book from early brainstorming phases to its completion. Finally, I am grateful to Gary Larson for creating over 4,300 timelessly funny and provocative cartoons.   •

Gary Larson
and
The Far Side

Introduction

As a slightly awkward preteen in the early 1980s—who probably resembled one of the iconic nerds in Gary Larson's work more than I would have wanted to admit—I was crazy about irreverent comedy. On any given day you would have found me doing something related to the consumption or performance of vaguely inappropriate humor: trying to memorize zany bits from Steve Martin's latest comedy album; acting out with friends one of Bill Murray's brilliantly stupid skits on *Saturday Night Live*; copying into a notebook one of Don Martin's wacky, farting figures from *MAD* magazine; or reciting, verbatim, a bit of cheeky dialogue from *Monty Python and the Holy Grail*. So I knew I had something especially potent—a comedic landmine of sorts—when I purchased my first *Far Side* book collection in the fall of 1982.

That subversive power was immediately evident as I opened its pages and shared selected cartoons (like the one featuring a matronly, romance-focused woman wearing a chainsaw [fig. 0.1]) with relatives at a large family gathering. I was struck by how Larson's comedy elicited such wildly different reactions: surprised and explosive laughter from some, reluctant smiles and disbelieving headshakes from others, blank stares of confusion from a good number, and expressions of genuine alarm and disgust from one or two. I wasn't focused on the demographic breakdown of those varying reactions at the time, of course, but looking back, it was clear that people were divided along some generational and cultural lines: older people did not seem to enjoy it as much, the especially earnest personalities in the group tended not to get it, and the most pious in the crowd thought it was offensive. As the evening wore on, a large group of siblings, cousins, and a few of the more irreverent-minded adults gradually gathered around me, all looking at the compact book together, eagerly anticipating the next cartoon. The laughter that followed the reading of each panel was loud, consistent, and contagious; in fact, there was a giddy undercurrent to the collective experience—the excitement that comes from finding (and sharing) something that is consistently funny and genuinely original.

In the following years I developed a preference for Larson's weird comedy above that of all other cartoonists: I clipped favorite panels out of the newspaper, avidly collected all of his books, purchased *Far Side* merchandise (posters, T-shirts—and, later, calendars), and mimicked his minimalistic style in sketchbooks—populating them with evil ducks, nerdy kids, and large women with outsized hairdos and cat-eye glasses. I was also eager to identify myself as a fan, finding that this affiliation won me a bit of cultural capital among peers who were also aficionados of irreverent comedy—or with hip older people who seemed to be connoisseurs of all things alternative in the early 1980s. Like a cartoon world equivalent of a Trekkie (a "Side-ie"?), I was so avid for all things *Far Side* that my worldview was shaped (and perhaps deeply warped) by Larson's absurdist take on life. I remember starting to notice, for example, that some people actually looked like characters from a *Far Side* panel (the pear-shaped body, rolled shoulders, and buffalo hump at the top of the spine); and weird social practices that I had previously taken for granted (like our tendency to eat some animals, while treating others like adopted members of the family) began to seem bizarre. The deeper philosophical dimensions of Larson's work, in other words, were actively informing my budding sense of humor—and perhaps even my critical thinking habits.

The Far Side may have been relatively unique among newspaper comics, in fact, in its potential to provoke this level of engagement, identification, and creative thinking among its most avid readers. Unlike typical cartoon panels that featured clichéd gags or predictable platitudes, Larson's work was consistently surprising and challenging, containing dense wordplay, ambiguous vignettes that required imaginative closure, self-deconstructive gags, and layered parodies. In fact, the regular unpacking of that kind of dense comedy might have trained the most invested readers to see the hidden assumptions, formulaic conventions, or unintentional ironies in other cultural texts. Moreover, in light of Larson's preoccupation with evolution, deep time, and science in general, *The Far Side* encouraged its most serious fans to see the world through a set of bracingly skeptical lenses: an irreverent questioning of conventional wisdom or religious pieties, a testing of comforting myths against the hard truths of scientific naturalism, and a rationalistic deflation of all things cutely idealized or pretentious in mainstream culture.

"Excuse me, Harold, while I go slip into something
more comfortable."

Fig. 0.1. Gary Larson, "Excuse me, Harold ..." *The Far Side*, Dec. 15, 1981.
(The dates here refer to the dates the comics were originally published;
in *The Complete Far Side* it appears in Vol. 1, p. 173—subsequent references
will cite only volume and page number, like this: 1-173.)

I recognize, of course, that smart younger people who have recently
discovered *The Far Side*—but who did not live through Larson's strange arrival on the newspaper comics page—might find it difficult to see, at least
initially, the subversive or profound qualities of Larson's work. That reaction makes sense when you consider that Larson's cartoons thrived on the
comics page for close to fifteen years and were merchandised aggressively
through calendars, posters, and T-shirts; as a result, *The Far Side* comes
across to today's observers as vaguely conventional or mainstream—albeit
with slightly less polished aesthetics and a wackier tone than your typical

Analyzing humor

Fig. 0.2. Gary Larson, "Analyzing humor," *The Far Side*, March 15, 1984 (1-374).

syndicated material. Moreover, it might be hard for contemporary readers to see philosophical depth in *The Far Side* after only a brief exposure to a handful of representative cartoons. The passage of time, in other words, caused the alternative qualities of individual *Far Side* panels to blur into the similarly rowdy look or feel of other comic texts that have populated our cultural landscape in the last three decades. A new reader might wonder, in fact, what is so weird about Larson's art and comedy when compared to the current offerings on Cartoon Network's *Adult Swim*, or to any of the unhinged webcomics that currently populate the Internet.

A study that answers that question—reminding readers of *The Far Side*'s groundbreaking irreverence, absurdism, philosophical depth, and cultural significance—is overdue. I begin that task by first describing in

Late at night, and without permission, Reuben would often enter the nursery and conduct experiments in static electricity.

Fig. 0.3. Gary Larson, "Late at Night," *The Far Side*, July 31, 1982 (1-230).

this introduction the cultural climate and media landscape in which *The Far Side* first appeared and thrived. Reestablishing that historical context helps to explain why Larson's comedy elicited such intense and varied reactions from early readers: some loathing it, to the point of sending indignant letters to editors, the syndicate, and Larson himself, and others adoring it, feeling compelled to clip out, post, reread, collect, and share their favorite installments. As the book continues, I explore other understudied or underappreciated aspects of Larson's work: the story of his unlikely success on the ridiculously competitive (and highly filtered) mainstream comics page, the variety of comedic tools that he used in the construction of his original gags, the genius of his awkward and minimalistic art, the behind-the-scenes business decisions and negotiations that created and sustained the quality of his peculiar work, and the larger social and philosophical meanings communicated through the whole of 4,300-plus cartoons.

I should note at the outset that Gary Larson might be uncomfortable with this kind of ambitious treatment of his work. As longtime fans are aware, he is an intensely private and self-effacing person, eschewing media attention and generally downplaying *The Far Side*'s cultural importance. In fact, he has largely avoided giving interviews throughout his career because of an almost pathological shyness and acute distress at the thought of having to appear "ebulliently witty and weird in that inimitable *Far Side*-ish sort of way" (Gumbel). In his panels he also poked fun occasionally at the idea of stereotypical academics studying cartoons and comedy. Two particular installments that caught my eye (and made me pause and think carefully about what I am doing in this book) include a self-important professor giving a dry lecture on the mechanisms of spontaneous, slapstick comedy while sporting a "kick me" sign on his butt (fig. 0.2), and a diagram that shows mathematical computations that every cartoonist should know and use in creating reliably funny jokes (8/7/92; 2–242).

There are elements of truth, of course, in these gags. Academics can sometimes be a bit pretentious and boring when discussing comedy, and freshly irreverent jokes can wilt like a fragile butterfly under the pressure of too much labored analysis. I know from personal experience, for example, that you can relish only once your mother's involuntary scream of laughter (and then disapproving shake of the head) upon first reading the *Far Side* panel about a janitor conducting clandestine static electricity experiments in a hospital nursery (fig 0.3). Acknowledging the fleeting qualities of freshly surprising jokes, nevertheless, should not necessarily deter fans from analyzing Larson's panels more closely. Additional layers of humor and intellectual pleasure can be enjoyed, for example, in revisiting this same joke about the janitor, perhaps years later, and thinking about the textual, social, and psychological reasons for why this weird cartoon elicited such a conflicted response from my parent (and mischievous delight from me).

As you will see, Larson only reluctantly helps his readers in this effort to unpack additional facets of humor and philosophy in his work; beyond declining to discuss the deeper significance of his cartoons, he sometimes found his own creative process to be mystifying and would say he was not sure where his ideas came from—wondering, perhaps, if they were simply burblings from his unconscious mind (Astor, "Larson Explores" 32). Thankfully, though, he was also willing to talk in detail about his craft in a number of personal essays that are included in his book anthologies. In those reflections we see a "rigorous and ruthless editor of his own work," a deep and sensitive thinker with satiric intentions, and a perfectionistic comedian and artist who honed and distilled his random epiphanies until they were genuinely funny to other like-minded people (Morrissey, "Introduction" ix). And thus despite Larson's general modesty and reticence, there is a rich complexity waiting to be explored in both his deceptively simple-seeming work and his reflections about the craft of making funny and profound cartoons. After seeing that complexity, readers might agree with me that Larson's cartoons are so robustly cerebral, deeply absurd, and timelessly funny that they can survive a careful deconstruction. They are less like delicate butterflies and more like sturdily constructed birds of prey: not only can they hold up well to vigorous inspection, but they might even give an additional, vicious comedic bite as we venture in for a closer look.

Eager to avoid having any "kick me" signs adhered to my backside, I do my best in the following pages to make this an enjoyable and intellectually stimulating reading experience. Specific moves to achieve that goal include putting specific examples of *The Far Side* at the center of every discussion, and pursuing a writing style that is neither too serious on the one hand, nor too self-consciously clever on the other. (It seems foolish for an academic to try to match in his diction the irreverence and absurdism of Larson's cartoons). In sum, this book is meant to be a respectful, readable supplement to *The Far Side*—a resource for anyone interested in the cultural significance of Larson's work, and the deeper reasons that his cartoons were so comedically and aesthetically effective. And while the following pages show or describe a healthy number of Larson's best panels, there is no better way to enjoy *The Far Side* than to simply go to the source: fifteen years' worth of daily cartoons published in Larson's excellent anthologies. (As a way of helping you find these cartoons in their purest form, I include parenthetical information about each *Far Side* panel I cite or describe, pointing to its original date of publication and the page number where it can be found in Larson's two-volume anthology, *The Complete Far Side*.)

The Far Side in Its Original Cultural Context

If we were to choose one *Far Side* cartoon that distilled how Larson's work first impacted the comics page and culture in general in the 1980s, it would have to be the iconic image of an impish python that has swallowed Garfield (fig. 0.4). While *The Far Side* was not radically countercultural or outrageously offensive when it appeared in 1980, it was genuinely original and

Fig. 0.4. Gary Larson, "Garfield devoured by a python," *The Far Side*,
December 16, 1983 (1-351).

slyly subversive—a sort of liminal work of alternative comedy that quietly
slithered onto the mainstream comics page, and then, against expectations,
thrived there, essentially "devouring" the cutely bland fare that surrounded
it. As the years passed, that python gradually grew to a gargantuan size,
alarming Garfield's figurative owners (the readers and cultural guardians
accustomed to the bland status quo of the funnies page) and mesmerizing
everyone else. Within a half dozen years *The Far Side* effectively moved from
being a cult favorite that seemed out of place among the traditional funnies, to becoming perhaps the most popular and successfully merchandised
cartoon in any print medium, running in 1,900 newspapers (the mostly
widely syndicated *panel* cartoon in history) and selling in book collections
that always topped the *New York Times* bestseller list.

My point here is that you have to go back in time a bit—to the early 1980s, when *The Far Side* was new and controversial—to fully appreciate Larson's originality and the seismic cultural impact of his work. This was an era when the media landscape featured radically fewer venues for subversive comedy (television was limited to a handful of conservative network channels, for example), and the mainstream comics page was notoriously intolerant of even mildly "inappropriate" content. Within that cultural context, Larson's cartoons had worldview-shifting potential for readers who were thirsty for comedy that was not vapidly cute or lamely clichéd. *The Far Side*, for example, contrasted with the professionally slick material that surrounded it on the funnies page in a number of ways: its aesthetics were intentionally awkward and minimalistic; its morbid humor was weird and bracing, introducing taboo subject matter like death, violence, and odd (but generally benign) perversities into mainstream newspapers; its consistent animal–human inversions were philosophically unsettling, highlighting a naturalistic (and explicitly evolutionary) view of life that challenged traditional Christian and anthropocentric (human-flattering) worldviews; and there was an absurd and oblique quality to Larson's jokes that kept even regular followers off-balance.

The combination of those ingredients in one cartoon elicited highly divergent reactions from readers in those early days. In comics page popularity polls *The Far Side* won both the "favorite" and the "most disliked" categories on a consistent basis (McCarthy). People who liked it, *really* liked it, actively cutting out favorite installments to put on fridges and office doors, collecting book anthologies, and buying *Far Side* merchandise. And those that disliked it seemed to detest it with a passion. A vocal minority of readers (and a few editors), for example, continually complained (and sometimes actively agitated against) its presence on the comics page, because it broke long-standing rules about what constituted safe or normal entertainment for a "family-friendly" medium. Their efforts resulted in a rich body of letters to the editor—and hate mail sent directly to Gary Larson—that chronicled in elaborately indignant (and sometimes comical) language their strong objections. Among a plethora of complaints, *The Far Side*, in their view, was "ugly," "demoralizing," "revolting," "dehumanizing," "insulting" (Harnisch 137), "sick," "obnoxious," "sadistic," "vile," and "not fit for exposure to children" (Keefe 14).

And then there were those readers who simply didn't get it. Larson's work for them was not necessarily too intellectual (the jokes were often too silly or morbid for that label); it had more to do with the cartoon's relatively bizarre tone and use of unconventional comedic devices. Most traditional followers of the funnies page were accustomed to decoding gags that were obvious, familiar, and comfortingly cute, as if the cartoonist were spoon-feeding the humor. Larson, instead, created layered, implied, or inscrutable jokes like the installment in which a flat-eyed bovine proudly stands next to a table with lumpy, vaguely useful-looking objects on it, accompanied by the simple caption "Cow tools" (10/28/82; 1–252). Concepts like that provoked confusion rather than laughter for many readers, spurring them to demand clarifications from Larson or their newspaper's editor. In addition, *The Far Side* featured a number of comedic/satiric devices that were unfamiliar and off-putting to readers who did not want to work too hard in the enjoyment of their daily dose of humor: nerdy wordplay; ironic incongruities; deconstructions of fairy tales, genre entertainment, and comics conventions; scenes that required readers to conjecture events that happened either before or after the gag; and deadpan tones and aesthetics that essentially asked readers to participate in the completion of the joke.

Some of these unconventional comedic devices had been circulating in alternative cultural texts since the 1960s: underground comix, antiestablishment films, satiric novels by writers like Joseph Heller or Kurt Vonnegut, experimental standup comedy, late-night television, and the work of a handful of iconoclastic magazine cartoonists that Larson admired: B. Kliban, George Booth, Gahan Wilson, and Charles Addams. Larson, however, was the first cartoonist to introduce successfully those brands of comedy onto the mainstream funnies page. And although the cultural importance of newspaper comics has declined precipitously in the last thirty years, it was a truly mass medium in the early 1980s, consumed avidly across most age and demographic groups. As a result, it might be difficult for us to overestimate how much Larson's success changed the geography of comedy and cartooning in the United States. *The Far Side*, in fact, qualifies as one of the key cultural texts (in addition to *MAD* magazine, David Letterman, and *Saturday Night Live*) from that period that effectively bridged the gap between alternative and mainstream comedy and that inspired fledgling cartoonists, comedians, and filmmakers to venture into less-conventional territory. In sum, it played a significant role in expanding the comedic palette of American readers and viewers during its fifteen-year run, helping to clear the path for other "alternatively mainstream" comics texts, such as *Bloom County*, *The Simpsons*, *South Park*, *Pearls Before Swine*, *Boondocks*, *Get Fuzzy*, and *Rick and Morty*.

After recognizing *The Far Side*'s significance in our recent cultural history, you might wonder how Larson achieved this unlikely success. And we should emphasize the word *unlikely* here, for reasons that were implied in the preceding pages: the intensely competitive nature of the mainstream comics page, draconian economic and editorial practices that effectively censored or undermined the vitality of innovative newspaper funnies for many years, and the seeming aesthetic and comedic limitations of the lowly panel cartoon. The following chapters answer that question in generous detail by following the unlikely arc of Larson's life and career, by exploring the aesthetic and comedic qualities of his cartoons, by looking closely into the business side of his success, and then by exploring how the *Far Side* brand as a whole connected with its core readers in profound ways. In sum, I will illustrate how Larson's work and career were counterdiscursive, challenging the norms of both the production and content of mainstream newspaper comics, and effectively reinventing his medium from within—pushing against, and often bursting past, its traditional institutional, aesthetic, comedic, and philosophical borders (Morrissey, "Introduction" viii).

Chapter Summaries

Chapter 1 is about Gary Larson's life and career. First we look into Larson's childhood in Tacoma, Washington, tracing the connections between his unconventional upbringing and the themes and jokes in his later cartoons (a pranking older brother, goofy parents, and almost unlimited freedom to explore the natural world). Then we chart his circuitous route toward a career in newspaper cartoons through a number of diversions and dead ends during his young adult years: studying communications in college, working at odd jobs, and indulging in peculiar hobbies like jazz guitar and snake collecting. The story of his ultimate break into comics (by way of local publications and then a "Hail Mary" trip to visit a syndicate in San Francisco) is especially fascinating, since it was achieved with so little awareness on Larson's part of what kind of profession he was pursuing. The fact that he succeeded at breaking into national syndication is also astonishing, because the odds were so clearly against him in light of the ultracompetitive nature of newspaper comics at that time and the rough quality and relatively weird nature of his work.

We can follow the initially slow but eventually exponential growth of the panel's popularity after its national syndication in 1980, highlighting along the way many of the accolades, controversies, and stand-out cartoons of Larson's early career. A key event in this progression was his switch from Chronicle Features Syndicate to Universal Press Syndicate in 1985—a move that helped him to secure copyright ownership, merchandising rights, and creative control of his work. As Larson's work transitioned from alternative to mainstream status in the mid-to-late 1980s, we consider how the resulting *FarSide*mania affected his professional and personal life, forcing him to retreat from the public eye on one hand, but encouraging him to further refine the quality and consistency of his work on the other. His arrival as a culturally significant figure was marked by several achievements: the ubiquity of his book collections and merchandising material, the unprecedented amount of fan and hate mail he received, and the way his work was embraced so avidly by niche reading communities such as scientists and academics. The first chapter concludes with a description of how Larson decided to retire *The Far Side* after only a fifteen-year run (while it was still popular) in order to go out on a high note and preserve his own sanity. Finally, his post–*Far Side* life is described; though highly private, he maintained for a time the popularity of his work while delving into a number of non-cartooning passions such as scuba diving, wildlife and habitat conservation, jazz guitar, and weird-pet collecting.

Chapter 2 explores the comedic devices and themes on display in *The Far Side*. First we look into Larson's working methods as a comedian, charting his process from free associative brainstorming into strategies of refining and clarifying his jokes, and finally receiving critical feedback from editors. Second, using specific cartoons as examples, we analyze the humor of Larson's work in relation to basic theories of what makes us laugh: surprising incongruities, irreverent treatments of taboo subject matter, and comic depictions of violence or misfortune that evoke in the reader mingled emotions of sympathy and schadenfreude (a sort of mild sadism). We then explore a number of the comedic devices commonly used in *The Far Side*, considering original ways that Larson modified or combined them. They included wordplay that literalizes figurative speech or tested the logic of clichéd maxims; in medias res (in the middle of the action) vignettes that require readers to complete a narrative; cross-overs between animal and human worlds; gothic or morbid deconstructions of comforting social myths; and cheeky parodies of a variety of genres, media, and discourses. Throughout the chapter I periodically break away from close readings of his cartoons to paint in broad strokes the larger philosophical meanings circulating around *The Far Side*, suggesting ways that his comedy often became pointedly satiric, borrowing from the philosophical traditions of naturalism, absurdism, and the carnivalesque.

The third chapter explores the art of *The Far Side*. To begin, I look at Larson's cartooning style with fresh eyes, unbiased by traditional frames that would readily dismiss his approach as simplistic or deficient. Using a more foundational set of objective questions as a starting point—Does it work? Is it funny?—I consider how his self-taught methods effectively became a strength within those focused goals. In practice, his seeming deficiencies allowed him to create especially funny imagery, communicate his jokes in efficient ways, and signal his alternative credentials (in contrast to the more slickly professional styles that surrounded *The Far Side* on the comics page). As a support in this exercise, I borrow ideas from Scott McCloud that highlight the underappreciated strength of highly distilled cartoon imagery—in particular, their ability to amplify ideas and essences through simplification, and invite high levels of reader engagement or closure. Secondly, I describe influences on, and precedents to, Larson's crude and intentionally unprofessional aesthetics: alternative magazine cartoonists like B. Kliban, minimalistic animation styles that emerged in the 1960s, and figures within the underground comix movement. The chapter concludes with an application of ideas borrowed from semiotics to understand the shifting connotations of a number of Larson's key aesthetic devices and symbols: affectless line work, a variety of eyeglasses, beehive hairdos, flat-eyed brows, pinheaded craniums, and shlumpy physiques. That exploration of the shifting comedic connotations tied to cartooning signs helps us to understand how Larson's aesthetics were so effective on one side (communicating key satiric ideas), and so derided as ugly and grotesque on the other (confusing uninitiated readers, or standing out as intentionally subversive and unprofessional to traditional guardians of the funnies page).

Chapter 4 looks at the business side of Larson's career, considering how he navigated the challenges of working in this highly competitive and intensively mediated field. Using a qualified version of the auteur theory as a starting point, I posit that Larson's success as a highly original cartoonist was contingent on his ability to protect his rights as an artist and satirist. We then assess how Larson almost accidentally stumbled into the role of the iconoclast but then effectively exerted the clout and independence of a genuine sateur (a satirically-minded auteur) with relative degrees of effectiveness as he negotiated contracts; interacted with syndicate bosses, newspaper editors, and reporters; made decisions about merchandising; and negotiated the pressures of celebrity. While these discussions of how cartooning auteurs deal with commercial and institutional pressures can be inherently interesting, they are especially fascinating in Larson's case because his success as a businessman was so unlikely. Given Larson's reclusive nature and general distaste for the commercial and administrative sides of being a syndicated cartoonist, it is a wonder that he made it onto the comics page in the first place, let alone became one of the most successful creators in the history of the medium. As we will see, nevertheless, it was often his lack of "professionalism" that ironically helped him—often intentionally, but sometimes unknowingly—to make decisions that would both protect the integrity of his work and amplify the popularity of his cartoon.

In the final chapter I assess the cultural significance of Larson's work within the closing decades of the twentieth century. To do this, I first question traditional views of newspaper cartoons as ephemeral gags that lack semiotic weight. I speculate, for example, on the level of emotional and intellectual investment of *Far Side* fans that collected and shared dog-eared anthologies, clipped out and posted favorite cartoons on doors and refrigerators, and proudly purchased and displayed paraphernalia like T-shirts and coffee mugs. Second, I consider ways of thinking about each *Far Side* cartoon as more than just an isolated joke; I posit, instead, that for core fans, Larson's best panels worked as small chapters in a sprawling, microserialized, years-long text that included over 4,300 installments. Read in relation to one another, and within a larger appreciation of Larson's worldview, they revisited a set of coherent themes: naturalism, evolution, deep time, contemporary devolution, and so on. They also articulate a set of consistent satiric ideas about the absurdity of the universe, the chronic myopia of individuals in civilized society, and the dangers of anthropocentric worldviews.

Finally, I suggest that while Larson's core satiric themes may seem a bit misanthropic or depressingly degenerative from a distance, when delivered in small, regular doses—via *The Far Side*'s distilled, endorphin-triggering gags—they may have performed bracingly astringent intellectual effects. In particular, the inherently skeptical, parodic, and deconstructive comedic gaming in Larson's work might have prodded his most devoted to readers to develop similarly critical ways of perceiving society, human behavior, and other mainstream cultural texts. In effect, the reading and rereading of Larson's thematically linked and satirically similar cartoons over years could have inoculated some invested readers against an array of blindered, romantic, or arrogant brands of thinking that plagued a highly (d)evolved species of primate at the end of the twentieth century. While much of my argument is speculative, since it is difficult to quantify the psychological and intellectual effects of decades-old reading and thinking practices, we can still document, nevertheless, in the final pages, vivid evidence of these effects and *The Far Side*'s lasting cultural impact from the recollections of everyday fans and some of Larson's cartooning and comedy-writing peers.

Chapter I

The Accidental Cartoonist

Larson's Life and Career

Larson's Upbringing and Family Life

We often expect our great comedians to come from dysfunctional roots (broken families, scenes of childhood trauma, economic hardship) that force the artist in later life to wield humor as a highly public coping mechanism. Larson gave a jokey nod, in fact, to that comedy truism in a 1989 book anthology; in the opening pages he showcased a series of pretend drawings from his childhood that illustrated demented beginnings: peeking out from behind bars on his bedroom window; sitting under the table at family dinner time with a rabid dog; tied to a tree by an oversized, torch-wielding brother; and being coaxed by his parents to run into the street to pursue some dangerously positioned chocolate chip cookies (Larson, "Fossil Record" 14–24). The reality of Larson's early home life was more benign, of course, disappointing our expectations of creativity-producing dysfunction. He grew up, for example, in the suburbs of University Place, Tacoma, Washington, a fairly bland-sounding locale, with his parents, Vern and Doris—a car salesman and a secretary—who were, by all accounts, loving and highly supportive of their two sons' interests. Moreover, Larson admired his older brother, Dan, with whom he was close friends throughout childhood and into adult life.

A minimal amount of probing just past this pleasant exterior reveals, nevertheless, a number of weird and unconventional (if not fully traumatic) aspects to Larson's early family life: traditions, dynamics, and incidents that might explain why he ended up creating something as consistently morbid as *The Far Side*, instead of a comfortably cute cartoon like "Ziggy or something" (Larson's words) (Larson, "Commencement"). For starters, when Larson was a small boy, his family had a perverse taste for strange pranks and dark humor—establishing a sort of "Theodore Cleaver Meets the Thing" dynamic in which Gary could be torn from a sense of calm normality into a panic of sheer terror at any given moment (Larson, "This Is My Brother's Fault" 1). His older brother, Dan, for example—though not inclined to inflict literal torture on his younger sibling, was a formidable antagonist who consistently "scared the hell out of him" (Weise). Larson explained that Dan "had studied me. He knew what scared me"; he was "some master from the Shau Lin Temple of Scaring Younger Brothers" (Larson, "Eye and I," 540). As an example, Dan would sometimes convince his younger brother to venture into the basement, and then proceed to lock the door on him and turn off the light; as Gary desperately tried to force open the door, his brother would chant, "It's coming, Gary, do you hear it? It's coming . . . hear it breathing?" (Larson, "On Monsters" 268; Sherr).

At other times Dan would capitalize on Gary's acute fear of monsters under the bed by hiding in the bedroom closet for hours, "just waiting for the golden opportunity to scare his sibling sick," and then slowly open the door, inch by inch, maximizing the sense of suspense and terror (Ferguson). Larson recalls one such incident leaving him with a scarring, "indelible memory." As the door opened inch by inch, almost imperceptibly, he was not able to take his eyes off the "black, vertical abyss" that surely contained a patiently malicious creature. He then let out a primal scream as "a single eye staring back" at him came into view—followed in the next moment by a smiling older brother who slowly revealed himself in a "very surreal fashion" (Larson, "Commencement" 1). Imagining such moments of real terror for a sensitive and imaginative kid adds a layer of poignancy to our reading of the dozens of "monster under the bed" cartoons Larson created—or to random gags about familial cruelty, like the classic where the father has rigged a contraption that intimidates his son into good behavior by simulating the knocking of a monster's fist on a closed basement door (1/6/87; 2–7).

Gary also had to be wary of parents who enjoyed subjecting their kids to unusually disturbing pranks. He remembers, for example, needing good peripheral vision, since they were inclined to slip "a small invertebrate into [his] glass of milk at the dinner table while [his] head was turned"; or they might simply jump out and surprise him at unpredictable moments. Looking back, he recalled that his parents were especially talented at this kind of playful, predator–prey comedy that provoked a sense of nervous laughter mingled with low levels of "fear and humiliation." Perhaps exaggerating a bit, he claims that they continually used "research, observation, psychology, biology" in "the quest to amuse" themselves at another family member's expense. Larson thus lived in a state of comedic anxiety as a young kid, always prepared to either scream or laugh as a parent or brother waited just "around any corner, in any room," ready to pounce. The average person might head for the therapist's couch to work through the cognitive dissonance of household dynamics equally tied to silliness and horror; Larson went a different route, chalking up these experiences as productive drills in a "*Far Side* boot camp." He effectively translated the lessons of that psychological teasing to the craft of cartooning, learning in his morbid gags to "study your prey, approach carefully, savor the moment, and then strike" (Larson, "On Dorothy" 4).

The celebration of morbid and juvenile humor was another unconventional aspect of the Gary's childhood. Larson described the lowbrow comedic tone of family conversations:

> Imagine your own father sitting at the Algonquin Round Table, surrounded by that famous group of New York intellectuals. Would he most likely attempt to use his verbal alacrity and facile mind to impress and entertain everyone? Or would he find a quiet moment and simply lean over and ask Dorothy Parker to pull his finger? (Sorry, Dad, but I know the answer to this one.) In short, the Larson Round Table was not a place where sharp dialogue and witticisms abounded. (Larson, "On Dorothy" 4)

He hastened to add that his parents (especially his mom) could be very smart and witty at other times but conceded that their jokes tended to be earthy and physical rather than cerebral; they liked to get down on their kids' level, relishing goofy wordplay, engaging in slapstick, playing with taboo subject matter, and making "offbeat" or "wacky" observations. And because the Larson household was so steeped in this kind of irreverent comedy (effectively normalizing it in Larson's mind), he often struggled as an adult to understand why some readers found his sense of humor to be so offensive or inappropriate (Gumbel).

Perhaps as compensation for all of the slapstick pranking, Larson's parents gave him an unusual amount of freedom to explore the natural world when he was young. In stark contrast to how today's parents helicopter over their kids in fenced-in backyards and groomed parks, Larson's parents allowed him and his brother "on any given day or night" to gather up their "boots, nets and collecting jars and head for the local swamps or tidelands

. . . on a quest for living treasure: the wetland fauna of western Washington" (Larson, "Syndrome" 180). Summertime expanded that range of
freedom as he and Dan stayed for days and weeks at his grandparents' farm
on Fox Island in Puget Sound just off the Tacoma shore. Larson describes
it as a "wondrous place" to explore—an island setting that "had a sort of
"Lost World" feel to it." Taking off from his grandparents' house—which
was set "in picturesque fashion . . . between the shore and a high bank
. . . overgrown with trees and leafy vegetation," they would venture into
untamed fields, [and] tidelands." Gary vividly remembers, in particular,
a small creek that fed into a "a textbook swamp" featuring "crystal clear
water," a sandy bottom, and "salamanders everywhere" (Larson, "Big Ungulates" 446; Weise).

It was these forays into the natural world that first inspired Larson to
think about becoming a scientist—and ultimately planted the roots of
some of the key themes of *The Far Side*: wildlife conservation, intersections
between animal and human realms, evolution, and a naturalistic worldview.
Larson thus had the sensibility of a zoologist from an early age; in his
words, he was continually "drawn to look under rocks, down holes, up trees,
under water . . . to capture and to hold, if only for a few moments, some
living, natural wonder, to observe it, examine it, have it touch your skin,
feel its heartbeat against your hand—to 'drink it in' before it once again
slips back over that invisible wall that separates Us from Them" (Larson,
"Syndrome" 180–181).

In addition to observing animals, Larson collected them. He and his
brother were continually bringing home bugs, lizards, and salamanders,
filling bedrooms and the family basement with terrariums. His parents
even allowed him to own a pet monkey for a time, and as he grew older, he
developed a fondness for snakes, eventually taking care of close to twenty
serpents (Kelly 86). The exotic nature of these pets sometimes got him into
awkward situations that sound vaguely like premises for some of his classic
cartoons. For example, his dad once discovered an eight-foot boa constrictor wrapped around his wife's sewing machine; and when Larson was a
young adult, he was forced to give away a fourteen-foot python when it
tried to eat him instead of a dead rabbit during a feeding session (Kelly 86;
Astor, "Larson Explores" 32). He admitted later in life that as a young boy he
had been unaware that most people considered these animals—especially
in those numbers—atypical or inappropriate pets: "Obviously, my social
life was a bit down at the time . . ." and "it took me a while to realize that
with an interest like that people are going to think there's something wrong
with you" (Gumbel). Imagining Larson's conflicted emotions as he tried to

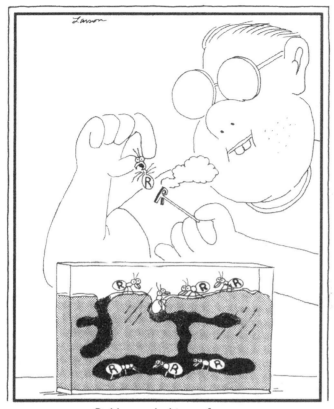

Robby works his ant farm.

Fig. 1.1: Gary Larson, "Robby works his ant farm," *The Far Side*, Nov. 7, 1986 (1-628).

reconcile his peculiar hobbies with conventional social expectations, you can see budding inspiration for the recurring theme of absurdly improper pets in *The Far Side*: a morose-looking giant squid cradling the family dog in the corner of a spare living room (4/14/86; 1–566); the alligator with an oblivious chicken perched on its snout, about to perform a violent party trick for guests in a suburban living room (3/8/86; 1–557); and the woman on the phone with her husband, patting her giant rhino on the head while holding the phone up to his snout, coaxing him, "C'mon baby . . . one grunt for Daddy . . . one grunt for Daddy (8/6/84; 1–410).

Themes of scientific experimentation in *The Far Side* can also be traced to these childhood exploits. Gary and Dan, for example, once commandeered an entire room of their parents' home to create a realistic desert ecosystem in which they could observe the natural behavior of their collected specimens. As you might guess, those informal studies would sometimes bleed into morbid territory, like when Gary became intrigued by the prospect of placing "two organisms . . . in a common jar" to see which one "would devour the other" (Barry D5). Based on these mildly gruesome vignettes, it is clear that Larson often embodied in spirit—if not in appearance—the chubby, bespectacled nerd in his cartoon who was continually doing half-scientific, half-horrific things with ant farms and other captured critters (fig. 1.1). Gothic themes also melded with science in Gary's memories of how he helped his dad work on odd, experimental projects in a home workshop. He remembers himself as the bumbling but eager assistant—the "Igor" to his dad's mad scientist. He would continually fetch the wrong tools, but his dad did not notice, or did not care, as he attempted, single-mindedly, "to bring life to a dead lawnmower" on a "stormy, lightning-filled" night (McCarthy).

The overlap of science and the supernatural was also a common theme throughout Larson's childhood. When not out exploring the natural environment, he was immersed in entertainment that was populated with exotic animals, monsters, or aliens. These interests had fairly tame beginnings, as he first enjoyed sweetly conventional stories about anthropomorphized animals: tales of Br'er Rabbit or Mr. Toad read to him by his mother. His animal-themed affinities took a fairly morbid and naturalistic turn, however, when he fell in love with one particular book—*Mr. Bear Squash-You-All-Flat*—and asked his mom to read it to him repeatedly. He recalled, "There was something so mesmerizing about the image of this big bear going through the forest and squashing the homes of these little forest animals. I thought that was the coolest thing in the world" (Sherr). That dark sensibility was fed and amplified in subsequent years when his regular babysitter, Mrs. Wetch, introduced him to more vividly supernatural fare: Dracula, Frankenstein, werewolves, the Mummy, and the Creature from the Black Lagoon (Larson, "Good Wetch" 122). Larson's taste in comics also fell within that borderland between the natural and fantastical. He liked stories of men mingling with apes—*Alley Oop* and *Tarzan*, in particular—and he would fixate on the details in these stories that appealed to his budding naturalist's mind, like Edgar Rice Burroughs' concocted dictionary of great-ape vocabulary. He memorized that entire glossary, in fact, and expanded his omnivorous reading habits to include other texts that satisfied his general interest "in wild animals, Africa and Nature" (Larson, "Jungle in My Room" 4).

Art was an additional creative outlet for Larson during these years, but he is quick to clarify that it should be "immediately obvious" that he never studied art formally while growing up—other than the random required class in grade school or junior high. On his own time he "loved to draw," filling notebooks with doodles plumbed from his imagination and the natural world (Barry D5). While his classmates were sketching "cool tanks and airplanes," he "preferred to draw dinosaurs, whales and giraffes" (McCarthy). This affinity for doodling persisted into high school, but during all those formative years he never once thought about (or was prodded toward) becoming a professional cartoonist. He explains that, "on Career Day in high school, you don't walk around looking for the cartoon guy" (Larson, "Tribute to Stephen Jay Gould" 57).

Larson's Teen and Young Adult Years

Later in life Larson shared scant information about his high school years. One can infer, nevertheless, that he was a bit of a social misfit who was more fixated on snakes and various nerdy occupations than stereotypical high school pursuits. In an honorary commencement address at his alma mater (Western Washington State University) in 1990, he explained that he was especially shy as a teenager but admired the unselfconscious kids who had the gumption to enter talent shows in high school: "I was really fascinated" by "the ones that got up there and made absolute fools out of themselves. It was like the equivalent of standing up in front of the entire student body and saying look at me everyone, I'm a nerd" (Larson, "Commencement"). Those impressions, in fact, seemed to inspire him eventually to pursue his own peculiar talents and passions; looking back, he said, "I realize though that those kids were pretty cool in a way because they were risk takers . . . they did something a little weird and it seems to me that we're all sort of in a talent show of sorts. I mean there's some point in our life that somewhere, sometime you're gonna have to stand up in front of some stranger and do your act" (Larson, "Commencement").

The outlines of Larson's future performance were still vague when he attended college at Western Washington State University from 1972 to 1976. On a social level he thrived among other "weird" students in a dorm that had the reputation for carrying the lowest grade point average in the entire college. Sounding like a secondary character in the movie *Animal House*, he participated in a number of zany extracurricular activities: enrolling in a karate class on a whim and breaking a finger; spontaneously taking a road trip to Spokane and coming back with a pet boa constrictor; lurking for a semester in a creepy attic with a friend, feeling like a pair of "mutated rats"; cruising a sled across the college's golf course after a freak snowstorm and landing in the hospital with a broken back; and—like a scene out of one of his more absurd cartoons—getting chased by an angry cow across a campus parking lot (Larson, Commencement).

Larson's efforts as a student were equally eclectic, though slightly less odd. Initially he majored in science, but after attending his first slate of classes, he had a crisis of confidence; he decided against becoming a scientist after encountering a latent "fear of physics" and wrestling with worries about low job prospects for a biology graduate (Bernstein 104; Ferguson). While still seeking out every natural history and science class he could fit into his schedule, he began to roam more broadly in his course-taking, venturing into random territory like the history of opera. He ultimately settled on a fairly pragmatic and bland choice of major: communications. Perhaps trying to add some exciting purpose and justification to that decision, he remembers imagining that he would someday "save the world from mundane advertising" (Kelly 86).

The prospect of a career in the corporate world, however, also gradually dissipated, amounting to another phantom act. Instead, he essentially "bounced around" for a number of years after college, careening from job to job without a clear sense of his talents or what he wanted to do with his life. Music was his most avid interest during those years, but the job prospects in that field were fairly limited, of course. He labored for a time in a retail music shop and founded a trombone-and-banjo-based band "named 'Tom and Larson,' which friends immediately dubbed 'two guys as exciting as their names'" (Weise). He also became enamored with the jazz guitar, seeking out any opportunity to study and play. This became a full-fledged passion, in fact, as he continued to pursue the craft throughout his adult life, later even devoting sabbaticals to studying with famous performers, and continually retreating into the world of jazz when not punching the cartooning clock. As an aside, it would be easy to see this affinity for jazz guitar as a separate, unrelated avocation from his cartooning, but perhaps we should not underestimate how the discipline and craft of mastering such an instrument—and the creativity required in playing it improvisationally—could mirror the construction of tightly distilled but still absurdly original cartoons.

Perhaps Larson's most *Far Side*-esque job during those young adult years was toiling for the Humane Society of Seattle. In typically morbid fashion he joshes (we can hope) that he ran over a dog on the way to the interview for that job; he stuck with it, nevertheless, because of his interest in, and love of, animals. You can imagine the plethora of comedic mental notes that were accruing in his mind (without him necessarily being aware of it) as he labored at this job, observing animal behavior, pet–owner relations, and other odd aspects of the animal–human overlap. As we will see, in fact, it was on duty as a Humane Society officer (while following up on a case of pony abuse with a *Seattle Times* reporter) that Larson achieved his first small break as a budding cartoonist (Bernstein 104).

The Beginnings of Larson's Career as a Cartoonist

It was during these post-college years that Larson embarked on a "sequence of random decisions, sporadic efforts, and lucky breaks" that gradually led him toward the unlikely career of a syndicated cartoonist (Ferguson). To begin, there had been the random, amateurish doodles in grade school and high school, and then some flirtation with full-fledged cartooning in college as he encountered the work of alternative magazine cartoonists like B. Kliban, George Booth, Edward Gorey, and Gahan Wilson. But un-like many of his later, professional colleagues, he did not see cartooning during these years as a viable career option, nor did he attempt to publish his drawings in the college paper. The decision to pursue the vocation seriously occurred in 1976, after college, while Larson was drudging as a salesman at a retail music shop. He recalls having an epiphany one day while on the job:

> As I stood next to the cash register, the sky seemed to suddenly open up over my head and a throng of beautiful angels came flying down and swirled around me. In glorious, lilting tones, their voices rang out, "you haaaaate your job, you haaaaate your job . . ." There was nothing really that terrible about it but, without prior warning, it came over me that this just wasn't what I wanted out of life. (We didn't even get good employee discounts.) I wanted something more. Insurance salesman, ice cream vendor, gravedigger—many things occurred to me, but I was pretty much rudderless. (Larson, "Fossil Record" 25)

In the wake of that revelation, "he took a weekend off to 'find himself,'" and after mulling it over "for 48 hours straight, he entered that special mental zone that exists somewhere between breakdown and epiphany. And in that heightened state of mind, Larson drew" his first set of six, polished, single-panel cartoons (Ferguson). Aesthetically the gags looked rough, but in tone they spoke with relative maturity and consistency; they echoed, in fact, the slightly off-kilter panels of Kliban and Wilson. They included, for example, crabs discussing the weirdness of human babies at the beach; a frog devouring a beautiful butterfly as it emerges from its cocoon; and an oversized, evil-looking Smokey the Bear on the verge of attacking a group of hunters loitering around a campfire.

Larson relished this creative adventure and dispatched those first cartoons to local publishing venues, probing for a way to make some money. To his delight, *Pacific Search*, a regional science magazine, accepted them for publication and paid him ninety dollars. A friend advised Larson to frame that first check rather than cash it, but finances must have been especially tight, since he was able to hold off for only about an hour before spending it (Larson, "I Remember" 450). Despite the modesty of that sum, Larson felt elated by a taste of success, repeating to himself, "You looooove cartooning, you looooove cartooning. . . ." It was enough encouragement, in fact, to compel him to quit his job and move back in with his parents to labor at cartooning with real focus and energy (Larson, "Fossil Record" 28).

His next round of cartoons, a batch that he titled *Nature's Way*, also found a publisher—*The Summer News Review* in Tacoma. The three dollars they paid him per cartoon, however, had a sobering effect on his dreams of doing this as a long term career. He was so discouraged by these meager financial rewards, in fact, that he stopped sending out his cartoons to new venues. Accepting defeat, he returned to the conventional working world, securing that job with the local Humane Society as an investigator. It was while performing this job, in 1979, that he had the chance conversation with a *Seattle Times* reporter that led him to unearth his cartooning dreams once again. On a whim, he asked for the contact information for that newspaper's comics editor and followed through in submitting a collection of his *Nature's Way* cartoons. The *Times* editor liked them well enough and allotted Larson a weekly slot that paid fifteen dollars per cartoon. (At that bargain, we can imagine the editor overlooking the rough art and morbid humor, rationalizing that there were probably some readers who might enjoy it.)

Despite the modesty of this new paycheck, Larson decided to revive his cartooning aspirations, and for a full year his weekly cartoons appeared in the *Times*. He was elated to get published regularly, but because this was the pre-Internet era (and also perhaps due to the busyness/laziness of the

Fig. 1.2: Gary Larson, "He says it's for good luck," *Nature's Way*, 1979.

staff at the newspaper), he received little information on how the editors or his readers felt about his work. He sent in his cartoons, they were printed, and he deposited his weekly paycheck. While that arrangement may seem less than ideal, in Larson's case a dearth of feedback was perhaps a strangely beneficial factor in his early development as a comedian and artist. Most professional comic strip artists endure a barrage of reader, newspaper, and syndicate feedback as they hone (and sometimes self-censor) their work on the road toward successful, national syndication; in contrast, Larson was allowed to work in a comedic vacuum of sorts, fully indulging his alternative sensibility and pursuing unconventional themes. As a result, his *Nature's Way* cartoons were especially hard-edged; they include the following morbid and often obtuse ideas: an awkward-looking, oversized rabbit with a human foot hanging around its neck (fig. 1.2); an alligator forcing a giraffe to re-tract its long neck by pulling violently on its tail; and a man at a restaurant berating a waiter because he ordered steak and received instead a giant, dead python between two pieces of bread. It is hard to imagine a typical, harried, syndicate or newspaper editor (full of anxieties about squeamish readers or the financial bottom line) looking through such cartoons and thinking, "We need more of that."

As it turns out, the *Times* had been receiving consistent feedback about Larson's work from readers; some of it was positive, Jim King, the managing editor explained, in an apologetic letter to Larson, "but the cartoon had been generating just too many complaints and the editorial consensus was to terminate it" (Larson, "Fossil Record" 36). The abrupt cancellation took Larson off guard; he explained, "I didn't realize I was working in a family medium" (Bernstein 104). That comment may sound sarcastic, but given Larson's lifelong track record of pursuing interests in a passionate but socially narrow way, it is plausible that he was largely ignorant about the limitations of this medium. He recalls, "I didn't really have too much of a notion about newspapers and newspaper comics. . . . The only thing I knew was there were some cartoons out there, mostly in magazines, that I did like and enjoy and thought were funny" (Morrissey, "Far Side of Retirement"). And since the magazine cartoonists Larson admired were enjoying an unusual amount of freedom and room for experimentation in the 1970s (thanks in large part to magazines like *The New Yorker* and *Playboy*), Larson might have had an inaccurate view of the latitude he might enjoy as a newspaper cartoonist. In sum, against all logic and evidence drawn from recent cultural history, he was on the cusp of engaging in a radical experiment: the exertion of the independence of a freelance, alternative panel cartoonist within the staid but lucrative field of newspaper syndication.

Larson's naive audacity remained an essential element in his next set of random decisions and sporadic efforts to begin his career in earnest. In the summer of 1979, while still unaware that the *Seattle Times* was about to fire him (that would come one week later), Larson listened to the urging of his then-girlfriend and drove 1,600 miles down to San Francisco in a Plymouth Duster. His vague goal was to sell his *Nature's Way* cartoons to more newspapers—to earn a real living somehow at this job. His expectations were low after making a cursory investigation of the funnies page at the time; he realized that 90 percent of the comics page was populated by strips (as opposed to single panels), and that his work felt decidedly "different" in tone and subject matter from established features. He fretted, as a result, that he would not "fit in" or connect with an audience (Morrissey, "Far Side of Retirement").

Looking back on those few critical days in San Francisco, he recalls doing "absolutely everything wrong," essentially stumbling into syndication (Larson, "Commencement"). First of all, based on his experience in Seattle, he mistakenly assumed that a cartoonist had to sell his work to papers individually, and so when he entered the offices of the *San Francisco Chronicle*, he did not realize he was courting *Chronicle* Features, a national syndicate that was affiliated with that paper (Miller 78). Secondly, Larson erred in preparing only one portfolio of his work, and so all of his chances hinged on that one contact with the *Chronicle*. Without an appointment, he simply dropped off his collection with the syndicate's receptionist. She was less than encouraging, warning him that the syndicate "rarely bought features from 'people who walked in off the street'" (Larson, "Fossil Record" 36). Several days passed without a response. As Larson stewed, he spent his time alternately bugging the receptionist from a makeshift phone-booth-office on Fisherman's Wharf, and wandering around, nursing his doubts (Larson, "I Remember" 450). Each time he called, there were no updates, and he was warned not to get his hopes up; he assumed he would soon receive the inevitable rejection. Near the end of his several-day wait he began "getting depressed and homesick," asking himself, "Who do I think I am?" (Larson, "Acknowledgments" xviii). For readers deeply attached to Larson's work, it is poignant to imagine what would have occurred if the receptionist's low expectations had been accurate: there would be no *Far Side*, since Larson admits, "If I had struck out with the *Chronicle*, I would have given the whole thing up" (Bernstein 104).

Luckily for Larson and his fans, there was a general manager at Chronicle Features Syndicate—Stan Arnold—with a sense of humor "as weird" as Larson's. He surveyed the portfolio and, in an unconventional move, descended into the lobby to meet Larson face to face (Larson, "Commencement"). Larson, who had anticipated rejection, describes the shock of this first encounter: "Arnold said, 'Are you Gary Larson?' I replied in the affirmative, and without hesitation, his next words were, 'You're sick!' There was a brief pause (during which my stomach rolled into a granny knot), and then he quickly added, 'I loved 'em!'" (Larson, "Fossil Record" 36).

Arnold then invited Larson into his office for a brief chat; the surreal quality of the encounter made it difficult for Larson to remember the details of the conversation, but he did gather that other editors would need to look at his work before they could talk seriously about the possibility of syndication. The additional colleagues must have readily concurred with Arnold's assessment, because several days later Larson was invited back to the Chronicle offices to discuss plans to promote his work on a national scale (Larson, "Fossil Record" 36). He recalled being timid and nervous in this first planning session, listening as Arnold discussed what he saw as the strengths and weaknesses of *Nature's Way*. From an editor's perspective, he thought the humor was great—if unusual—but had doubts that it could succeed as a panel cartoon. Arnold was biased, in fact, toward strips and tried to cajole Larson into switching the format of his cartoon, since "people like to see characters they recognize." The continuity, he explained, builds familiarity, fondness, and brand loyalty (Larson, "On Dorothy" 4, 6). While Larson admired the work of strip artists, he knew his limitations—that he was incapable of creating well-rounded characters (or of being able to render them the same way from panel to panel). In contrast, his limited strength, he knew, consisted of creating stand-alone gags—getting in and getting out quickly with a mind-bending joke. And so not knowing how to respond, Larson just perched there, holding his breath and remaining silent. Perhaps reading Larson's muteness as stubborn, artistic independence, Arnold eventually backed away from the suggestion, shrugging his shoulders and saying, "OK, we'll do it your way" (Larson, "Acknowledgments" xviii; Larson, "On Dorothy" 4, 6).

National Syndication of *The Far Side*

In the wake of that twenty-minute meeting, Larson was given a development contract and informed that his panel would be called *The Far Side*. Elated by this news, Larson reckoned, "They could have called it 'Revenge of the Zucchini People' for all I cared" (Larson, "Fossil Record" 36). The *Chronicle* offered no guarantees that his cartoons would make it into newspapers, but Larson still had a significant foot in the door. For the next several months he had to prove to the editors that he could keep up with the demands of syndication; that meant creating seven to eight, high-quality cartoons per week. Initially Larson succeeded at this task in terms of quantity but faltered a bit when it came to creating art and comedy that were consistently sharp. He remembers that "one week I submitted eight cartoons and they rejected seven" (Weise). Arnold's main problem with these early submissions was that they featured subject matter that most readers would find arcane or obscure. Worrying about how Larson would take rejection and criticism, he sent along careful notes with encouraging, "line-by-line explanations" of "which ones were almost there" (Weise).

At the end of this gestation period, Arnold and the other editors were satisfied with what they had seen and offered Larson a contract. As part of the official launch, they emphasized the peculiar name of the panel— *The Far Side*—a clear indication that they were intent on promoting it as something new and weird that stood out from the surrounding fare on the comics page. But given that only thirty papers picked it up initially, there were probably few people in Arnold's office who believed it would amount to anything more than a niche novelty, not likely to survive more than a year or two. Larson was pessimistic too; the paycheck from his first month of syndication was only about one hundred dollars, and he recalls thinking it would "be exciting if I ever got up to the level where I could pay my rent" (Bernstein 104).

Larson eventually garnered that amount, millions of times over, of course, but the inevitability of that success was not initially clear. The trajectory of *The Far Side*'s rise in popularity, in fact, followed the classic arc of exponential growth: gradual at first—only getting up to eighty papers after three years of syndication; building to two hundred by 1985; and then effectively shooting off the charts after that, reaching 1,900 papers at the height of its popularity in the early 1990s (Ferguson). Looking back at mid-career on all of the serendipitous breaks that gradually led to his unlikely blockbuster success, Larson marveled that it was "a Cinderella-type story." He elaborated, suggesting that instead of embodying the "assertive and aggressive" Horatio Alger–style go-getter who persisted through defeat and failure, he resembled the naive outsider who fell into this career on a half-hopeful whim. After being in the comics business for a number of years and seeing just how competitive and unforgiving it could be, he mused, "If I hadn't gotten lucky as soon as I had, I probably wouldn't have been a cartoonist. I don't think I could have withstood the rejection" (Astor, "Larson Explores" 32).

As an aside, that sense of accidentally falling into a charmed life that he didn't fully deserve haunted Larson throughout his career. In a mid-career interview he sheepishly admitted that he still had a "disquieting feeling" that there had "been some kind of mistake, and the other shoe would soon drop since "most cartoonists pay more dues than" he had; he worried, jokingly, that one day "someone's gonna show up and say, 'There's been a big mistake. The guy next door is supposed to be drawing the cartoon. Here's your shovel'" (Bernstein 105). At times that sense of guilt about the ease of his job, in fact, seemed to take on almost existential dimensions. He fretted, "Maybe it's my blue collar background, but work meant to me you come home covered in sweat. Now I just have to brush away the eraser shavings"; and, "I can't imagine drawing cartoons in a Third World country" (Kelly 86; Bernstein 104). Clearly Larson did not suffer from hubris; if anything, he was neurotic and self-questioning to a fault.

A more immediate insecurity hung over Larson head's during the first months of national syndication: he wondered if he would even be physically and intellectually capable of producing a quality cartoon every day going forward. He remembers it as

> a very formidable task in front of me when I first started doing it: How was I going to do this day after day, week after week—and then, of course, month after month, year after year? And I thought there was no way I was going to be able to do it, but I wasn't going to tell anyone that. I would just go until it stopped and I'd say, "Well, thanks, everyone, but I'm done." (Morrissey "Far Side of Retirement")

You can sense that anxiety at times when reading through some of the earliest, least-polished *Far Side* cartoons. The art, for example, was occasionally rough and inconsistent: fussy line work and distracting crosshatching; overly manic-looking characters; awkward, joke-obscuring compositions; and too much distracting detail. Comedically, there were also some weaknesses: too many clichéd expressions like "Egad!"; morbid topics treated with too much realism; gags that occasionally felt too similar to the work of his idols Kliban and Wilson (either archly weird or too cornily gothic); and too many jokes that relied on lame or predictable puns reminiscent of the gags enjoyed by junior high schoolers.

Larson kept at it, nevertheless, feeling a sense of "Ha, I did it again" every time he was able to dispatch another five or six cartoons (Morrissey, "Far Side of Retirement"). And the relentless demands of creating so many panels, week after week, exerted a powerful, ameliorating effect on his work. At approximately the four-month mark, in fact, he was beginning to solidify his own distinctive aesthetic style and develop some original comedic strategies. They included an awkwardly distilled drawing method with economical use of shading and line work; a "less is more" strategy in communicating the inner life of his characters (impassive expressions, eyes hidden behind glasses, phlegmatic postures, etc.); jokes that required mental completion by the reader, imagining before-and-after implications or consequences; absurdist twists on traditional gags, or deconstructive treatments of classic fairy tales; the use of understatement and implied horror or violence in his darker installments; and a greater clarity—both visually and verbally—in the delivery of the cartoon's central gag.

Those strategies of restraint, toning down emotional affect, and using visual ellipses, would become especially critical as he learned to make his core, gothic themes funnier and more palatable. In perusing his first half-year of cartoons, it is bracing to see how many gags deal with the subject of death or the prospect of serious violence. In a representative, two week

Fig. 1.3: Gary Larson, "Eyeglass testing area," *The Far Side*, March 28, 1980 (1-25).

sampling from the first year, we can identify seven out of eight cartoons that place humans in dire straits, often as the prey of sharks, bears, aliens, giant bed bugs, a desert island monster, and a malevolent mailbox. In the weakest ones, the violence is too vivid, the victims too emotionally distraught; as Larson improved, however, the reader was allowed to imagine the trauma as something that was about to unfold, or that had just concluded. That small degree of distance allows you to laugh rather than cringe at cartoons like the woman who has just opened the window to an empty, gently swinging window washer's perch (5/15/80; 1–35), or another one in which a scientist is running full speed into a brick wall to test out a pair of eyeglasses (fig. 1.3).

Larson also found ways to make morbidity funny through absurd premises and slapsticky imagery—like the panel in which enterprising squirrels

"Andrew, go out and get your grandfather . . . the
squirrels have got him again."

Fig. 1.4: Gary Larson, "Andrew, go out and get your grandfather," *The Far Side*,
September 9, 1980 (1-62).

try to stuff an old man into the hole of a tree by (fig. 1.4). Despite the
cleverness of all of these distancing modifications, nevertheless, it is no
wonder that sensitive readers and touchy editors were often scandalized by
the relentlessly dark subject matter coursing through his early work. They
were asked to witness Santa threatening to turn his reindeer into venison
(12/22/80; 1–88); polar bears reveling in the pleasures of "crunchy on the
outside—chewy on the inside" igloo snacks (9/29/80; 1–67); and a shifty
looking bull in a trenchcoat slipping into a meat locker containing human
corpses hanging upside down from hooks (fig. 2.18).

The slow but steady build of Larson's success was perhaps ironically
linked to the preponderance of those dark images and themes in his panel.

On the comics page in the 1980s, real estate was limited and in high demand, with each syndicate continually pestering newspaper editors to fill one or two free spots with the latest budding talent. In order to beat the competition, syndicate reps would actually crisscross the country, showing up in local newspaper offices to make person-to-person pitches about their company's newest offerings. You can imagine, therefore, that given *The Far Side*'s inconsistent quality in its early months—and Larson's budding reputation for creating morbid and confusing jokes—that it must have been especially daunting for a *Chronicle* salesman to present Larson's work to skeptical and cautious business people.

As it turned out, however, the dark and unusual qualities of Larson's work gradually became a unique and powerful selling point, since *The Far Side* contrasted so starkly with the relatively bland and conventional offerings of other syndicates. First of all, Larson's cartoons were guaranteed to catch an editor's attention, prodding him or her take a second look, or spend more time dwelling on the panel's long-term potential if they were to publish it. And secondly, because Larson eventually developed techniques for deftly understating or disguising the most egregiously offensive jokes, *The Far Side* seemed to intrigue editors who were perhaps getting bored (like many of their readers surely were) with the squarely cute comics that crowded the funnies page. Stuart Dodds, one of those *Chronicle* salesmen, provided a vivid picture of those first meetings in a report to his bosses back in San Francisco:

> The initial response to this cartoon has been quite funny and un-editor-like . . . all of a sudden, with Larson on their desk, what human sparks emerge! What has made this interesting to me is not knowing as I travel from one place to the next what *kind* of response to expect—the reactions are so diverse, unpredictable—even from editors I know fairly well. I don't know if I am going to be offered another cup of Sanka or shown the door. There is a lot of outright laughter—and then there is some deep groaning, a miserable sound to hear. (Dodds, "Memo" 55)

He continued, recounting some of the varied reactions he encountered:

> "I hate it, it's sick."
> "Oh dear, OH DEAR!"
> "The best thing since *Doonesbury* as far as I am concerned. And they're *all* good!"

"What a mind this man has. He's brilliant!"

"He's insane!"

"Jesus . . . Jesus Christ!"

"It might go over in San Francisco . . ."

"This is *not* a Buffalo product."

"I don't know what this is but it's not for us."

"This is an excellent feature you have."

"This is the strangest thing I have seen in my life."

"Funny as hell."

"Who is this guy?" (Dodds "Memo" 55)

It is tempting to imagine Larson taking mischievous glee at the thought of upsetting the more squeamish editors in this mix, but the reality was more mundane; he was simply grateful for the growing accolades and support he garnered from those newspaper people who were willing to give him a chance in these early, tenuous days. Looking back, he said,

I must deeply thank those newspapers that did not recoil when they first saw my work. Indeed, a handful even embraced it. When you draw a cartoon that may, for example, show a nerdy kid walking toward the front of his class for "show" 'n' tell," carrying a jar with a human head in it [8/19/81; 1–145], then you definitely need some folks around you who aren't afraid to shake things up a little, or at least are willing to look the other way once in a while. During the first year or two that I was drawing, these papers essentially paid my rent and kept me in ink. (Larson, "Acknowledgments" xviii)

Larson joked that he realized his strip had turned a corner, and he had finally embarked on a genuine career, when he was able to purchase a new electric pencil sharpener (Larson, "I Remember" 450). In fact, there were no moments of clear breakthrough in the early years; syndication numbers grew gradually from 1981 to 1984, and although his initial fans embraced *The Far Side* with fanatical devotion, they still amounted to only a large cult following. In 1985, however, Larson entered into the exponential curve of his career trajectory, achieving professional success and mass popularity in a number of ways. First of all, he was recognized for the brilliance of his work by his peers, garnering the first major award of his career: the Best Newspaper Panel Cartoon Award by the National Cartoonists Society. Second, his book collections were selling so well by this point that they became a significant part of his income—as well as important vehicles for distributing his work and growing the size of his audience. With sales fueled by enthusiastic, word-of-mouth publicity, the collections received a great deal of cultural buzz and started topping the *New York Times* best-seller list. It would be difficult to trace the grassroots pathways through which Larson's work effectively went "viral" at this mid-decade mark, but it is likely that much of it originated with the published collections—lethally concentrated doses of *The Far Side* virus that were avidly purchased and spread by thirteen-year-old kids like myself and other followers of offbeat comedy.

The Switch from Chronicle Features to Universal Press Syndicate

Finally, Larson's arrival as a superstar cartoonist was signaled (and perhaps amplified, moving forward), when he switched syndicates from Chronicle Features to Universal in 1985 and signed a new contract that both protected his rights as an artist more clearly and assured his financial success more emphatically. Up until that point Chronicle Features had generally treated Larson well, and he remained grateful to them throughout his career for how they had opened the door to syndication and nurtured and promoted his unusual work. In typically neurotic fashion he had worried in those early years, nevertheless, that his career would be short-lived. And thus when his first contract expired, he felt compelled to capitalize on his budding popularity by switching to "a bigger syndicate with a larger sales force" (Piraro).

Reading between the lines in interviews, it also appears that Larson was generally unhappy with the structure of his first contract with Chronicle Features. Like most fledgling cartoonists, he had been required to sign off on a deal that was unbalanced in the syndicate's favor and unfriendly to an artist's long-term, creative independence (no copyright ownership of the work, lack of control over merchandising and other ancillary uses, and no guaranteed rights to sabbaticals or retirement on the cartoonist's terms or timetable). Given Larson's understandable frustration at these arrangements, Universal Syndicate was an inviting alternative, since they had developed a reputation in the industry for being especially progressive in respecting artists' rights and for finding and nurturing "difficult," alternative cartoonists like Garry Trudeau (*Doonesbury*). True to that track record, it appears from Universal's accounts of the contract negotiations that Larson gained ownership to his cartoons, garnered a greater cut of the profits from syndication and book sales, and could exercise an unusual degree of control over the content of his work (Heintjes).

Universal was also a logical partner for Larson because he had developed a healthy and lucrative relationship with them as publishers of his early book collections. The profitability of that facet of Larson's work, in fact—combined with the prospect of additional monies that could be earned through ancillary merchandising—seems to have been the motivation behind Universal's willingness to give Larson such generous terms. Their expectations were more than satisfied, of course. As *The Far Side*'s popularity continued to grow into the late 1980s, the book collections topped sales charts (selling over 12 million copies), his syndication numbers grew to over eight hundred newspapers, and fans enthusiastically embraced a line of merchandise that included greeting cards, postcards, posters, T-shirts, and cartoon-a-day calendars (Astor, "*Far Side* Cartoonist" 37).

Larson was grateful for the immense income that flowed from these additional *Far Side* products, but he would always harbor queasy feelings about his participation in feeding what he called the "merchandising monster." Specifically, he worried that the unique humor of the panel might eventually be eclipsed by the paraphernalia, and that he would lose his special rapport with fans if they grew to believe he was only "in it for the dollar" (Sherr). In addition, showing that he understood the significance of his reputation for being "alternative," he fretted that all of the secondary products would give the impression that he had sold out, essentially going "mainstream." Ultimately he attempted to avoid the pitfalls of overexposure and egregious misuses by not allowing his syndicate to create atomized, decorative versions of his imagery and characters (such as dolls); the products, in other words, had to be pure reiterations of the cartoons themselves (Sherr).

While some core fans might have felt disenchanted in observing the parade of merchandise that Universal sold in the latter part of Larson's career, there was surprisingly little public backlash about those ancillary activities. In fact, the immense popularity of *Far Side* calendars, T-shirts, coffee mugs, and so on underscored how avidly core readers engaged with Larson's work on a personal and social level. Unlike many newspaper comics that were read superficially, prompting a passing smile, Larson's work was dwelled upon, collected, and purchased in book form; fans also posted favorite installments on office doors, passed books among themselves, or showed off T-shirts and coffee mugs featuring the most iconic panels. In sum, perhaps because Larson's work had emerged as a grassroots phenomenon—with people often discovering it through friends or co-workers—it still felt like a precious resource (despite the massive merchandising) that could be shared, talked about, and celebrated in a variety of ways beyond the comics page.

Controversial Cartoons

As Larson's popularity widened in the late 1980s, effectively achieving blockbuster proportions, the detractors who found it offensive became more vocal. A minority of editors still occasionally complained to Universal about "inappropriate" installments that were disrespectful toward God and religion, that were too scatological, or that "played to the humor of violence" (Bernstein 104). In addition, special interest groups sometimes sent in complaints to newspapers, asking that the cartoon be dropped; at times those letters were sent to Larson directly, demanding that he apologize for inappropriate jokes or begging him to avoid particular types of gags in the future. Amnesty International, for example, wrote a letter of complaint each time Larson created a cartoon about dungeons and torturing; and mental health professionals were often upset that he made light of serious psychological disorders (McCarthy). There were also unofficial protest groups among everyday readers—cat people, dog people, or pious defenders of all things religious—who were predictably provoked whenever a particular cartoon lampooned what they held dear.

Among these constituencies Larson considered "Cat People" to be his "dreaded enemy" because they were easily provoked by any panels about pranks or cruelty involving felines. He ran into trouble with this group on a regular basis, of course, since one of the key themes in *The Far Side* was the introduction of real violence from the natural world into mundane suburban life. Examples include the classic of the dog trying to lure a cat into a dryer with poorly drawn signs promising "FUD" (fig. 1.5); the pathetic image of a cat with two front peg legs looking resentfully at a piranha in a fish bowl (fig. 3.10); or the panel with the kitty delivered to the doorstep of a weirdly excited woman who was actually a dog in disguise (5/24/84; 1–394). On one occasion—when Larson depicted a cat tied upside down, suspended, outside a living room window—the reaction from feline advocates was so strong that he felt compelled to offer a rare explanation and apology (1/16/87; 2–11). He wrote, "Let it be known, it is the dog—in a mafia-like gesture—who had done this to the cat. The humans are innocent—this time" (Larson, "To Whom" 11). As a side note, it is interesting that there were no complaints forthcoming when Larson joked about the

Fig. 1.5: Gary Larson, "Oh please, oh please," *The Far Side*, March 30, 1985 (1-470).

cruelty committed by cats in the real world—like the classic of the feline literally playing with a mouse (by tossing a ball back and forth) before eating it (9/11/84; 1-417); or the one with the petulant cat who is prevented by his master from bringing a whole wagon full of dead prey into the house (4/29/92; 2-400).

Other cartoons that spiked the number of letters of complaint included grotesque happenings in hospital nurseries, like the one in which a nurse good-humoredly shoos an alligator out the door of a roomful of helpless infants, saying "Get, you rascal! Get!," and then calling to the other nurse, over her shoulder, "Heaven knows how he keeps getting in here, Betty, but you better count 'em" (4/1/85; 1-471); references to pornography, even if it only involved amoebas (6/5/86; 1-580); and any installments that depicted God engaging in mundane activities: unsuccessfully trying to create

Acts of God

Fig. 1.6: Gary Larson, "Acts of God," *The Far Side*, December 5, 1991 (2-367).

a chicken in his bedroom when He was a young boy (9/24/85; 1–616), rolling out snakes with Play-Doh (1/11/91; 2–302), and performing corny vaudeville acts (fig. 1.6). In retrospect, Larson understood why these particular cartoons rankled conservative readers, but occasionally he would be caught off guard by vehement reactions to an installment that he considered fairly innocuous. He was perplexed, for example, that a large number of readers were incensed by an image of "Dog Hell" in which naughty canines were condemned to scoop up doggie doo-doo for eternity (6/8/86; 1–582).

In sum, the hate mail Larson received was steady and voluminous, perhaps more than any cartoonist had earned in the history of the medium—enough to fill a room in his house by the end of his career (Reagan xx). Playing upon the name of the feature, everyday critics regularly declared, "This time he really had gone too far," "Larson has gone well beyond the so called 'far side,'" or "This time he's really over the deep end" (Hanson 367). Indignant readers also questioned his sanity, his morals, his sense of humor, his level of taste, etc. Common to many of the letters was the charge that Larson was flouting the rules of this "family medium" and thus should be removed or censored. Anticipating those complaints, a handful of editors did occasionally drop *The Far Side* for a day if they sensed their readers would find a particular installment to be too offensive, but rarely did they cancel Larson's work once it had established a hold in their papers. The immense popularity of the feature effectively protected it from being removed; editors knew, essentially, that the protests they would endure from die-hard fans in the wake of a cancelation would far outweigh the grief they got from the random (albeit, vehemently indignant) armchair critic.

The Difficulties of Celebrity

As Larson's public notoriety grew, he struggled with a significant contradiction at the center of his career: the disconnect between his perceived public persona as a morbid trickster figure on one side, and the reality of his shy and neurotic character on the other. For example, as much as one might want to imagine Larson taking glee at provoking sensitive readers—as if he had the agenda of a taboo-flouting rebel—the reality was that he was genuinely shocked (at least initially) by the volume and tone of the hate mail he received. It surprised him "just how upset some people could be" since he never consciously sought that controversy. He explained that his default assumption was that "everyone in the world has the same sense of humor" as he and his close friends (Cook). He elaborated in an interview on ABC's 20/20 in 1986 (his one national TV appearance): "I never set out to offend anyone. I would never consciously . . . I don't say, 'Gee I wonder if I can ruffle some feathers.' I just end up doing it" (Sherr).

As Larson's fame grew, nevertheless, journalists tended to focus on the morbid and controversial side of his work, reinforcing the general impression that he was a cartooning rebel. His syndicate also learned how to leverage the controversies surrounding his work in their favor, selling the feature as something that would shake up the comics page and generate reader interest. Promotional materials adhered to this script, reinforcing the notion that Larson was a goofily warped individual—a perpetually juvenile-minded prankster hiding behind a bland-looking, bespectacled facade. That strategy was especially evident in book collections that featured odd photos of Larson (such as trapped in an animal display case), jokey exaggerations of his traumatic childhood, or blurbs and liner notes that highlighted excerpts from some of the more pious and ridiculous-sounding letters of complaint (e.g., "Do these [cartoons] come from inmates of prisons & are sold to him [Larson] which he in turn sells (them) to you?") (Lewis 203). The constructed persona of Larson as demented, unhinged, morbid, and so on, effectively became a prominent facet of the *Far Side* brand—a clear indication to fans that they were enjoying a subversive work of popular culture that defied the rules of its square medium.

Vivid public-persona construction has always been a common practice in the comics industry, of course, and one can see how it played a key role in the career of one of Larson's principal idols, Charles Addams. Working as a gothic cartoonist with a capital G, Addams's promotional photos often depicted him in dark Victorian surroundings replete with animal skeletons or other morbid debris. He played up the act too, eagerly sharing exaggerated stories of being married in a graveyard or having perverse family traditions. Larson and his syndicate never went to those extremes, largely because he was almost pathologically reclusive and self-effacing throughout his career. He hated being interviewed, was embarrassed by attention from fans, and hated being recognized in public. Friends and observers who grew to know the real Larson tended to highlight his self-critical, almost neurotic qualities:

> He has a "slight ego and a massive self-awareness. He doesn't need to be idolized, but he doesn't want to be thought of as lame." (Stein)

> In person, I found Larson to be surprisingly shy and modest; he does not try to impress you with his brilliance or overwhelm you with his ego. (Reagan xx)

> I don't think he considers himself a failure, but he is reflexively self-deprecating. (Apello as quoted by Barry, D5)

> Larson "is his own worst critic. He's never been comfortable or complacent. He's like a kid always worrying how long he's going to stay up on his bike, when he's been riding for a long time." (Morrissey as quoted by Barry, D5)

There were some downsides to these anxious, introspective tendencies, as you might imagine. For example, he floundered in television interviews. After being asked a tricky question at a local Ohio station, he had a debilitating panic attack; he recalls, "I couldn't think of anything to say. I was rooted to the spot, like the proverbial rabbit caught in the headlights" (Gumbel). Things went only marginally better in his national television appearance on 20/20 in 1986; in that interview he continually second-guessed his answers, apologized for earlier comments, and berated himself for dithering. As an example, when he was asked if it gave him pleasure to make other people laugh, he responded, after a long pause, " . . . yeah, yeah, I guess it does. Let me think about that . . . Yeah, I guess the answer would be yes, it does. Hell, I'm a cartoonist. What *would* be the answer?" And then later, when he was asked if it were true that he respected animals more than humans, he responded, "Yes. Yes, it would be. . . . well, I don't know if I really believe that or not . . . I guess down deep inside . . . No, I don't. But I don't know . . . I've never met an Irish Setter I didn't like" (Sherr). That chronic self-reflexivity could also emerge in print interviews—like his response to the question about whether he considered himself "normal." After initially saying no, he added, "Who's normal? I have some friends that make me feel pretty normal. I guess everybody's normal and nobody is at the same time. Yeah, I guess I am pretty normal" (Morrissey, "Far Side of Retirement").

There were positive aspects to Larson's self-consciousness, nevertheless. Unlike many cultural celebrities with big egos or a sense of entitlement, he was never mean or intimidating in social situations. At the height of his fame, he still looked and acted like a normal, mild-mannered guy. In addition, his clothing of choice remained consistent throughout his career: T-shirts, jeans and running shoes. And he never displayed any vanity about his glasses, balding pate, and unkempt hair (Kelly 86). Moreover, if he ever received special attention in a social situation—like when he was given a grand tour of the Natural History Museum in Washington by its curators—he behaved modestly. His guides on that occasion described him as reticent, cordial, and shy, only making the occasional "little cryptic comments, full of wit and intelligence" (Barry D5). Colleagues and editors also appreciated his humility, noting that in person he was unfailingly reasonable, apologetic, and kind; and his correspondence was "pithy, astute and self-deprecating" (Morrissey, "Introduction" viii).

Larson's deep-seated humility could have also been a contributing factor in the consistent quality of his work through the full length of his career. Rather than believing his own hype or coasting on his accomplishments, Larson never stopped pushing himself or questioning the quality of *The Far Side*. He explained, "I think one thing that's important to maintain is a sense of fear, always doubting yourself. . . . A good dose of insecurity helps your work" (Holguin, "Gary Larson's Farewell" 5H).

While chronic insecurities and shyness were conducive to the craft of perfecting pithy cartoons in private, they did not help when it came to dealing with the public side of *The Far Side*-mania that took off in the mid-to-late 1980s. Larson grew increasingly annoyed during these years with overly enthusiastic fans that accosted him in stores or took pictures of his house. He lamented, "It used to be simple. . . . Draw the panels and send them out. Now it's too showbiz" (Bernstein 105). Larson's idol, the alternative cartoonist B. Kliban—who gained unexpected fame with his *CAT* cartoons and book—gave some perspective on how this attention can grate on an artist:

> The ego hit is there for maybe an hour a day. It's like getting physically stroked. It feels nice at first, then after a while you think maybe they could lay off a little, and it gets irritating, and then it actually becomes abrasive and even painful. "I don't want it. It doesn't feel good. People will bug you." (Kliban 50)

To avoid being overwhelmed by his increasingly eager fans, Larson initially got an unlisted phone number and stopped doing media appearances in Seattle; he hoped this would result in fewer local people recognizing him in public (Larson, "I Remember" 451). Later he became even more cautious, refusing to appear on television again or have his picture taken (Stein). This helped restore some anonymity, but he was still such a household name that cashiers would sometimes get agitated when seeing his identity on a credit card. Larson admitted that in these cases he would often lie, insisting that he was not *that* Gary Larson (Stein). Two especially harrowing experiences with fans finally cemented his resolve to retreat completely from the public eye. In the first encounter, a female stranger "learned where [he] lived, knocked on [his] door, and asked for an autograph. [He] went to a room in the back of the house to get a pen, turned around, and there she was, standing right next to [him] . . ." (Larson, "I Remember" 450). The second one occurred at a book signing:

> a woman, dressed in a rabbit suit, showed up . . . and hit me with a cream pie. (I think it was actually intended to be a "friendly" pie-in-the-face, but the episode was a little, well, awkward.) And since I had to leave directly for the airport and the pie had actually missed my face but not my shirt, on the flight home I'm sure everyone around me thought I was wearing banana cologne." (Larson, "I Remember" 450)

Larson joked about these awkward moments in later years, but in the moment he was genuinely rattled and used the lingering trauma as a justification to stop doing promotional tours or mingling with readers in any context. At about that same time (1988) he also drastically cut back his interview schedule—deciding to open his door only on rare occasions if he could promote animal conservation or talk about one of his other non-cartooning interests. From that point on he ceased attending professional meetings as well—even to receive his Reuben Awards in 1991 and 1995. It was clear that the psychological and social demands of being a famous comedian were too much for him to endure in perpetuity. Foreshadowing his advocation of periodic sabbaticals and an early retirement, he predicted as early as 1985 that the hubbub would eventually force him to "pull the plug" completely on cartooning in order to preserve his sanity (Bernstein 105).

Larson's Working Methods and Collaborators

While Larson struggled from the mid-1980s onward with the public side of being a superstar cartoonist, he handled the day-to-day pressures of creating excellent cartoons with growing confidence and professionalism. Perhaps in part due to his reclusive nature (and the fact that he had no children to distract him), he had established a highly effective working routine. For starters, he would sit in his studio on the second-floor of a Tudor-style home, surrounded by such artifacts as a stuffed warthog head and a fossilized mastodon tooth given to him by his grandmother (Bernstein 104). And then staring alternately at a blank page and the natural world outside his window, he would drink coffee and free associate, following stray recollections from childhood, watching for stray burps from the unconscious realm, or mulling over tired conventions or clichés from genre entertainment, fairy tales, popular maxims, etc. That raw material would then be filtered and shaped at the intersection of three seemingly contradictory philosophical frames peculiar to Larson's life experience and worldview: scientific naturalism, gothic morbidity, and comic absurdism. In terms of creating original gags, that tension between the rational, the dark, and the silly was highly productive, resulting in cartoons that contained surprising incongruities, nerdily original wordplay, and mind-bending animal–human crossovers. It also produced gothic glosses on mundane moments, irreverent treatments of sacred cows (both figurative and literal, in some cases), and literalistic deconstructions of empty platitudes.

Despite the raw brilliance of these brainstorming methods, the key to Larson's long-term success was his ability to shape carefully his stray ideas into distilled, iconic images and jokes. Fans might have imagined Larson as the cartooning equivalent of an improv virtuoso—spontaneously delivering fully formed gags directly from subconscious realms—but the reality was more banal (but perhaps equally fascinating): like the cartooning world's version of Ernest Hemingway, he had a special talent for revising and refining his raw, unformed comedic impressions down to a powerful essence. Friends and editors, in fact, marveled at his patient and dogged craftsmanship—his ability to rework an idea, eliminating unnecessary words or superfluous details. One observer said that he was "ferocious in guarding against mediocrity and a perfectionist about his art . . . unrelenting when it comes to making his work as good as it can be" (Reagan xx). That level of care can be attributed to a number of factors in Larson's own life and personality: his scientific worldview, always observing and testing the cultural data that passed through his mind; his unusually reclusive nature—a propensity that allowed him to spend long hours happily and patiently distilling his work; and perhaps a sense of humble responsibility to make the most of this unlikely career—to live up to his growing reputation, week after week, as a brilliant comedian.

Larson's collaborators during these years of great success deserve credit as well. He relied on his wife, Toni, for objective feedback, and his key editors (Stan Arnold at Chronicle Features, and Jake Morrissey at Universal, in particular) were essential to the refining process that gave his cartoons potency and clarity. While many syndicate editors in the industry favored family-friendly jokes and bland, cutely merchandisable characters to a fault, a few of the best editors—Lee Salem, Jake Morrissey, and the late Jay Kennedy at King Features Syndicate—were actually fans of antiestablishment comedy. As a result, they advocated for greater artistic and comedic diversity on the comics page and committed themselves to being effective mentors to the quirky talents they discovered. They were still businessmen too, of course, and realized that pragmatic concessions had to be made in translating "weird" material for mass consumption; but they were ultimately devoted to shaping and editing cartoons in ways that did not damage the essence of the creator's work and worldview. Larson, in fact, would have never emerged from obscurity without that help. For example, exchanges between him and his favorite editors reveal that he was insecure at times about his ideas and needed opportunities to bounce them off an objective and intelligent critic; he did not always trust his own ability to see when his gags were too obscure or his references too arcane. In effect, his ability to shape his "alternative" art and comedy into consistently readable, high-quality cartoon packages was contingent on the healthy collaboration he established with these editors.

Dealing with Long-Term Success

By midcareer Larson had established the clout and productive working conditions that allowed him to create consistently original and often stellar cartoons. He had also found ways to overcome the narrative limitations of the single-panel cartoon medium by linking jokes, revisiting a set of core themes, and establishing and distilling a set of iconic character types: the chubby preadolescent nerd; the petty and vindictive scientist; the oblivious and judgmental matron; the everyman cow; the evil duck; the aspiring caveman; the opportunistic and enterprising dog; the pragmatic chicken; and so on. These figures became so familiar to fans, in fact, that they worked as icons of the *Far Side* brand; Larson gradually canonized the types by including them repeatedly in "group photos" in spot illustrations, on book covers and in various promotional materials (fig. 4.1). And thus, beyond serving effectively as recurring characters from cartoon to cartoon, they performed extratextual functions as well, solidifying fans' attachment to the sum of his work, and reinforcing some of the satiric or philosophical ideas articulated in the best installments: chronic human foolishness or myopia, the bracing implications of a naturalistic philosophy, the limitations of anthropocentric worldviews, and the absurdities and indignities of everyday life.

Given the massive output of material required in syndicated cartooning, it was inevitable, perhaps, that the quality of Larson's work would decline, or that he would discover ways to avoid creative burnout as the years passed. We can, in fact, identify a couple of fallow periods in the course of Larson's career—one in 1987 and another in 1990—when *The Far Side*'s quality was less consistent, and Larson tended to rely too heavily on overused tropes or tired puns. But that seems like a petty quibble when one compares the sum of his work to other panel cartoons like *Marmaduke, Dennis the Menace*, or *Ziggy*—features that unapologetically rehashed a handful of formulaic scenarios year after year. In contrast, Larson both employed a much more expansive repertoire of characters, situations, and comedic tropes, and created a greater number of uniquely original comedic ideas than anyone who had ever worked as a panel cartoonist in this daily published medium.

Perhaps one key to maintaining that unusual level of variety and quality was Larson's success at taking the occasional break from his relentless
schedule. Due in large part to Larson's and Garry Trudeau's promptings,
Universal Syndicate adopted a practice in the late 1980s of giving their star
cartoonists a one-month vacation each year. Larson took full advantage of
these regular breaks and also negotiated a full-fledged sabbatical in 1988.
For fourteen months he left the drawing table to go on extended trips to
Africa and the Amazon with his wife, Toni Carmichael (the two had married
the year before); he also moved to New York City for four of those months
to study jazz guitar with one of his heroes, Jim Hall (McCarthy). Larson
relished his freedom from the demands of daily syndication, avoiding "the
drawing table like the plague." By the end of his sabbatical he felt "fresh
and recharged" and so far removed from the grind of cartooning that he
joked about needing to do "50 finger pushups every day for a week" before
he could reengage. The return to full-time joke-writing was also eased by a
new arrangement with his syndicate in which he had to produce only five
cartoons (instead of seven) per week moving forward (McCarthy).

In *The Far Side*'s remaining six-year run (until 1995), Larson enjoyed success and accolades on a grand scale. In 1988 he was again awarded the prize
for best Newspaper Panel Cartoon by the *National Cartoonists Society*, and
in 1990 and 1994 he garnered the Reuben Award for best overall cartoonist in the nation. The popularity of *The Far Side* also spread beyond the
conventional reach of the traditional funnies page, because of the widely
distributed book collections and daily calendars; in a pre-Internet era,
these repackagings served as cartoon meme carriers, penetrating social
ecosystems in which people did not read the daily newspaper. Moreover,
teachers and businesspeople began peppering their presentations with
Larson's work, capitalizing on how his cartoons could soften an audience
by introducing a topic in a creative way or by titillating them with just the
right amount of morbidity or weirdness. Scientists, academics, and people
in technical fields also festooned their office doors with their favorite installments, creating their own sort of idiosyncratically curated *Far Side*
galleries. Beyond entertaining the casual passerby, these ragged collections
could effectively say a great deal about the people behind the doors: the
rough outlines of their personalities, the general nature of their research
interests or nerdy preoccupations, and the quality (or at least, existence)
of their senses of humor.

Larson's popularity within professions traditionally seen as nerdy became a big talking point in the latter part of his career. Scientists, in particular, came to feel that they had found a comedic spokesperson—someone

who saw the world with similarly curious or skeptical eyes and repeatedly tackled topics of interest to them. The *Natural History* magazine made it official, dubbing him the "cartoonist laureate of the scientific community" (Weise). Other groups paid tribute to him in even more inventive ways. Two newly discovered insect species, for example, were named after him: an owl-biting louse was dubbed "Strigiphilus Larsonlarsoni," and a butterfly was labeled "Serratoterga larsoni." The curators at the Dinosaur National Monument also named the tail spike of stegosaurus a "Thagomizer," in reference to a cartoon in which some cavemen invent that word in honor of a recently departed hunting colleague named "Thag." Finally, the California Academy of Sciences honored Larson by creating an exhibit of four hundred science-related *Far Side* cartoons that traveled to natural history museums around the country (Weise; McCarthy; Ferguson). About the louse tribute, Larson joked, "I considered this an extreme honor. Besides, I knew no one was going to write and ask to name a new species of swan after me. You have to grab these opportunities when they come along" (Ferguson).

A number of famous scientists also chimed in with generous praise. Don Kennedy, the editor-in-chief of the journal *Science* effused, "I find him inordinately clever. . . . There's something wonderfully sardonic about the human characteristics he gives to animals. There are so many particular circumstances in science that can be perfectly illustrated by a wry single frame" (Weise). E. O. Wilson, a prominent scientist from Harvard, described eagerly reading fresh *Far Side* cartoons each day and admired how Larson so accurately identified "the foibles of scientists in an affectionate way" (Weise). And then Stephen Jay Gould marveled at Larson's brilliance, dubbing him in the introduction to *The Far Side, Gallery 3*, the "national humorist of natural history" (Gould 10). Larson returned the compliment, writing a tribute to Gould in *Natural History* in which he esteemed Gould to be "one of the most remarkable scientists of our time" and then related the fantasy of serving as his Igor-like assistant (complete with white lab coat and enormous hump), eagerly "fumbling with crania and enraging Gould by mixing up the Homo habilis and Homo robustus skulls" (Larson, "Tribute to Stephen Jay Gould" 57).

There were also the occasional awkward episodes in his dealings with his scientific cohorts—especially when it came to those individuals who insisted that all of his cartoons reflect the natural world with complete scientific accuracy. Behaving somewhat like the fussy pedants Larson skewered in his cartoons, these academics would send corrections on anachronisms or other minor inaccuracies in his depiction of the natural world. Errors

"Well, well — another blond hair.... Conducting a little more
'research' with that Jane Goodall tramp?"

Fig. 1.7: Gary Larson, "Well, well—another blond hair," *The Far Side*, August 26,
1987 (2-80).

they noticed included cavemen appearing alongside dinosaurs, polar bears
interacting with penguins (they live at different poles), or a particular
animal behaving out of its natural character (like a male mosquito doing
the biting rather than the female). Some of these errors were the intentional distortions of comedy, of course, but the occasional unintentional
misstep would distress Larson. As one observer put, he "did not take his
gaffes lightly"; they got under his skin because he was also, to a degree, a
"perfectionist—and a scientist—by nature" (Ferguson).

Perhaps Larson's strangest—but ultimately most rewarding—interaction with a scientific celebrity was when he delved into the world of
Jane Goodall's primate studies in 1987. The hubbub started with a cartoon

Larson published in which a female gorilla, wearing Larsonesque cat-eye-glasses, comments disapprovingly about her simian spouse doing more "research" with that Jane Goodall "tramp" after finding a blonde hair on his back (fig. 1.7). Without Goodall's awareness or approval, one of her top assistants—the chief officer of the Goodall Foundation—wrote an indignant letter of complaint, demanding an apology:

> I was appalled when I saw Larson's *The Far Side* cartoon. . . . To refer to Dr. Goodall as a tramp is inexcusable—even by a self-described "loony" as Larson. The cartoon was incredibly offensive and in such poor taste that readers might well question the editorial judgment of running such an atrocity in a newspaper that reputes to be supplying the news to persons with a better than average intelligence. The cartoon and its message were absolutely stupid. . . . "Tramp"? Hardly. The irresponsibility of *The Star* in choosing to run such an obscenity is disgusting. In fact, any woman should be insulted by the reference that the female—in this case, a typical Larson eyeglass wearing animal—would be unaware of what Dr. Goodall's research really is, its seriousness and the assumption that a female only would have the mentality to look for sexual implications. (Engel 80)

Larson and his people were initially a bit rattled, assuming that this person spoke in an official way for Goodall herself; the reality, however, was quite different. Goodall had been out of the country when the cartoon first appeared and did not even know about her assistant's angry letter until months later. She had long been a fan of Larson's work, and when she did finally see the cartoon in question, her reaction was wholly positive: She guffawed and said, "Wow! Fantastic! Real fame at last! Fancy being in a Gary Larson cartoon!" She was understandably distressed, then, to learn about her employee's earlier letter to Larson. She made plans to write an apology, but other work distracted her, and she never found the time to do it. The situation was finally resolved a year later when the National Geographic Society sought permission to publish this infamous cartoon in the pages of its magazine. After initially being denied reprint rights by Larson's syndicate—the editors were afraid of being sued by Goodall's foundation—the Society looked deeper into the matter. After checking in with Goodall, the misunderstanding was resolved, the two camps forged friendly ties, and the magazine was able to feature the cartoon.

Goodall and Larson eventually met several years later, when he accepted her invitation to spend some time at her research facility at the

Gombe National Park in Tanzania. Despite the goodwill between them, there were still aspects to this visit that were traumatic and absurd—as if drawn directly from the annals of *The Far Side*. Larson and his wife, for example, were determined to rough it in the outdoors when they got to Africa—despite the option of staying in a comfortable guesthouse like the other celebrities (such as Jack Lemmon) in attendance that weekend. He and Toni spent the first afternoon quietly struggling to figure out how to put up a tent, not wanting to bother anyone; meanwhile, the other guests had been enjoying a relaxing swim and drinks while watching the sunset. Then, as if the universe were conspiring against Larson, the tent they'd worked so hard to construct collapsed the next day from young baboons sliding down its roof (Goodall 5).

Later during the visit, while on a hike, Larson was also attacked by Frodo, a chimp that Goodall described as the resident bully. The assault was so intense that Larson had to protect himself by hugging a tree. No serious harm was done, but he sustained a vivid set of bruises and scratches (Goodall 6). Imagining the disturbing, slapstick qualities of this scene, you cannot help but draw a connection to the recurring theme of interspecies competition and conflict in Larson's cartoons. It was as if Frodo were the agent of some kind of cosmic karma, bringing one of Larson's dark jokes to life. Only positive feelings emerged from this trip in the end, nevertheless, and Larson later gave Goodall permission to sell T-shirts with his "tramp" cartoon printed on it, and in 1995 she wrote the introduction for *The Far Side Gallery 5* (Vol II p. 80).

Retirement from *The Far Side*

Through the 1990s Larson's work continued to gather fans and acclaim. *The Far Side* had effectively become a lucrative mini-industry, with 1900 papers around the world subscribing to his daily panel, calendars and merchandise selling briskly, and popular book collections consistently reaching the top of bestseller lists. In light of Larson's solitary disposition and neurotic perfectionism, however, it was inevitable that he would at some point completely retreat from all of the busyness of his career. That date arrived earlier than his syndicates and most of his fans would have liked; in 1995 he bucked the trend of popular cartoons persisting in perpetuity (even if their creators passed on) and retired the strip after a fifteen-year run and over 4,300 cartoons. This move ran counter to the contracts and traditions of his field; perhaps the only other superstar cartoonist to retire both himself and his strip at the same time successfully was Bill Watterson (*Calvin and Hobbes*), in that same year. Larson explained, looking back, that the decision was made much less difficult because of the "unforeseen nature" of his luck-riddled career. Unlike other highly successful cartoonists, he had not aspired to and struggled for that kind of fame and wealth. He was grateful for it, for sure, but he would not miss it; he could let go without regret (Larson, "Final Thoughts" 525).

Some of Larson's explanations for the early exit were jokey and flippant: "You should always leave the party 10 minutes before you actually do," and I have "pushed the rock up to the top of the hill" (Holguin, "Voice from the Far Side"; Stein). In other interviews he was heartfelt and vulnerable, expressing ambivalence and explaining that he had begun struggling from "simple fatigue and a fear that if I continue for many more years my work will begin to suffer, or at the very least ease into the Graveyard of Mediocre Cartoons" (Astor, "Widely" 45). He elaborated: "It was 15 years of deadlines. . . . It can be torture. The clock is ticking on the wall and I'm thinking 'Where is this going?' and staring at a blank sheet of paper. . . . Every week when my batch of weekly cartoons would go to FedEx it felt like a small miracle. Then in a few days, it's 'Here we go again'" (Weise). A drift into complacency seemed to be his greatest fear: "You have to retain a little dose of fear with it, to keep your edge, to feel like every day is show time. . . . You can just start coasting a little bit. I didn't want that to happen. I wanted to bring it to an elegant conclusion" (Cook). In sum, he did not want to become one of "The Drawing Dead . . . You know, those cartoonists where you think 'Isn't he dead?' or 'Shouldn't he be dead?'" (Weise).

The outcry of disappointment from fans was intense, and some colleagues struggled to understand why anyone would want to abandon the good fortune and privileges that come with that level of success. Bruce Beattie, a political cartoonist, griped, "It's a shame that someone with his level of talent doesn't enjoy the work enough to keep on going. If he's not happy, who is!?" (Astor, "Larson Fans" 36). Larson must have worried about appearing spoiled or ungrateful, because he underscored in each interview that the decision was difficult and bittersweet, making him feel wistful and melancholy (Holguin). Moreover, he acknowledged that he had been supremely lucky to earn a good living at a job that did not pose any "serious, life-threatening difficulties"; he elaborated, effusing that it "was just a wonderful experience for me. It's hard to imagine that happening to anyone—to draw cartoons for a living and have all that success follow. It was surreal" (Larson, "Second Most Asked Question" 222; Astor, "Gary Larson and Life" 34).

Even years after Larson's retirement, many fans still held out hope that he would return to the comics page someday. While not making any promises, Larson said, "never say never," and wondered if he might "need to exorcise some ghosts" by returning to the drawing table at some point. He elaborated that one thought still haunted him:

Not every day, and sometimes not for weeks, but sooner or later it creeps into my brain, stays a while, and leaves a lingering sadness after it's gone. It is this: What else didn't I draw? What other ideas and characters are doomed to remain everlastingly in my inkwell, never to have *The Far Side* marquee hoisted over their heads, left to wander forever in the Land of the Undrawn? (Larson, "Final Thoughts" 525)

Longtime followers had to content themselves in the subsequent years, nevertheless, with daily calendars, reruns, book collections featuring previously unpublished work, and iterations of *The Far Side* in other media. Two of the more substantial offshoots included two animated films (*Tales from the Far Side* and *Tales from the Far Side II*) that were created in 1994 and 1997, and a children's book titled *There's a Hair in My Dirt!* The contents of the animated specials—disjointed vignettes that were an undiluted distillation of some of the weirder aspects of his comedy—satisfied core fans but were perhaps too obtuse to please a broad audience. *There's a Hair in My Dirt*, published in 1998, was equally bracing in its reflection of Larson's unconventional and undiluted worldview, but perhaps a bit more accessible. Turning traditional fairy tales upside down in a variety of ways, it follows the adventures of a young princess, Harriett, from the perspective of a family of earthworms. With her head full of ignorant and romantic ideas about the natural world, she blithely skips through an ecosystem, misreading everything she sees. That naiveté ultimately results in her death, as she catches a dangerous virus by kissing an infected mouse she has saved from the clutches of a king snake. While the book is drawn in Larson's goofily appealing style, the story was quite dark and unusual for a children's book. It worked well, nevertheless, as a darkly funny cautionary tale about the brutal realities of the natural world; readers were effectively encouraged to move beyond fairytale visions of nature—replete with cutely magical creatures and inflated romantic predicaments; instead, it suggested they should embrace a more naturalistic worldview that recognizes the existence of pathogens, the competition of species, and the reality of death. Larson added that what he wanted to show was how arbitrary our judgments can be of what is beautiful and what is ugly in nature . . . There's a form of prejudice at work. People get very passionate about saving the whale, but when something like a Florida indigo snake is endangered there are not a lot of people out there holding up placards. (Gumbel)

In fact, that goal of promoting an informed, scientific worldview and championing wildlife and habitat conservation came to dominate Larson's post-cartooning career. Newly retired, with more time on his hands, he often found "himself staring at the walls, wondering how things could have gone so terribly wrong for our planet" (Weise). The acuteness of that concern was sharpened after a couple of eye-opening experiences. One seminal moment came when he returned as an adult to his grandparents' swamp—the place where he had learned to love animals within a complex ecosystem. He reported that

Today the swamp is gone. . . . Filled in and a house or two now stands there, and the creek is just a landscape feature through someone's yard. But the other creepy thing is that, while the drift line is obviously still there, the lizards are all gone. I've gone looking for them, walking among the driftwood on a warm, lizardy kind of day. Not a one. . . . And that's the problem. Everything is getting filled in, dug up, overrun and generally made uninhabitable for everything but humans. Places where animals can live in peace, or at least live, are being destroyed at an increasing rate. (Weise)

Projecting that specific example to larger, planet-wide trends, he lamented, "I can't imagine how we'll be remembered by future generations if we allow this to happen. . . . It's a holocaust, only instead of killing off people, we'll be 'the flora and fauna Nazis'" (Weise).

The second significant epiphany came appropriately—given Larson's interest in Darwinian ways of seeing the world—on a scuba-diving trip to the Galapagos islands in 1996. While there, he was introduced to a nonprofit organization (Conservation International) that could help him to channel his frustrated energies and monetary resources in productive ways. He and his wife both became donors and activists for the group, explaining that they made the commitment because this NGO "flew under the radar," doing real "conservation in the trenches" rather than in glossy magazines (Weise). To elaborate, while some of the most prominent conservation efforts fixated on "charismatic megafauna"—like the World Wildlife Fund's fetishization of endangered pandas—Larson preferred supporting efforts that were more holistic, protecting entire ecosystems and less flashy species like newts (Weise). In addition to donating funds to conservation efforts, Larson created a calendar in 2006, the sales of which were channeled to support similar causes.

On a more personal level, retirement allowed Larson to fully indulge the "demon" that kept chasing him throughout his adult life: learning to play the jazz guitar (Cook). He admitted that one "red flag" for him that it was time to retire was the amount of time he was spending playing music instead of working (Holguin, "Voice from 'The Far Side'"). Given his private and anxious nature, it is no wonder that he turned continually to a pastime that had always allowed him to "forget everything else"—a place where "all your problems are gone," and "you're immersed in another world" (Astor, "Gary Larson and Life" 34). Over the years he had taken advanced lessons from two famous guitarists—Remo Palmier and Herb Ellis—but he still considered himself a neophyte in his retirement years. Perhaps to remedy that situation, Larson constructed a small-scale home studio and began devoting hours of his more open schedule to poring over complicated musical theories (Holguin, "Voice from 'The Far Side'").

In addition to the guitar, Larson turned his attention to scuba diving and the care of a substantial number of pets: two bull mastiff dogs, several snakes, and a carnivorous frog from Argentina. In appropriately morbid fashion, Larson kept a freezer full of "pinkies" (packaged dead mice) to feed his frog. He joked, "Let's just say you don't automatically reach for the vanilla ice cream at my house" (Bernstein 104).

Retreating into favorite hobbies did not result in a complete cessation of work related to *The Far Side*, nevertheless. Because of the immense and ongoing popularity of his work, he created FarWorks Inc., a company to handle ongoing merchandising and image licensing endeavors. With his wife, Toni, acting as a business manager, he added a number of assistants to keep track of business deals, to run interference between him and overly friendly fans, and generally to police misuses of his copyrighted materials (Gumbel). That level of organization ultimately allowed him to think less about his old cartooning life, spending perhaps only a few hours each week dealing with business-related concerns. Indeed, given the quasi-corporate environment of the FarWorks offices in downtown Seattle, it is no wonder that he would want to limit his time within a steel-and-glass-encased sixth-floor office, dealing with employees, scrutinizing merchandise numbers, or worrying about improper uses of his cartons. Despite his immense and unlikely success in the world of mainstream comics, and his significance as a cultural icon, he remained a shy and modest fellow. Moreover, if he had the choice between the public and private sphere, he would always choose to be by himself, playing guitar, or out in the natural world with animals— perhaps someplace similar to the untamed tidelands of his youth, looking under rocks and logs, always alert for the next cool snake or stray newt.

Chapter 2

Deadpan Irreverence with Cosmic Proportions

The Comedy of *The Far Side*

I sometimes got frustrated as an adolescent when reading mainstream panel cartoons such as *Family Circus* or *Ziggy*. Easily bored by gentle humor, I often felt like rattling the pages and yelling, "Be funnier!" As an aspiring cartoonist myself, I knew that comics could be an especially powerful medium for challenging comedy; the unique combination of distilled art, conceptual gags, and pithy language could create humor that was both intellectually stimulating and viscerally surprising. That potential was clear, in part, because I experienced comedic epiphanies on a regular basis when reading *MAD* magazine or coming across the occasional head-trippy panel by Sam Gross or George Booth in *The New Yorker*. It irritated me, then, that most of the real estate on the comics page seemed zoned for clichéd platitudes directed at sweet grandparents or easily amused dog lovers.

Thus conditioned to expect so little surprising funniness from the funnies, I remember feeling sucker-punched, in a good way, upon coming across certain *Far Side* panels for the first time—like the one titled "Early Experiments in Transportation" (fig. 2.1). Trying to recall the particulars of that original encounter, it probably took me a moment to get my bearings because of the unconventional qualities of Larson's work: the dry, straight-faced presentation—like a sober book report or public service announcement; the minimalistic construction of the panel (no dialogue, flat facial expressions, and little movement within the figures); the relatively bland art; and the implication (rather actual depiction) of the impending accident. In sum, this kind of deadpan, conceptual, in-the-moment gag

Early experiments in transportation

Fig. 2.1. Gary Larson, "Early experiments in transportation," *The Far Side*, October 23, 1984 (1-427).

required a bit more mental energy than your typical installment from *Family Circus* to decode. The rewards for that effort were generous, though: the involuntary bark of laughter as I put it all together, and then perhaps a sense of rueful sympathy as I imagined the surrounding narrative (the poor guy's bad luck at drawing the short straw, eager cajoling from his comrades, nervous anticipation, and then crushing [cough] disappointment).

After a number of similarly rewarding encounters with Larson's panels, I was curious: Who was the brilliant weirdo behind these gags? How in the heck did his morbid cartoons make their way onto the bland comics page? And, was this *Far Side* thing too original, too dark, and too funny to last? Partial answers gradually emerged as Larson's fame/notoriety grew, and *The Far Side* not only endured but thrived—despite the fact that there were also a good number of readers who were not amused by his cartoons. Some of those grandmothers and dog lovers (the self-appointed custodians of "family-friendly" humor on the comics page), in fact, probably also felt sucker-punched (in a bad way) upon first encountering Larson's irreverent and challenging panels.

At that time I did not need an academic approach, of course, to understand the basic reasons why Larson's comedy delighted me and confused or provoked others: it was morbid, irreverent, and often absurd, and it featured complicated wordplay and parodies. Years later I am still fascinated, nevertheless, by the deeper social and psychological mechanisms at work in Larson's comedy; I want to understand how his cartoons work as self-contained panels combining visual and verbal ingredients in clever ways, and as cultural texts that made such a controversial splash in that venue, at that historical moment. In addition, I am intrigued by the philosophical dimensions of Larson's comedy—the way that reading his cartoons over time in book collections and on calendars encouraged a person to ponder the unsettling naturalism of the universe or the obliviousness of humanity. This chapter features those explorations, as we delve into the deeper textual, cultural, and philosophical dynamics of Larson's work. We assess more deeply, in other words, what made *The Far Side* funny and intellectually satisfying for fans, and distressing or confusing for its detractors. Moving from basic building blocks to larger cultural meanings and uses, I explore Larson's comedy from a number of different angles: in light of his pragmatic working methods, with the help of basic theories of humor, according to his use of specific comedic tools, and within an understanding of some long-running satiric and philosophical traditions.

Larson's Working Methods

Examining Larson's nuts-and-bolts methods for constructing comedy is a good place to start. He reported that fans were always curious about how he came up with his jokes; they often asked him, predictably, "Where do you get your ideas?" (and often followed that up with "*Why* do you get your ideas?"). While appreciating their interest, he was generally exasperated by this line of questioning, because it implied that there was an easy answer or that there was a "secret tangible place of origin for cartoon ideas"— like (as he once said) a dusty old book in his grandparents' attic with an embossed cover and gold script that read "Five Thousand and One Weird Cartoon Ideas" (Barry D5). Larson also resisted giving elaborately detailed descriptions of his methods because he did not completely understand his own creative process (and perhaps wanted to preserve some of the mystery surrounding the construction of his jokes). Shaking his head, he would say things like, "I don't know," "Not sure," "I have no idea why I drew this or what it means," "It just happens," or, "I sort of let it come out." (Barry D5; Kelly 86; Morrissey, "Introduction" viii; Astor, "Larson Explores" 32). Most elaborately, he described a vague method of free association: I "reach down into my own brain, feel around in all the mush, find and extract something from my persona, and then graft it onto an idea" (Larson, "On Dorothy" 5).

By 1989, however, Larson was more generous in discussing his strategies, even including detailed descriptions of how he brainstormed and refined specific cartoons in his *Prehistory* collection. Drawing from those pages and other late-career interviews, we can stitch together a fairly elaborate understanding of his methods. To begin, he acknowledged that from childhood his imagination was active and free-wheeling—especially in a visual sense—and that he was hyper-aware of the random impressions that struck him as odd or funny (Astor, "Larson Explores" 32). An early observer reported that Larson was spontaneous and open to gathering those ideas wherever he happened to be, always carrying a sketchbook for doodling images or "jotting down phrases" (Kelly 86). Larson later clarified that he was generally more deliberate about the process, scheduling late-night brainstorming sessions in which he would drink coffee, listen to jazz, and confront an empty drawing table:

> I don't have ideas that are coming left and right . . . I'd sit down and go to work. And I would let that part of my mind loose and start to come up with things, start to sketch things. I'd get the juices flowing and then hope something would happen. I don't drive around or go someplace and have thoughts like, "Oh, that would be a good cartoon," or "That's a strange thing; I should remember that." Usually when I sat down to draw a cartoon, it would be more of a reflection of things in my past. Or it could be something I had experienced that morning, or that week, or something I might know that's part of my background. (Morrissey, "Far Side of Retirement")

Given the pressing deadlines Larson continually faced, he was surprisingly unrushed in this process. He recalls investing a lot of time "in just sitting, staring, and thinking," to the point, sometimes, that he wished a "Lou Grant–type person" would burst into his studio once in a while to say, "Larson! Draw!" (Larson, "Second Most Asked Question" 222). He was also flexible and patient in allowing his random impressions to gradually morph into something usable. One of his former editors explained that he

> begins with the seed of an idea, which often doesn't feel traditionally funny, and then tends it a bit to see what takes root . . . [and] sometimes what sprouts isn't what anyone expects, least of all Gary: He plants what he thinks is a carrot and it turns out to be cabbage. (Morrissey, "Introduction" viii)

In sum, the key ingredients of Larson's process seemed to be caffeine, a jazz soundtrack, open-ended time, a distraction-free environment, doggedness, and a flexibility of mind. If the elements came together effectively, Larson relished the process and reported often being able to enter that flow state enjoyed by many artists "where time is a disconnect" and the work unfolds in a pleasurably stress-free manner (Larson, "Second Most Asked Question" 222).

If Larson became occasionally stymied during the early, brainstorming phases of his process, he would give himself a particular subject as a starting point—perhaps a fairy tale, a conventional maxim, or a random subject: "aardvarks or toaster ovens or cemeteries or just about anything" (Larson, "Creative Process" 42); then he would make "strange juxtapositions," perhaps reversing animal or human roles or testing the literal meaning or logic of a conventional saying to its breaking point (Kelly 86). Observers of this strategy were especially impressed with his ability to make those odd connections in such an uninhibited way. Jake Morrissey, his editor at Universal, said he was "struck by how open [Larson was] with his own creativity, how willing he [was] to be guided by it" (Morrissey, "Introduction" viii).

In fact, highlighting Larson's independence of mind during this process may be a key to understanding the originality of his humor. Early in his career he was inspired by the work of a handful of alternative magazine cartoonists, but otherwise he was untutored in the rules and joke-telling practices of the funnies page. His route into syndication preserved much of that productive ignorance. In effect, his backdoor approach—through a local paper and then with a syndicate willing to take a chance on something different—allowed him to avoid the pressures that encourage mainstream cartoonists to create jokes that anticipate demographic tastes or reader sensitivities. And then once Larson gained a foothold in national syndication, he intentionally (and sometimes unknowingly) continued to nurture his originality in a variety of ways: remaining aloof from the professional meetings in his field, engaging with fans from a distance, and renegotiating his contract so that he had more control and ownership over what he created.

Intent on protecting that comedic independence, Larson was naturally inclined to cater to his own sense of humor, rather than trying to anticipate predictable, crowd-pleasing gags. He said that his driving impulse was to make *himself* laugh, recalling, "I was just in tune to myself, in tune to my sense of humor. I feel I always had a really direct link with that part of

me—pretty unfiltered in that sense" (Morrissey, "Far Side of Retirement").
He elaborated that being true to his own sense of humor and worldview—
rather than trying to appease others—was critical to maintaining the quality of his work:

> I think it's vital to be honest with yourself. You do have to satisfy
> yourself first. If you're drawing something, you have to ask yourself
> if it's something you genuinely think is funny. Or is it starting to
> fall into just a category, just kind of a shtick thing? I think it's im-
> portant for all cartoonists to be honest with themselves about their
> own sense of humor and what they're doing. (Morrissey, "Far Side
> of Retirement")

Controversy was another outgrowth of that determination to channel
his own interests and humor so purely. Readers who were unfamiliar with
his comedic strategies, or unsympathetic toward his worldview, were usually confused or offended by his relatively weird gags. Interestingly, these
negative reactions tended to surprise Larson; he was so deeply engaged in
listening to his own impulses—and unable to shake the habit of assuming
that everyone in the world shared the same sense of humor as he and his
"six closest friends"—that he felt blindsided at times by especially negative reactions (Cook). Fortunately, he was never so deeply bothered by the
pushback as to change course; showing a quiet and tenacious resolve, he
essentially remained true to his own idiosyncratic muse (who surely had
big hair and wore cat-eye glasses) for fifteen years.

Shaping and Editing Ideas into Polished Cartoons

While Larson preserved many of the original facets of his comedy through
a strategy of isolation, he was still deeply committed to pleasing his core
readers by making a quality cartoon each day. And the final stages in his
cartoon-construction process reveal how carefully he tried to finalize his
quirky ideas into accessible, highly polished comedy landmines. That hon-
ing process included revising ideas, distilling captions and imagery, and
collaborating with a spouse and editors who could objectively "proofread"
his work.

First, let us understand his methods for shaping raw ideas into coherent cartoons: Once Larson had the inkling of a concept, he would then try
to shape it into a funny cartoon in a holistic sense, imagining from the

Chicken nudist colonies

Fig. 2.2. Gary Larson, "Chicken nudist colonies," *The Far Side*, January 8, 1987 (2 10).

start the final, overall comedic effect of the entire rectangular "canvas." That holistic shaping included tethering the image and text to the same purpose; distilling the caption and characters down to their most efficient essences; making sure that the final product communicated a funny and original stand-alone joke; and fitting the entire gag into the overall tone or (il)logic of the *Far Side* universe. This end-oriented approach differed, it should be pointed out, from the way many panel cartoonists tended to approach their process—beginning with either a funny doodle (and then searching for a joke), or starting with a comedic caption that just needed an illustration. By not atomizing the parts of his craft in that way—by keeping his sights set on the big picture of both the individual panel and the cartoon as a brand—he effectively distinguished *The Far Side* from the majority of magazine panel cartoons that seemed to serve as neutral windows opening onto a series of unrelated gags. In contrast, Larson's square space always revealed the same strange but coherent universe; each cartoon, in effect, was built according to a distinctive "attitude" and contributed to a consistent (albeit always absurd and surprising) worldview (Larson, "On Dorothy" 5).

To see Larson's methods of refinement and distillation at work, we can trace the development of his classic cartoon about a chicken nudist colony that he allowed a television crew to film as it was under construction (fig. 2.2). First, the kernel of Larson's idea for this cartoon showed comedic promise because it ventured into vaguely taboo territory (nudity) in a way that was also inherently goofy (at a private colony—a place readers might associate with less-than-attractive individuals who cavort about in awkward ways). And then Larson's free-associative process led to a productive juxtaposition (an animal–human crossover) that delivered a surprising but weirdly logical incongruity: if chickens were to appear nude, they would have to lose their feathers, right? And wouldn't that require some uncomfortable plucking? The humor in the implied answer is heightened by Larson showing us only the aftermath of what must have been a painful process: bare chicken bodies covered in stubble and the occasional stray feather left behind.

In terms of visual distillation, Larson amplified the humor (and perhaps underscored the animal–human overlap) by reducing the chickens to a clumsy, iconic essence: flightless, round, and stubby, they are the sedentary schlubs of the bird kingdom. He also gave them minimalistic and dispassionate demeanors—eyes hidden behind human glasses, flat-eyed stares, and fairly static poses—thus making them appear jaded and bored at what should be a relatively festive event. An earlier draft included a shack at the center of the action; Larson replaced it with a volleyball net, thus allowing for some funny imagery of flightless birds playing an unlikely sport. But even the individual chickens involved in that game seem to be exerting only a minimal effort, just going through the motions. The overall blandness of the partying and the simplicity of the drawing effectively gave the cartoon a straight-faced tone, thus inviting the reader to participate in constructing the humor.

The textual elements in the cartoon were also refined down to the most effective essences. The caption, for example, could be considered high-concept, since everything you need to know is contained in three words—"chicken nudist colonies." A less perfectionistic cartoonist might have ended up overexplaining the idea, writing something like "If chickens had nudist colonies . . ." or "Nudist colonies in the animal world." Larson actually gave in to that impulse to overdescribe in his first draft of the sign planted within the frame itself; initially it read, "Happy Grove Featherless Beach," redundantly emphasizing the comic aspects of the plucked chickens. In the final draft it stated succinctly and cryptically, "No Ducks." That adjustment added a weird depth to the overall cartoon, suggesting a larger history to the place (with disturbing scenes of earlier nude chicken–duck disputes, perhaps), and engaging in a bit of commentary about human nature (the impulse to divide, classify, and ostracize).

This rare glimpse of Larson's process illustrates the perfectionism described by editors like Jake Morrissey; he explained that

Larson is a rigorous, even ruthless, editor of his own work, writing and rewriting his captions so the flow of the words matches the cartoon's art and tone. He understands that the heart of a successful cartoon lies in the writing. Good writing can save bad art, but good art can never save bad writing. That is why Larson willingly reworked captions word by word to get them right. . . . (Morrissey, "Introduction" ix)

At times this drive to hone and perfect became slightly neurotic or obsessive, with Larson fixating for too long on a minor detail, allowing it to grow out of proportion to its real significance (Larson, "Final Thoughts" 524). Morrissey reported, for example, once having "six different phone conversations in one day about a single word in a caption" (Morrissey, "Introduction" ix).

Despite the advantages of doing much of the early drafting in protective seclusion, Larson clearly needed objective help at the later stages. His wife, Toni, was the most immediate resource; he described her as a "reliable editor" and appreciated her capacity to look at something he'd "worked really hard on, and then, with eyes full of love, gaze into [his] and softly say, 'That's not funny'" (Larson, "Acknowledgments" xviii). He also trusted a handful of syndicate editors to help him see when ideas weren't working or to suggest ways to fix a problem. Realizing that many of his cartoons could be obtuse, Larson would often include jokey notes to his editors like this: "Do you get it, and did you get it right away? This is a test. Do not attempt to ask someone else" (Morrissey, "Far Side of Retirement"). At the start of his career, when he was with Chronicle Features, the editorial feedback he received was fairly blunt at times, amounting to rejections of ideas that were too confusing or disturbing; as the years passed, however, and Larson got better at his craft, editors served more like collaborators—objective ears for testing and refining the nuances of a cartoon. As an example, Larson remembered Morrissey's help as "invaluable":

Let me say this about editors in general: Not having a good one is like doing brain surgery with a butter knife—you can do it, but you're always paranoid the other surgeons are rolling their eyes when you're not looking. What a relief to have someone standing next to you hand you a sharp scalpel and just say, "Cut that thing, Gary! Right there! Cut it, damn you!" (Larson, "Acknowledgments" xviii)

For someone as neurotic as Larson, it must have been comforting to have an editor who was not just serving as a gatekeeper (ruling out odd

or offensive installments) but also willing to jump in as a real collaborator. Morrissey remembers that on Monday mornings they would look at a
week's worth of work and "discuss each cartoon, addressing the points he
raised in the notes he attached, editing language or modifying art when
we agreed it was necessary" (Morrissey, "Introduction" ix). And because
Morrissey was committed to protecting the weird and unique qualities of
Larson's comedy, he would sometimes think and behave in very un-editor-
like ways. As an example, he would occasionally wonder to himself, "Should
we release a cartoon that not everyone would understand, or use one that
more people might understand but that might not be as funny? More often
than not, funny won out" (Morrissey, "Introduction" x).

After seeing the amount of care and labor that went into Larson's process, it should make sense that he often bemoaned the pressures of coming up with so many cartoons, day after day, year after year. Moreover,
while other newspaper cartoonists made that challenge easier by relying
on narrative continuity (thus efficiently stringing together a number of
related cartoons), and establishing recurring characters (who could suggest ready-made gags based on their personalities), Larson had to create a
wholly original, stand-alone, comedic gem each day. A few colleagues and
fans may still begrudge him his early retirement, but this description of his
especially thoughtful and exacting methods should leave us with a sense
of amazed gratitude that he pursued the craft for as long as he did (fifteen
years) and that he knew when to stop, while *The Far Side* was still great.

Theories of Humor and Laughter Applied to *The Far Side*

Moving into more academic territory, we can explore Larson's comedy
with the help of five traditional theories used to explain how jokes elicit
humor and laughter: relief, superiority, recognition, incongruity, and play.
To begin, Larson's work regularly featured jokes that included "inappropriate" subject matter or that reminded of us our physical, animal nature. In
his carnivalesque world it was implied that heavyset middle Americans
have weird sex lives (fig. 0.1); that aliens might accidentally be shaped like
human butts (and have the bad luck of making first contact with a herd of
goats) (9/21/85; 1–512); that people are slaves to their physical appetites in
vivid ways (like the heavyset woman desperately holding on to a parking
meter while being torn by gale-force suction into a candy shop) (1/12/82;
1–254); and that we have to beware of odd recluses like Doug (fig. 2.3). Some
of that material seems mild in light of the cavalcade of unhinged comedic

Fig. 2.3. Gary Larson, "Beware of Doug," *The Far Side*, March 26, 1983 (1-290).

texts that dominate our cultural landscape today, but within their original venue and historical moment—the highly tame, thoroughly filtered mainstream newspaper comics pages of the early 1980s—the relative irreverence of these cartoons was either delightfully surprising or disturbingly inappropriate.

The Relief Theory

To understand those vivid and varied reactions we can first look to the relief theory of humor. This model conjectures that we laugh at jokes that feature taboo material or involve some aspect of human behavior that we usually repress or deny (the fact that we all pass gas, for example). According to Freud's view of our conflicted, unconscious psyches, we go through life experiencing a low level of psychological tension: on the one side, we have our animal appetites urging us to seek out immediate pleasure or to behave in uncivilized, often aggressive, ways; on the other side, our fatherly superegos (steeped in the rules of religion and civil society) inhibit us from doing or saying all kinds of "inappropriate" things. A comedian like Larson is given the license to provide temporary relief from those bubbling tensions by finding artful ways to express repressed impulses or hostilities, to bring up taboo subject matter, and to poke fun at our flawed, biological nature.

Of course, Larson did a lot more to provoke laughter with these cartoons than just break the etiquette of respectable society or flout the unwritten rules of the comics page. If his gags had simply spilled over with crude humor day after day, core fans would have quickly grown bored, and Larson would have potty-humored himself right off the comics page. What made the irreverence palatable and funny was Larson's artful coding of the dicey subject matter into clever wordplay, resonantly familiar situations, and a coherent worldview about the awkwardness of our physical bodies. Consider, for example, Larson's panel about the dog going to the vet to get "tutored" (fig. 2.4): first of all, jokes with inappropriate material work best if they come at a person indirectly and abruptly, perhaps couched in a Freudian slip or the misuse/misunderstanding of a word, as in this case. And then there's additional humor evoked in this panel by the irony of the reader knowing more (sadly, a lot more) than the naively enthusiastic canine. And by anthropomorphizing the dog—by essentially making him act like a human child—the joke is given a familiar, resonant ring, reminding a reader, perhaps, of a time when he or she misread the world and its complicated words in an embarrassing way. Finally, the juxtaposition of the dog's cheerful ignorance against the harsh realities of life (a common trope in Larson's universe) gives the joke a poignant aftertaste.

Moving on, we can speculate about why irreverent jokes elicit such divergent reactions at different moments among different crowds by triangulating a few key factors: the venue in which the comedy is featured, the worldview of the persons receiving it, and the cultural moment in which it takes place. If a person, for example, in an accidental trip of the tongue, announces to a few friends at a private dinner that she feels a deep emotion with "all of my fart" (instead of "heart"), everyone has a good chuckle. If the same verbal slip, however, is delivered at a site where expectations of propriety are elevated—over a pulpit in a church, perhaps, with hundreds of people reverently paying attention—the resulting laughter might be especially explosive. In addition, the reactions within that congregation

"Ha ha ha, Biff. Guess what? After we go to the drugstore and the post office, I'm going to the vet's to get tutored."

Fig. 2.4. Gary Larson, "Ha ha ha, Biff," *The Far Side*, May 25, 1985 (1-485).

might be radically different—with some churchgoers gasping in shocked dismay instead of laughing—based on their relative capacity to tolerate a bit of unscripted irreverence. Finally, the historical moment in which the taboo comedy appears has to be considered. A mildly off-color joke about a baby's soiled diaper, for instance, might have triggered a cascade of manic laughter among students in an early 1940s classroom (while scandalizing their authoritarian teacher), but the same joke might provoke only an isolated giggle or two in a typical classroom today, where kids are already addled on *South Park* gags or *Captain Underpants* wordplay.

Applying these ideas to Larson's cartoon about dog tutoring, we can imagine that the joke would have seemed tame, or even a bit bland, in a venue that regularly featured taboo-busting zaniness—the pages of *MAD* magazine, for example. Moreover, in our current historical moment, in which we are awash in irreverent comedy, it also strikes one as almost sweetly discreet in its layered wordplay about castration. When we place it back in its original venue and moment of arrival, however—the aggressively censored, family-friendly comics page of the mid-1980s that was policed by an older generation of sensitive pet lovers raised with stringent notions about social etiquette—the panel's original, concentrated potential to provoke either surprised delight or shocked disgust becomes evident.

In some settings "inappropriate" joking can also perform vaguely subversive political functions. This brand of comedy is often called "carnivalesque" because of its roots in traditional folk-festival traditions; it works as a type of bottom-up social expression where the genteel and restrictive rules of everyday "first life" are replaced during a temporary "second-life" experience (or text) featuring rowdy inversions, scatological joking, celebrations of the grotesque, and overindulgence in satisfying bodily appetites. On a basic level, the festive laughter created by this kind of irreverent comedy can challenge restrictive codes of thinking and behavior or question hierarchies of privilege; according to Mikhail Bakhtin, it provides a sort of working-class victory over supernatural awe, the sacred, death, authority figures, upper classes, and "all that oppresses and restricts" (Bakhtin 92).

At the same time, because carnivalesque comedy traditionally tends to be temporary and ambivalent in its attacks (both denying *and* renewing what it mocks), it cannot be considered wholly subversive in terms of its long-term impact on a dominant culture. Consider, for example, an earthy play that might have poked fun at local town elders within a sanctioned carnival in a medieval European community. Because of the temporary nature of that cheeky performance on one isolated festival day—and the overarching permanence of the "first-life" social hierarchy and belief systems during the rest of the year—that brand of sanctioned irreverence might have even reinforced, to a degree, the values and power of cultural authorities. Perhaps it worked, to a degree, as a figurative safety valve that released pent-up social discontent or psychological tension in a largely harmless manner (Bakhtin 9–13).

The potential for taboo-challenging humor to have lasting, democratic political effects might be increased, nevertheless, if we update the context to the United States in the twentieth century. In particular, accessible modern media like cinema and newspapers allowed for carnivalesque texts to become a lasting part of the cultural landscape and people's everyday lives. And thus a film by Charlie Chaplin that mocked genteel cultural guardians from a working-class perspective—or a rowdy newspaper comic like Walt Kelly's *Pogo* that took on the rigid tenets of midcentury McCarthyism— might have amounted to genuine brands of grassroots subversion. These popular texts had the genuine potential to change viewers'/readers' world-views in progressive ways, using unbridled laughter to challenge cultural dogma, mock inflated authority figures, and bind disparate audiences in a democratic acknowledgment of our shared, flawed humanity (Dale 11, 16).

While Larson's subversive brand of joking lacked the topicality of Kelly's satire, his cartoons did feature a consistent, artful irreverence that had vaguely ideological dimensions and effects. For example, as a core fan encountered one of Larson's more famously inappropriate cartoons, he or she might have experienced another layer of amusement at the thought of Larson breaking the rules of a rigid comics page and upsetting reaction-ary readers. And then as they observed Larson get away with that kind of cheekiness month after month, he achieved in their minds the status of an antiestablishment prankster who ran counter to the staid conven-tions of his medium and challenged the normative values of mainstream culture. Moreover, as they read his book collections and identified larger philosophical patterns in his work (such as naturalistic deconstructions of religious myths and anthropocentric worldviews), Larson might have even graduated in their minds to the role of cosmic satirist—a social critic in clown's clothing who used seemingly inconsequential and indirect potty humor to articulate a bracingly subversive worldview.

The Superiority Theory

According to the Superiority Theory, comedy sometimes serves as a weap-on, provoking laughter among likeminded people as they read or listen to jokes that tap into repressed hostilities or mock (and sometimes scapegoat) individuals or groups that they view as inferior. In its most malignant form, superior humor can be bigoted, attacking groups of people based on falsely constructed stereotypes related to ethnicity, gender, or class status. A brief perusal of comedy throughout American cultural history confirms that this kind of condescending laughter thrived in a number of eras and settings—particularly in mainstream media like comics and animated films during the first half of the twentieth century.

Superior humor can also take on benign or socially useful forms when the targets of the comedy deserve the reader's contempt: officious bureau-crats, greedy opportunists, or ignorant blowhards. In determining whether *The Far Side*'s brands of mockery were bigoted or justified, two traditional criteria are helpful: first, we can ask whether Larson's targets were being mocked for willful foolishness (bad thinking or behavior that they chose to commit) or for inherent cultural, gender, or ethnic traits (neutral qualities over which they had no control). And second, we can consider whether the joking about characters' physical flaws (obesity or bad eyesight, for example) was simply shallow, superior mockery ("You're fat, haha . . .") or a type of metaphorical joking that was more complex (pointing to larger, justifiably mockable, moral failings) (Swift 529).

Larson's work generally passed these tests with a few qualifications. A majority of the fools who paraded through *The Far Side* deserved the reader's laughing contempt: matronly women who chose to see the world through critical lenses, forever judging others inaccurately or reading a situation with dogmatic narrowness; arrogant and immature intellectuals, prone to pedantic squabbles or wrongheaded experiments; shlumpy, officious bureaucrats; self-made idiots whose foolish thinking or behavior invited the universe to bite back; and mean kids who conducted sadistic experiments on insects and small animals. From a distance, nevertheless, some of the physical deficiencies of these characters might initially seem undeserving of mockery; what's fair about poking fun at their thick glasses, plus-sized profiles, or bad postures? A careful application of the second criterion (physical flaws needing a metaphoric connection to moral failings) suggests that these exaggerated traits often pointed to larger satiric meanings. For example, thick lenses connoted cultural myopia; cat-eye glasses, with their slanted angle, signaled ossified attitudes and knee-jerk disapproval; obesity and rolled shoulders registered laziness and cultural complacency; and pinheaded craniums might have represented devolution—a sign that the culture was squandering its intelligence on lame entertainment or narrow intellectual pursuits. In light of that assessment, we might feel justified, for example, in laughing at the pathetic image of a fat kid with glasses at the Midvale School for the Gifted pushing fruitlessly against a door that explicitly says PULL (fig. 2.5).

Perhaps the greatest misuse of superiority-driven humor in the history of comics media was the scapegoating of ethnic minorities. In the decades straddling the start of the twentieth century, entire cultural groups—the Irish, Jews, African Americans—were often reduced to caricatures based on the specious theories of eugenics, and reflecting a set of anxious, condescending lies about that ethnicity's essential nature (Bhabha 66). In subsequent decades those racist practices coexisted with more complex and progressive uses of ethnic humor—characters, for example, who wore the outward shell of a stereotype but behaved in more sympathetic ways,

Fig. 2.5. Gary Larson, "Midvale School for the Gifted," *The Far Side*, January 1, 1986 (1-634).

embodying trickster figures, wise fools, and downtrodden everymen. Under pressure to make their cartoons more politically correct and "polysemically flexible" (and thus more commercially viable), cartoonists also migrated those deeply established ethnic stereotypes into animal proxies such as mice, cats, and possums (Gordon 62; Sammond 218). By the 1960s, blatantly racist material had largely disappeared from the comics page, and even vestigial ethnic caricatures in animal form were uncommon or largely separated from earlier, bigoted codings. For better or worse, by the time Larson began his career, ethnically themed comedy was essentially taboo territory for newspaper comics, and the few ethnic minorities that were featured in newer comics were often boring and two-dimensionally admirable.

So how did Larson's comedy fit into that conflicted tradition? For starters, like a lot of comics from that era, *The Far Side* tended to avoid

ethnicity-based humor altogether. The majority of Larson's human characters were doughy, white Middle Americans. During the cartoon's fifteen-
year run, we can identify approximately a dozen gags related to a character
being black, Italian, Irish, or Jewish, and none of those installments relied
on tired stereotypes to get a laugh. In addition, while earlier cartoonists
like George Herriman (*Krazy Kat*) and Walt Kelly (*Pogo*) used anthropomorphized animals to address issues of race and class in allegorical ways,
Larson's animal–human crossovers felt largely aracial—their codings being
more about interspecies dynamics than coded depictions of caste systems
within human society. The one exception might have been the periodic use
of anthropomorphized Holstein cows to represent a brand of repressed,
overweight, white, Protestant Americans.

On one level, this strategy of general avoidance was a sensible way of
escaping the tired practices of golden age cartoonists who seemed incapable of resisting the impulse to create racist jokes and stereotypes. On
another level, the dearth of ethnic-themed jokes in *The Far Side* seems
like a missed opportunity to be edgy in an additional way (since Larson
was otherwise willing to approach taboo material from original angles).
It is fun to imagine, for example, how he might have explored jokes about
passive brands of racism or misuses of insider-oriented ethnic humor. In
fact, traces of that potential to deconstruct stereotype-driven comedy
could be seen in Larson's occasional parodies of how traditional comics
and genre films represented Native Americans or members of "primitive"
tribes. In these cases Larson usually inverted the predictable tropes and
stereotypes of classic Westerns or old *Tarzan* movies; in one panel we
encounter a "primitive" tribal war party consisting entirely of chanting
lawyers with briefcases (7/29/92; 2–418), and in another, Native American
warriors irritate the U.S. cavalry by shooting rubber suction-tipped ar-
rows (3/4/80; 1–20). The best cartoons in this vein take the parodic inversions into more fully deconstructive territory and show a sophisticated
awareness of the lasting sore spots and ironies of a postcolonial world;
consider the installments, for instance, where first world explorers are
alarmed to see their "primitive" pursuers pass them easily with the help
of an outboard motor (fig. 3.14), or the cartoon in which a tribal leader
tells everyone to hide their modern-day conveniences when they see the
arrival of "Anthropologists!" (fig. 2.6).

Another long-standing misuse of superior humor in twentieth-century
comics was the crush of patronizing jokes about, and sexist typing of,
women. While each generation had exceptions to the rule—for example,
female cartoonists who created "girl" strips like *Brenda Starr* (Dale Mesnick)

"Anthropologists! Anthropologists!"

Fig. 2.6. Gary Larson, "Anthropologists! Anthropologists!" *The Far Side*, July 10, 1984 (1-404).

or *Cathy* (Cathy Guisewite) that addressed gender roles in playful ways—the majority of comics produced by men tended to stereotype women into a handful of reductive roles: air-heady nymphs, controlling wives, and doddering grandmothers. And while the worst brands of *ethnic* typing had faded to a large degree in the medium after the 1940s, sexist humor persisted well into the 1960s and 1970s in strips like *Li'l Abner* (Al Capp), *Beetle Bailey* (Mort Walker), and *B.C.* (Johnny Hart). The key female characters in *Bailey*, for example, consisted of Miss Buxley (a skimpily dressed, hourglass-shaped secretary), Private Blips (another secretary who is supremely unfeminine and competent), and Martha Halftrack (the domineering and heavyset spouse of General Halftrack). In *B.C.* the reductive typing was unapologetically on display as the two main female characters conformed to (and were reductively named after) physical types: "The Fat Broad" and "The Cute Chick."

It is worth noting that these chauvinistic practices amounted to a strange blind spot in an industry that prided itself on policing inappropriate content of all varieties, whether the material deserved it or not. On the one hand, political satire and irreverent humor were disallowed, but sexist depictions of women were seen as harmless or as natural reflections of societal attitudes. It would be interesting to see if the persistence of those practices was abetted by the dominance of syndicate and newspaper editorial offices run by men with old-school mind-sets; those backward-looking attitudes were certainly encouraged up into the 1970s within the joshing clubbiness of the male-dominated National Cartoonists Society. As an example, there was a long-standing tradition from the 1950s into the early 1970s of the yearly convention newsletter including nude drawings of various artists' female cartoon characters.

By the time Larson arrived on the comics page, those unthinking traditions were beginning to be challenged by cartoonists like Garry Trudeau (*Doonesbury*) and Lynn Johnston (*For Better or Worse*). Trudeau, for example, boycotted the NCS for a time because of its chauvinistic traditions, and he and Johnston both avoided the hyperbolic gender typing common in older strips. They did this comedically by avoiding stereotypical gags, and aesthetically by depicting the body and facial types of men and women as only nominally different. In the few cases where constructed gender identities became a prominent part of Trudeau's comedy—as with storylines featuring the image-obsessed cheerleader/actress Boopsie—he effectively parodied the practices of older cartoonists or satirized a culture invested in shallow notions of beauty and celebrity. Finally, Johnston and Trudeau still found ways to include gender-oriented comedy in progressive ways, featuring screwball battles between the sexes that unfolded according to naturalistic, and sometimes even feministic, perspectives.

Larson's methods of female typing fell somewhere between the old-order traditions and the progressive moves of Trudeau and Johnston. On one side—in concert with the older professionals within the NCS—Larson relied heavily on some reductive female types: crotchety grandmothers and large, domineering mothers/wives. In a vein similar to Trudeau and Johnston, however, he did not engage in winking objectification of younger female characters, and he tended to parody (rather than lazily repeat) assumptions about stereotypical gender roles/identities in his panels. This mildly progressive orientation, for example, is on display in his treatment of middle-aged married couples. According to traditional, sexist practices, the large, battle-axe wife was paired with the "little man"—a nebbishy husband who was emasculated both at the office and on the domestic front. While this male character was also a reductive type, the comedy in those older cartoons tended to favor his worldview and sympathize with his complaints; in particular, jokes tended to rehash hoary conceits about modern wives being unattractive, uninterested in sex, and determined to limit a male's freedoms and manhood. Larson avoided those regressive conventions in several ways. First of all, husbands in *The Far Side* matched their wives in size, physical profile, and general foolishness; second, gags about dysfunctional marriages avoided privileging the male's worldview. Finally, Larson's approach to drawing the faces and eyes of bickering couples prevents us from favoring one figure's experience over the other's; the motivations of both were usually left inscrutable—hers hidden behind opaque cat-eye glasses, and his within the slit of a vacant brow.

In some cases Larson exaggerated the stereotypical qualities of the domineering wife to an absurdist breaking point, effectively moving into deconstructive territory. The following panels, for example, feel like self-aware parodies of the previous generation's sexist jokes about the abuse endured by the poor Walter Mittys of the world: a heavyset woman in spectacles and safari gear orders a stressed-out husband to tickle the belly of an alligator as it violently upends their canoe (10/21/82; 1–249); a similarly proportioned wife berates her spouse for embarrassing her as he's being eaten by a crocodile at the zoo (10/2/80; 1–68); and in another, the wife screams at her mate in self-righteous panic, insisting that he's about to kill them both because he turned into a quiet parking lot via a lane that is clearly marked with a one-way arrow going the other direction (7/27/83; 1–317). In a few cases the woman and man are engaged in romantic, rather than combative, relations, but even those installments tended to subvert traditional conventions, depicting the couple in birdlike mating behavior (fig. 3.15), wearing an armory of sharp tools on an intimate date (fig. 0.1), or playing a ridiculous game of "swing me in a circle" in a bland living room (fig. 3.12). In sum, sexuality and gender difference were still facets of these marriages and various male–female encounters in *The Far Side*, but Larson approached them like a dispassionate (albeit, slightly demented) anthropologist, emphasizing biological imperatives, highlighting mundane realities, and mocking absurd cultural practices.

Schadenfreude, humor evoked by the pleasure of seeing bad things happen to other people, is often linked to the superiority theory. It was clearly evoked by many of Larson's cartoons since violent mishaps routinely

It was an innocent mistake, but nevertheless,
a moment later Maurice found himself receiving
the full brunt of the mummy's wrath.

Fig. 2.7. Gary Larson, "It was an innocent mistake," *The Far Side*, December 12,
1993 (2-521).

befell his characters; in his words, they regularly "got crunched, speared,
shot, beheaded, eaten, stuffed, poisoned, and run over about twice a week.
Tastefully, of course" (Larson, "On Dorothy" 6). It is conjectured that we
laugh at this kind of morbid comedy primarily because we are relieved
that these unfortunate things are not happening to us (a bit of low-level,
self-interested sadism, apparently). But only the most perverse reader
would laugh at scenes of undiluted tragedy, of course; thus, the comedian
must frame unfortunate incidents with enough distance—or through the
filter of a comic tone—to make it funny rather than tragic. This idea is also

expressed in the maxims "Comedy is tragedy viewed from the wings" and "Tragedy plus time equals comedy."

According to Larson's detractors, he didn't get the equation right. They charged that his jokes were "sick" and that he "too frequently" played "to the humor of violence"—creating jokes, for example, out of torture, hangings, and death at the jaws of wild animals (Bernstein). Those critics may have had a valid point if you focus on Larson's earliest work. During his cartoon's first year in national syndication, he often depicted violent events *in process* and showed the vivid panic on the victim's face (bugged-out eyes, sweat drops flying, lines of agitation around their figure); as a result, readers were not given adequate distance to be amused rather than horrified. But with time, Larson realized that showing violence as it unfolded was a "tad grotesque" and thus learned a number of techniques to create that essential shift in tone or proximity. He would often imply the prospect of tragedy by presenting the scene that either preceded, or immediately followed, the violence. As an example, consider the fairly static "before" image where a guy in a neighboring bathroom stall accidentally mistakes a wrathful mummy's stray wrappings for toilet paper—fig. 2.7. Other times he would give the victim a distant, faceless anonymity, or tamp down the display of movement or emotion at the critical moment, thus giving the scene a deadpan, ironic flavor (Larson, "Creative Process" 45). Combined, these practices underscore a key reason Larson chose the genre of single-panel cartoons rather than strips: he didn't want us to get too attached to his characters, given the misfortune they'd routinely experience (Larson, "On Dorothy" 6).

The Recognition Theory

Despite the pervasive morbidity in Larson's humor, the feelings of schadenfreude evoked by his comedy were not always wholly cruel. The recognition theory, in fact, provides a way to add some nuance to the emotional dynamics at work in many of the *Far Side*'s more pathetic panels. According to this frame, a comedian provokes laughter by drawing our attention to the common indignities of everyday life in a clever way (think of Jerry Seinfeld's typical stand-up opener, "Did you ever notice? . . ."). The artful exaggeration of typical frustrations provokes laughter and, at times, catharsis: we are relieved to see that others share our same challenges. In fact, by emphasizing commonalities rather than differences among readers, this brand of joking is seen as more democratic and inclusive than those associated with the superiority theory.

Suddenly, Professor Liebowitz realizes he has come to the seminar without his duck.

Fig. 2.8. Gary Larson, "Suddenly, Professor Liebowitz," *The Far Side*, February 29, 1984 (1-369).

In the most conventional panel cartoons that were featured on the comics page—works such as *Family Circus* or *Marmaduke*—the mechanisms of recognition were clearly on display as the reader was invited to smile knowingly at the cute things kids say or the predictable behavior of mischievous pets. In *The Far Side*'s case, the reader was invited to identify with decidedly more sour experiences: mind-numbing tasks, stupid inconveniences, bad-luck injuries, and the treacherous nature of our own bodies (always tripping, falling, or enduring more serious indignities) (Dale 11). The schadenfreude of *The Far Side*, then, when filtered through recognition humor, takes on more layered qualities, often mingling with a sense of sympathetic identification—especially in those installments that dial back the morbidity a bit. Examples that invite those layered emotions include the one where a distressed scientist in the audience realizes he's the only one who forgot to bring his duck to the seminar (fig. 2.8), or the installment in which a guy in the science lab obliviously drinks a glass of amoebic dysentery with his lunch (12/21/87; 2–116). In these cases we laugh in part because the scenes evoke common anxieties and memories of similar (albeit slightly less absurd) dilemmas.

Even within some of Larson's more luridly tragicomic gags, we might feel a sense of collective identification. We laugh ruefully, for instance, at scenes where the universe seems to conspire against a hapless fool: the lone palm tree falling on the guy stranded on a desert island (7/24/81; 1–140), the Eskimo getting his tongue stuck on ice right as a polar bear appears on the scene (9/3/86; 1–610), or the condemned guy repeatedly falling through the gallows floor without injury (yet), because the hangman is still trying to figure out the knot (11/5/81; 1 164). The sad figures in these cartoons serve as everyman fools—representations of the unlucky nerd we often see in ourselves. And the bad-luck dilemmas they continually faced articulated a bracingly absurdist worldview that many of us sometimes suspect is true: not only are there no supernatural forces watching over and protecting us, but the universe itself has a slightly malevolent sense of humor and is determined to bring us down in darkly comical fashion.

The Incongruity Theory

Another foundational theory of humor posits that we enjoy laughing at surprising incongruities. Conditioned to see predictable patterns and outcomes in the world around us, our minds are delighted by playful deviations that contain bizarre logic, ironic twists, or absurd conclusions. As a cartoonist with an "alternative" reputation, Larson was naturally inclined to wield this brand of comedy, starting in familiar territory and then challenging readers with subversive twists. He also benefited from the stand-alone quality of each panel cartoon installment; unhampered by narrative continuity and character development, Larson was free to start each day with a fresh conventional premise in need of an absurd inversion.

Fairy tales and genre entertainment were especially productive starting points for these kinds of *Far Side* jokes. Because readers were so thoroughly steeped in the character types and narrative conventions of traditional stories, they essentially did half the work for Larson—teeing up in their minds a specific set of expectations. And then when Larson's gunfighters,

"Oo! Goldfish, everyone! Goldfish!"

Fig. 2.9. Gary Larson, "Oo! Goldfish, everyone! Goldfish!" *The Far Side*, September 8, 1983 (1-328).

marauding Vikings, and dowdy princesses sharply deviated from the script or played against type in a bizarre but logically justifiable way, the reader experienced a sense of surprised hilarity. As an example, consider the cartoon where a burly Visigoth urges his companions to notice the cute goldfish in the moat as they attack a castle (fig. 2.9). The joke in this case is especially effective, since the incongruity is both reasonable *and* absurd. A person could be expected to admire a cute fish in most circumstances, but definitely not at that particular moment by that kind of individual.

Larson also used everyday platitudes, conventional myths, and cheesy maxims as fodder for his jokes of incongruity. In one example, a chubby, white-haired Einstein drives a ball into the paint on a basketball court,

"Ha! Ain't a rattler, Jake. You got one of them maraca
players down your bag—and he's probably more scared
than you."

Fig. 2.10. Gary Larson, "Ha! Ain't a rattler, Jake," *The Far Side*, October 3,
1984 (1-423).

allowing Larson to exploit a common narrative turn found in many famous
persons' biographies: "Unbeknownst to most historians, Einstein started
down the road of professional basketball before an ankle injury diverted
him into science" (1/1/87; 2–12). In another installment in which a cowboy
lifts the cover of a buddy's sleeping bag, Larson twists the conventional
wisdom about the vulnerability of seemingly dangerous animals: "Ha! Ain't
a rattler, Jake. You got one of them maraca players down your bag—and
he's probably more scared than you" (fig. 2.10).

Larson's understated, deadpan approach to logically illogical humor
amplified the payoff of these jokes. Other cartoonists might have tried to
advertise the incongruities more vividly, exaggerating the dynamics of the

scene or the appearance of the character. A less funny version of the rattler cartoon would feature a maraca player with a big, stereotypical smile—and the cowboys reacting with agitated alarm; and the Einstein cartoon would simply be corny if he were athletically dunking the ball, dominating his opponents, and staring down the reader with bulging eyes. Instead, Larson tamps down the emotions of all the characters, keeps the aesthetic flourishes in check, and delivers the parodic twists with a straight face. In fact, because so little comedic sign-waving takes place in these scenes, the reader enjoys the added pleasure of connecting the dots, teasing out the bizarre logic of the vignette.

The Play Theory

A final theory of humor helps to explain the appeal and benefits of engaging with comedy that invites a high level of reader engagement. Echoing some aspects of both the relief and the incongruity frames, the play theory suggests that we enjoy mental games that feature odd juxtapositions of ideas, fresh treatments of conventional wisdom, or irreverent inversions of hierarchies. Consumed in moderation—perhaps in regular readings of the newspaper funnies or a cartoon-a-day calendar—this kind of imaginative play gives us a break from psychological tiredness or tension (in a Freudian sense) and fosters flexible critical thinking skills. To elaborate, a *Far Side* reader might develop a nimbleness of mind if tasked with regularly teasing out the absurdly logical implications of animal–human crossovers, the layers of wordplay in tragic misunderstandings, or the implications of literalizing figurative maxims; they might develop, in fact, a tolerance for ambiguity, variety, and multivalence. In terms of real-world benefits, the reader could gradually become more adept at creative problem-solving, at using outside-the-box thinking strategies, and at seeing challenges from multiple, shifting perspectives. Given the ubiquity of those intellectually playful devices in Larson's comedy, it makes sense that *The Far Side* was embraced so avidly by scientists and intellectuals—and that his cartoons appeared commonly in business presentations that invited attendees to innovate or revise traditional practices.

Evolutionary psychology (a field that might find a soft spot in Larson's heart) gives additional ways of imagining the social uses and benefits of intellectually challenging, playful humor. The thinking goes that because we have had to adapt over the centuries to complex social structures where opportunistic strangers might want to hurt or take advantage of us through deceitfully layered word and action, we gradually developed strategies for identifying and eliminating those dangers. Joking gossip or pointed satire, for example, became informal methods for highlighting dangerous people's subtle lies, specious logic, or manipulative behavior. And thus comedy like Larson's, that satirizes a variety of social and psychological foibles that make individuals vulnerable to the machinations of others—myopic thinking, dogmatic behavior, naive beliefs in inflated cultural myths, and so on—might encourage readers to foster in themselves a safer approach to social interactions: a kind of world-wise, moral thinking that increases one's chance for figurative (and maybe literal) survival in contemporary society.

Comedic Devices at Work in *The Far Side*

Wordplay

Moving from overarching theories to particular methods, we can explore a number of comedic devices in *The Far Side*: clever wordplay, in medias res jokes, human–animal crossovers, gothic themes, and parodies. To begin, one of Larson's signature moves was wordplay: clever puns, inverted platitudes, malapropisms, and double entendres. Perhaps the primary appeal of word gaming is its ability to challenge our expectations about the conventional workings and meanings of language. We are so inundated with clichéd maxims in everyday conversations and readings, in fact, that any kind of incongruous departure from that flow of bland information can elicit pleasurable surprise. If a comedian's wordplay is too thoughtless or predictable, however, we groan rather than laugh, of course; tired puns neither stun us nor provide any new ways of thinking about the subject. At the start of his career, Larson had the tendency to fall into this clichéd pattern, creating gags based on the kind of knee-jerk wordplay that we associate with preteens who are overly impressed with their ability to spot homonyms or to highlight the literal meanings of figurative language. For example, during his first months of syndication, Larson engaged in some cringe-inducing installments: a physically tiny lady was a man's "little woman" (2/6/80; 1–15); a cowboy "drifter" floated several feet off the ground as he headed through town (9/12/80; 1–63); and a "camelot" was a place for selling used camels (3/31/80; 1–25).

As Larson's comedic sensibility sharpened over time, the obvious puns gave way to wordsmanship that was genuinely creative and sometimes

Fig. 2.11. Gary Larson, "Virginians," *The Far Side*, November 30, 1986 (1-635).

intellectually provocative. He discovered, for example, that some of the following conditions could heighten the effectiveness of this kind of humor: an incongruous departure that takes the reader into vaguely morbid or taboo territory, accidental wordplay (malapropisms—the ignorant misuse of words or a Freudian slip); puns that were original, absurd, or displayed a demented logic; or verbal jokes that had something clever to say about human nature, society, or the instability of language in general. As an example, Larson's cartoon about two bland-looking women in glasses who are thrilled at the special treatment they're receiving from a primitive tribe meets a number of these conditions (fig. 2.11). At the center of the joke are two words, of course, with similar sounds (*virgins* and *Virginians*). The confusion is especially funny for several reasons: there is comic/dramatic irony in the reader knowing more about the situation than the sweetly naive women, the dark reality of the moment is so out of sync with the women's cheerful expectations, and the ladies' proportions and personalities are deeply incongruous with the character types normally featured in this clichéd scenario about sacrificial maidens. Additional examples of effective and original word-based gags include the explorers in an Egyptian tomb who are shocked at the sight of their discovery carrying a red handbag: "Oh my God, Rogers! . . . Is that? . . . Is that? . . . It is! It's the MUMMY'S PURSE!" (9/3/91; 2–346); the old guy telling "Gross Stories" to mesmerized kids seated around a campfire ("And then, he slooooooooowly lifted the bucket of lard to his lips, and with a low, guttural sound, began

"Oh, wonderful! Look at this, Etta — another mouth to feed."

Fig. 2.12. Gary Larson, "Oh, wonderful!" *The Far Side*, May 11, 1987 (2-46).

to *drink!*") (1/13/86; 1–545); and the suburban couple who watch in horror as their panicked guests are slowly absorbed into the floor, the caption reading, "And down they went: Bob and Francine—two more victims of the La Brea Carpets" (2/15/90; 2–234).

You can imagine a less savvy comedian communicating these kinds of jokes in a fashion that would feel too wacky: "Look at this outrageous twisting of words I executed here!" Larson avoids that impression by creating a universe that seems unfazed by absurd juxtapositions. Consider, for example, the emotionally neutral manner in which Larson presented bizarre scenes like the matronly woman calmly walking through a dark forest corridor with a household vacuum (nature abhors her appliance, she belatedly realizes) (10/19/92; 2–437). She is like all of the characters featured in Larson's panels who consistently respond to the bizarre logic of their situations with dispassionate expressions. In other scenes, guests do not seem disturbed, for example, when their hosts ask them if they've met "met Russell and Bill, our 1.5 children?" (3/14/88; 2–146), and a middle-aged fellow is merely irritated (rather than horrified) when he looks in the mirror and discovers he has inexplicably grown a second set of lips and teeth—another mouth to feed (fig. 2.12). We would probably be less amused if the man registered alarm; his bland expression and misdirected frustration, in effect, amplify the resulting humorous pleasure for the reader as he or she unpacks the strange logic of the scene.

Finally, we could argue that Larson's wordplay was so consistently inventive that it gradually took on philosophical dimensions for its core readers. In *The Far Side* words tended to have multiple, shifting meanings; characters continually confused terms and concepts; vapid sayings were upended to see if they have any substance; and figurative phrases were made literal, or the literal was made figurative. The generosity of that verbal slapstick placed Larson within the camp of other great language and dialect-obsessed cartoonists like George Herriman (*Krazy Kat*) and Walt Kelly (*Pogo*). *Krazy Kat* was especially ambitious in its playful use of miscommunication and invented dialects to deconstruct hierarchies of race and gender; Herriman's jokes, in fact, worked as a sustained exposé of the futility of communication—or, as Krazy put it, the idea that language exists so we can "misundestend each udder." In *Pogo*, Kelly used ethnically derived dialects and vaudevillian verbal slapstick to satirize the ideology of McCarthyism—a discourse that, in contrast, used language in oppressive ways, categorizing, stereotyping, inciting fear, establishing authoritarian hierarchies, and so on.

Larson's wordplay was perhaps less consistently subversive than Herriman's, but it certainly reached a larger audience, given the limited cult popularity of *Krazy Kat*. In comparing Larson to Kelly, we could say that word-gaming in *The Far Side* lacked the satiric topicality of the jokes featured in *Pogo*, but it often pointed to provocative ideological implications. Larson highlighted, for example, as one critic put it, "that language is not a neutral medium of optimum communication, but also a reservoir of illogic, cultural chauvinism, and literally senseless cliché" (Gould 10). In sum, in consistently enjoying Larson's creative wordplay, readers were perhaps encouraged to adopt a flexible view of our ability to communicate effectively and a wariness toward manipulative uses of language in other cultural texts.

In Medias Res Cartoons

Single-panel cartoons are often looked down upon by comics professionals and scholars because they seem (at least from a distance) to be especially limited in their narrative and comedic vocabulary. The artist, after all, has only that one small box in which to condense a great deal of comedic information. The best cartoonists in the history of the medium nevertheless found ways of expanding and amplifying the power of that lone frame. Larson, for example, was especially good at executing jokes that throw the reader into the middle of the action so that she or he had to imagine the scene within a larger context and flow of time. We were shown a narrow vignette that could appear confusing or enigmatic at first but upon closer inspection, revealed a handful of telling details about what has happened before, or will happen immediately after, that particular moment. Examples include the cartoon with two bland-looking jumbo-jet pilots calmly looking out the front window of the plane, wondering aloud what that mountain goat is doing way up here in this cloud bank (2/2/83; 1–277); the image of leopard in a tree full of old tourist cameras opening his eyes abruptly from a nap as a sedentary-looking safari-goer in the near distance audibly clicks a photo of the animal (7/13/82; 1–225); or the installment where we see in the distance, through a kitchen window, a cow sitting on the fence in a cocky manner, saying to his friends, "Look, if it was electric, could I do this?" Meanwhile, in the foregrounded kitchen, a farmer is about to hit the on-switch for that soon-to-be electrified fence (2/24/93; 2–463).

A common element of these "in the middle of things" cartoons was the implication or foreshadowing—rather than literal depiction—of serious violence. In addition to creating some essential emotional distance, the relative placidity of the "before" scene created a sense of schadenfreudic anticipation as the reader visualized the weird chaos that would soon arrive. Especially effective examples of that dynamic at work include the cartoon with two heavyset, nerdy boys tossing a bear cub about in the sight-line of its mother (11/2/83; 1–340), and the panel where a guy is explaining to his fellow elevator-riders that his pet lion won't hurt people—unless it gets startled—while not noticing, unfortunately, that his pet's tail is trailing between the soon-to-close elevator doors (fig. 2.13). The sensations felt while reading one of these charged vignettes are similar to the dramatic irony a viewer experiences in watching a good farcical play; you know more, and can see more, than the pathetic players involved in the dilemma onstage and can only cringe in anticipation of the approaching chaos.

"Don't be alarmed folks . . . He's completely harmless unless something startles him."

Fig. 2.13. Gary Larson, "Don't be alarmed, folks," *The Far Side*, June 4, 1981 (1-130).

A comparison can also be made between Larson's panels drawn in medias res and cinema. Most contemporary readers are prepared to interpret the before and after of panel cartoons because they are already adept at decoding sequential comics and popular film (Carrier 15). The single-panel cartoon, in effect, communicates its information like a highlighted excerpt from one of those more expansive narrative forms. Many *Far Side* scenes feel like the pivotal moment from a slow-motion sequence in a deflated blockbuster movie; one of Larson's classic dog vs. mailman panels, for instance, evokes the filmic methods of a psychological thriller: both figures stand like statues, and the caption reads, "The can of Mace lay where it had fallen from Bill's hand, and, for a moment, time froze, as each pondered the significance of this new development" (7/6/85; 1–494). Similar panels burlesque the climactic reveal from an espionage thriller or horror movie—like the scene in which we peer over a farmer's shoulder, discovering two startled cows on their knees, creating a diagram of the different meat cuts for a human body (fig. 2.14).

In some cases Larson intentionally complicated the readability of these cartoons by using slightly unconventional filmic methods, many of them borrowed from New Wave cinema. They include first-person perspectives, disorienting jump cuts, or isolated, minimalistic shots that emphasize narrative ambiguity. A vivid example is the cartoon in which we see, from a disorienting first-person point of view, a circle of Native American faces

Farmer Brown froze in his tracks; the cows stared wide-eyed back at him. Somewhere, off in the distance, a dog barked.

Fig. 2.14. Gary Larson, "Farmer Brown," *The Far Side*, February 12, 1986 (1-551).

wearing war paint, looking down on the reader with menacing smiles. The minimalistic caption reads, "Custer's Last View" (fig. 2.15).

Because Larson varied his techniques so inventively with his "in the moment" cartoons, they kept readers on their toes. In fancy reception-theory lingo, they worked as dialectical texts that provided only half of the essential information; the reader had to finish connecting the dots, and then a synthesis occurred in which the humorous meaning emerged. Some installments heightened this dynamic by requiring the reader to discover an especially small, revelatory detail. In the cartoon featuring the pet lion in the elevator (figure 2.13), for example, we have to notice the beast's

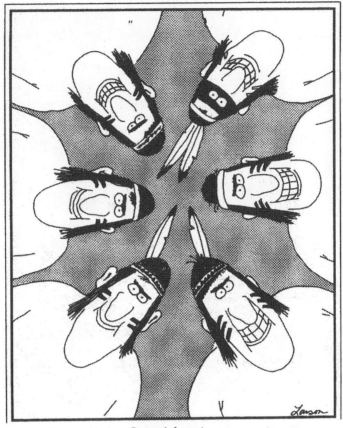

Custer's last view

Fig. 2.15. Gary Larson, "Custer's last view," *The Far Side*, March 29, 1986 (1-562).

tail, trailing nonchalantly between the closing elevator doors, before the cartoon delivers its comedic punch. Similarly, readers get a secondary jolt of humor in the human-as-meat-cut-diagram cartoon when they notice an arrow pointing to the farmer's head with the awkwardly written note, "THROW AWAY" (fig. 2.14).

For newspaper readers accustomed to the more obvious gags of the traditional funnies, the puzzle-like density of some of Larson's panels might have been slightly alienating; one or two encounters with a cartoon that required extra mental energy to decode might have been enough to steer them away from his work in the future. Even readers invested in his work occasionally found some of his "in the moment" jokes to be inscrutable. The following fan seemed on the verge of going bonkers in the effort to imagine the before and after of the cartoon in which a small poodle is attached to a leash that trails, pathetically, under the gargantuan body of King Kong (9/6/84; 1–431):

> We don't feel that it can be as simple as "the gorilla fell on the dog's master, so what is the dog going to do now?" We are assuming that the gorilla is King Kong, but why is he lying down? What is that little thing his head is lying on (a parking meter)? Is there something missing, some punch line that we are not getting? Did you put in a cartoon that you knew no one could figure out on purpose just to boggle our minds? This is driving us crazy. (Holt 431)

At other times, Larson's intentionally ambiguous vignettes worked like warped, comedic versions of Rorschach inkblots, eliciting unintended, but equally funny interpretations. As an example, Larson got this letter inquiring about the cartoon where a cow is staring in shock at the contents of a kitchen freezer; the caption reads, "While Farmer Brown was away, the cows got into the kitchen and were having the times of their lives—until Betsy's unwitting discovery" (8/8/83; 1–320):

> Please help us settle this minor family dispute. My son maintains that Betsy's unwitting discovery was finding steaks in the freezer. My husband and I believe that Betsy found Farmer Brown's supply of frozen bull semen. Which of the above is the right answer—or, are they both wrong? Did you have something more delightful in mind? What? We can hardly wait for your answer. (Dinerman 320)

Animal–Human Crossovers

Cartoons with cows venturing into the human world also point to one of Larson's most reliable comedic devices: animal–human crossovers. On the surface this trope was fairly straightforward, with Larson applying the customs of one kingdom to the other and imagining the strange results: a grown man involuntarily jerking his leg while being rubbed on the belly by his pet dog (4/15/82; 1–206); a captive rhino in a zoo talking with his mate through a phone on the other side of a glass window, as if he were in a human prison (10/21/93; 2–507); a doomed guy obliviously positioning himself between a mother grizzly bear and her cub in an office-building elevator (5/9/90; 2–251); or an "animal nerd" derailing an impending attack

That evening, with her blinds pulled, Mary had three helpings
of corn, two baked potatoes, extra bread, and a little lamb.

Fig. 2.16. Gary Larson,"That evening," *The Far Side*, September 10, 1987 (2-83).

by his fellow wolves by abruptly showing up and saying, "Hey! Hi, you
guys! What's going on?" (10/18/84; 1–427). Much of the humor in these
gags emerges from the absurd but reasonable logic of the overlay. It makes
sense, for example, that grizzlies would always behave according to their
most primal impulses, even if they were inexplicably coexisting with humans in corporate settings. And if there are sweetly intentioned but socially
awkward nerds within the human family, why not within other animal
species?

At times these cartoons also evoke more poignant layers of humor in
a variety of ways: by getting us to see human behavior with fresh eyes, by
challenging our humanity-flattering worldviews, and by reminding us of

the unsentimental, naturalistic laws that seem to govern the universe. For example, we see the foolishness of treating pets like human children when that practice is taken to a logically absurd extreme in cartoons like the one where a faithful dog is berated by its owner for doing a poor job of mowing the front lawn (10/7/83; 1–333). In similar panels we are reminded of our essential animal natures after seeing human mating behavior or self-defense practices in parallel with the instinctive impulses of other species—as in the cartoon where a timid-looking fellow in an alley attempts to scare away muggers by flaring the "eyespots" on the top of his bald pate (12/23/91; 2–369).

As Larson's career progressed, he expanded the comedic and philosophical functions of these cross-over cartoons by creating a spectrum of overlapping types of anthropomorphism (animals taking on human characteristics) and zoomorphism (humans taking on animal qualities). To begin, because the practice of anthropomorphizing animals has a long history in fables, children's literature, and animation, Larson could readily parody established conventions and clichés; in most cases this was achieved by applying a naturalistic worldview to the sentimental cuteness of fables in contemporary children's literature and animation that feature comforting myths about the natural world and the special place of humans in the universe. Classic *Far Side* burlesques of that brand of entertainment include a woman horrified to encounter a room full of Looney Tunes–style cartoon animal heads taxidermied and mounted on a wall (5/18/88; 2–170); the jaded-looking woman who is stuck with a house full of polliwogs after falling for the "kiss a frog" fantasy (1/12/81; 1–96); or the especially bracing installment in which a heavyset Mary from the children's rhyme is eating at a kitchen table, above the caption, "That evening, with her blinds pulled, Mary had three helpings of corn, two baked potatoes, extra bread, and a little lamb" (fig. 2.16). The combination of aggressively deconstructive parody and naturalistic overlays effectively push these cartoons into satiric territory, questioning the arbitrariness of lines between cute pets and consumable livestock, and undercutting comforting myths about the animal world.

Larson's treatment of the human–cow divide led into some especially unstable points along the animal–human spectrum. At times his iconic Holsteins simply served as metaphors for bland, Middle Americanness; they are slow, heavy, similar in appearance, and generally naive about the world beyond their own provincial lives. The image of the cow family dutifully and passively posing upright in front of the Grand Canyon embodies well that notion (11/20/84; 1–434). At other times their relative human/

"For crying out loud, gentlemen! That's us! Someone's
installed the one-way mirror in backward!"

Fig. 2.17. Gary Larson, "For crying out loud," *The Far Side*, May 20, 1985 (1-482).

cow status was in disturbing flux. For instance, in some panels they are
inappropriate pets, wheeling about the house in a giant hamster bubble
(9/25/86; 1–616); in others they behave like sentient livestock, discovering dark secrets about their larger purpose in the kitchen freezer (8/8/83;
1–320); and in some cases they are fully equal to humans—such as the
panel in which the cow in a life raft is fantasizing in a thought bubble
about his human companion as an edible field of grass and flowers (7/8/85;
1–496). In a few vignettes the cow's status was so confused that it served
several conflicting roles at the same time. An especially morbid example
depicts a group of doctors operating on a cow in a hospital setting; the lead
surgeon says, "Well, we've done everything we can; now we can only wait

and see if she pulls through . . . If she doesn't, however, I got dibs on this porterhouse right here" (8/8/88; 2–194).

Larson's methods of zoomorphism (putting humans into the animal roles) were also subversive to different degrees. In some instances the roles were inverted in a sort of temporary, carnivalesque way—like the cartoon that speculates on what it would look like if horses pulled humans around in trailers on the highway, their big butts protruding awkwardly out the back window (1/7/87; 2–6). In other cases the crossover feels more unstable, like we've entered into liminal territory with no going back. Examples include the panel in which a primitive kid is proudly showing his family tree at school, pointing to grandparents who are rodents, lizards, and fish (9/4/86; 1–609); and a nebbishy-looking guy on a date with a sheep at a fine restaurant alarmed at the sight of another sheep named Doris that he apparently dated in the past (3/9/92; 2–389). In the midst of all this inter-species mingling, hybridity reigns, hierarchies are in flux, and the borders between species are porous.

I especially like the panels in this genre that mess with the barrier between scientists and animals in lab settings. As examples, there's the one with a group of sober nerds in white coats dispassionately testing whether a variety of other species kiss by performing the act on the animals themselves (and occasionally getting slapped by their indignant subjects) (12/10/85; 1–534); or the one in which chagrined primate researchers discover that they've been staring for months into a one-way mirror (fig. 2.17). These jokes might have prodded devoted readers beyond nervous laughter to recognize their own evolved, animal nature; to question their self-congratulatory, anthropocentric worldview; and to consider the inconsistent ways that we treat other animals—arbitrarily nurturing some like cherished family members and consuming or performing experiments on others.

Gothic and Morbid Comedy

Larson's jokes based on gothic themes were also varied in their comedic meanings and uses. For starters, his depictions of horror were fairly tame when he riffed on the predictable tropes of genre entertainment: jungle explorers being impaled with spikes, torture scenes in dungeons, and a plethora of jokes about classic movie monsters like Frankenstein's monster, Dracula, werewolves, or mummies. The clichéd familiarity of those jokes effectively distanced readers from the realities of literal violence or death. Larson's jokes entered more profoundly disquieting territory, however, when he depicted horrible accidents happening to everyday fools: a forlorn astronaut staring down at a note from his companions who decided that he'd waited too long to show up (6/29/81; 1–134); or the middle-class couple emerging from a bunker to confront a landscape devastated by a nuclear holocaust, with the husband exclaiming, "Thank God, Sylvia—We're alive!" (12/8/81; 1–72).

The origins of this kind of everyday black comedy can be traced in part to the midcentury philosophies of existentialism and absurdism. If the traditional Christian notion of a benevolent God is simply a comforting fantasy—as these worldviews posited—then humankind is either left to impose its own meanings and morality onto an uncaring world and corrupt society (existentialism), or flail against perversely malevolent natural forces in ineffectual ways (absurdism). Without the prospects of divine intervention and authority in life, moreover, the resonance of traditional comedy (with its redeeming marriages and reconciliations), and tragedy (with its cathartic meting out of justice in the end), also dissipates and the two genres are left to implode into each other. The resulting offspring of that pathetic, collapsing embrace were hybrid, tragi-comic genres like black comedy and absurdist theatre.

By the 1960s, this kind of bleak but intellectually bracing humor migrated from highbrow plays like Samuel Beckett's *Waiting for Godot*, into popular cultural texts like Joseph Heller's *Catch-22*, Stanley Kubrick's *Dr. Strangelove*, and later, the television sitcom *M.A.S.H.* Underground and alternative-magazine cartoons by artists such as R. Crumb and B. Kliban also featured darker tones, but mainstream newspaper comics were a conservative holdout against such pessimistic (or maybe realistic) worldviews. You could argue that traces of existential realism/pessimism peeked between the cracks of cuteness in 1960s standbys like *Peanuts* (Schulz) or *B.C.* (Hart), or in the topical, real-time naturalism in *Doonesbury* (Trudeau), or *For Better or Worse* (Johnston), but these examples were anomalies among the unrelenting cheer that dominated the rest of the page. Until Larson arrived in 1980, the funnies were largely dominated by comforting vignettes of suburban safety, cutely tame and anthropomorphized animals' hijinks, inconsequential slapstick violence (even in ostensibly war-related cartoons like *Beetle Bailey*), and strips that did not even allow characters to age, let alone die. As a result, Larson's morbid themes felt fresh and genuinely subversive within that context, and at times echoed some of the themes of absurdist theater: that without God, humans are merely ineffectual fools trying to make sense of an unfathomable existence; that the search for order or meaning brings us into conflict with the universe—which often

Fig. 2.18. Gary Larson, "Freezer Locker 37," *The Far Side*, December 29, 1980 (1-89).

tends to bite back in perverse ways; and that individuals are often stymied by bureaucratic institutions with rules that are arbitrary and cruel.

Larson also added an original, satiric twist in many of these darkly absurd installments by depicting his fools being tripped up by their naive understanding of the uncaring, naturalistic forces of the animal kingdom. In cartoon after cartoon people seemed continually surprised that animals were inclined to "sting, bite, spit, stab, suck, gore, or stomp" (Larson, "Creative Process" 76). The best, most absurd variations on this theme featured humans inviting that violence upon themselves by holding too tightly to romantic notions of the human qualities of pets or by being too insulated within civilized comforts. In other cases people were blinded by arrogant, academic stupidity—as in the one where a time-traveling scientist is about to trigger his own violent demise by using a giant rectal thermometer to do a firsthand test of whether dinosaurs were warm-blooded creatures (12/26/87; 2–118).

Perhaps Larson's most provocative cartoons in this morbid vein are those that depict violence as a banal feature of everyday life. Scenes from butcher shops, in particular, were especially useful in exploring brutalities that have grown mundane. I still get a bit of a dark chill down my spine, for example, when I see the panel in which a bull in a trench coat is entering a meat locker full of humans suspended by their feet (fig. 2.18); and I laugh nervously when I reread the one where a jaded-looking butcher concedes to a shady-looking customer that he'd let his plus-sized teenage assistant go for about $1.99 a pound (7/9/81; 1–136). The implications of violence in these cartoons are more than mere reflections of the unsentimental realities of competition for survival in the animal kingdom; instead, they are slight distortions of the mundane but disturbingly ambitious ways that humans can use and abuse most species in the animal kingdom (including their own).

Parody

An analysis of Larson's use of parody gives us a final illustration of how *The Far Side* rewarded its most attentive readers—or frustrated the uninitiated. By its nature, parody requires a significant effort from readers to decode, because it is both intertextual (quoting other works of art and entertainment) and layered (adopting a mocking tone in some cases, and a vaguely celebratory note in others). To elaborate, in a typical newspaper comic, the characters are stable, the situational dynamics remain constant from cartoon to cartoon, and the jokes are delivered in a relatively straightforward manner. With *The Far Side*, however, readers had to reorient themselves from one cartoon to the next, discerning new contexts, shifting character dynamics, and subtle changes in ironic tone. And because a great number of Larson's cartoons were parodic, it was also critical that the reader have a familiarity with the conventions of the text or genre being lampooned in the joke. Examples of that layering include the panel with a matronly woman dressed in contemporary clothing pulling a medieval sword from a stone, while her female companion says, "Put it back in the rock, Barbara— you couldn't even slice a tomato with that old thing" (7/28/81; 1–140); the image of General Washington and his soldiers heroically (but stiffly, like figures in a painting) crossing an everyday street (10/15/86; 1–622); and a fog-shrouded chicken shed pictured above this caption: "The rooster stared back at me, his power and confidence almost overwhelming. Down below, a female paused warily at the coop's entrance. I kept the camera running. They were beautiful, these 'Chickens in the Mist'" (3/7/90; 2–238).

For culturally literate people most of these references were fairly obvious, of course; once oriented to the context (e.g., the legend of King Arthur, or the famous image of Washington crossing the Delaware), it was easy enough to compare the conventions of the original text to Larson's parodic twist. We should not underestimate, however, the difficulties that preteens or a newspaper subscriber from a different cultural background might have encountered when trying to decipher these kinds of intertextual jokes. The "Chickens in the Mist" cartoon, for example, referenced a fairly obscure biopic from 1988 starring Sigourney Weaver as gorilla researcher Dian Fossey. When this cartoon was first published, in 1990, educated, adult fans would have easily made the connection to the film. The joke's meaning, on the other hand, probably remained obscure for younger readers at the time or for older demographics less tuned in to the latest Hollywood fare. With the passage of time, references like that became even more inaccessible, reducing the gag in a typical reader's mind, perhaps, to a heavy-handed "heroic chicken" premise.

Beyond requiring a moderate level of cultural literacy to decode, Larson's parodies also assumed that readers could read the nuances of ironic tones. Once again, the facetious quality of Larson's parodies may seem obvious to a fan of satiric comedy, but we are occasionally reminded that some people are unprepared for or uninterested in deciphering that kind of subtle layering. For example, the fact that many casual television viewers assumed that Stephen Colbert was an earnest pundit speaking for people on the far right of the political spectrum—rather than a constructed persona who was burlesquing pompous newscasters like Bill O'Reilly—attests to the instability of meaning in the reception of that kind of joking (Baumgartner and Morris 622). In fact, misunderstandings of this kind occurred with Larson's work regularly during his career. As an example, Larson confused some younger readers with his parody of the classic children's magazine game in which readers are asked to find hidden objects. The *Far Side* version asks you, in a deadpan tone, to identify 127 "hidden kitchen appliances" in a forest setting in which only a handful of obvious examples are in view (11/1/87; 2–102). Larson's ironic tone was so convincingly straight-faced in this case that it elicited a letter from a grade school teacher and her fifth- and sixth-grade students that read, in part, "We would like to know how you got the answer 127 major appliances. . . . We would appreciate it if you could let us in on the puzzle" (Hurst 102). Larson's editor, Jake Morrissey, made the cartoon's facetious intentions explicit in his friendly response: "Gary's cartoon was a parody of those puzzles that are full of hidden pictures. His cartoon had such clumsily hidden objects (kitchen appliances) in it, and such an outrageous answer (127), that it was not meant to be taken seriously" (Morrissey, "Dear Mrs. Hurst and Class").

I remember becoming acquainted with the layeredness of parody at about the same age as these kids, encountering sarcastic humor in *MAD* magazine, *Saturday Night Live*, *Late Night with David Letterman*, and *The Far Side*. Research shows, in fact, that it is during that formative period that young people learn to identify irony, and so those preteen years may be the ideal time to peel apart the shifting tones of parody in a cartoon like *The Far Side* ("Getting Sarcastic with Kids"). Regular engagement with that kind of joking might train a young reader to see the constructedness of a comedian's persona (especially when it's deadpan) and begin to think critically about the manipulative conventions at work in more earnest cultural texts.

Although I was not fully conscious of this at the time, *The Far Side* was perhaps more effective than *MAD* and *SNL* at using its parody in satiric ways, and in prodding a young reader to think critically—even deconstructively—about mainstream entertainment. To support that argument, we can assess the relative satiric potency of Larson's parodies according to a rubric outlined by the scholar Linda Hutcheon. First, she establishes that because parody relies on a reader's familiarity with the targeted cultural product, and inevitably repeats many of the core elements of that original work, it "always implicitly reinforces even as it ironically debunks"; in other words, the dynamics of repetition and recognition end up denigrating *and* celebrating the comedy's target (Hutcheon xii). She adds, nevertheless, that all not all parodies are alike in their ideological effects; some approaches are better than others at actually satirizing targets in a substantial way. And we can assess that potential by placing the comedy along a spectrum of tones and intentions—from "respectful to playful to scathingly critical"—and by assessing how well each parody repeats the elements of its target "with critical distance," emphasizing the "difference rather than similarity" from what it is mocking (Hutcheon 6).

In the most egregiously shallow cases, parodies are considered a form of "pastiche," a flippant quoting of other cultural works with little distance or difference; they essentially have nothing critical to say. Many postmodern design products and music videos amount to this kind of shallowness when their parodic quoting feels randomly eclectic or pointlessly ironic. In other cases, a significant degree of comedic distance is achieved in the parody's joke, but the *difference* is essentially erased as the comedy is harnessed to commercial rather than satirical purposes. Key examples might include commercials that lampoon advertising conventions in general as a way of selling particular products more effectively by preempting the consumers' derision. Consider the Sprite commercials from 1997, for example, that mocked other soft drink commercials' conventions and then asserted "Image is Nothing, Thirst is Everything." The pose of knowing, hip parody effectively allowed those ads to camouflage their commercial intentions.

As we move up the scale toward greater comedic/satiric bite, we can identify conflicted texts like *MAD* magazine and *Saturday Night Live*. *MAD* parodied mainstream cultural texts in consistently irreverent ways, but its parodies of popular films and television shows often ended up celebrating—as much as satirizing—their targets, because the editors were so heavily motivated by the pressure to sell more copies of the magazine. They chose their targets in an opportunistic fashion, gauging the best way to grab a buyer's/reader's attention by scanning the popular landscape to "see what's on and what's coming out soon, trying, as best as they [could], to gauge what's going to be hot" (Evanier 122). As a result, the magazine's treatments of television shows like *Charlie's Angels* felt like vague celebrations of key elements from the original text, such as the packaging of its protagonists as sex objects. It was as if they were saying to thirteen-year-old boys, "Here's a clever treatment of more of what you already like." I can remember, in fact, enjoying *MAD*'s playful parodies of movies like *Star Wars* largely because they were simply another iteration of something that I unabashedly loved.

In *Saturday Night Live*'s case, a good deal of distance and difference from targets was achieved because the writers, producers, and performers perceived themselves as cultural hooligans who used the loosened standards of late-night television as an opportunity to mock political culture and the square values of mainstream entertainment. Performers like John Belushi, Gilda Radner, and Bill Murray carried the aura of unhinged carnival clowns, and guest stars like Steve Martin enhanced their antiestablishment credentials by performing in live, parodic skits that always felt like they had the potential to go off the rails. That genuinely subversive dynamic had a directionless, scattershot orientation at times, nevertheless, for several reasons. First, the show's comedy was created by a committee of writers (rather than a lone satirist with a coherent worldview); second, because the sketches were sometimes tailored to flatter the interests and egos of star performers; and finally, because the show's satire often had more to do with what was culturally hot that particular week than what actually deserved critique on the cultural landscape. In sum, the show's comedy was generally irreverent and antiestablishment in tone but usually lacked a coherent or consistent satiric vision.

The Far Side fares better when measured by Hutcheon's rubric. To begin, Larson behaved like an independent-minded cartooning auteur in the way he pursued his career, concocting an idiosyncratically grotesque drawing style that helped to create distance and difference from the targets of his comedy. In addition, the sum of his comedy and art reinforced a set of philosophical worldviews with subversive implications. As a result, some of Larson's most effective parodic methods were genuinely satiric. They included reducing the spectacle of genre entertainment to a mundane level, filtering the romantic myths of our culture through a naturalistic lens, and deconstructing the mechanisms of the comic strip medium itself.

That first strategy—deflating mainstream spectacles—can be seen in the plethora of cartoons that revisit inflated scenes of genre entertainment: a group of menacing Vikings pausing before a battle to do the lame kind of stretching we associate with suburban joggers (12/26/84; 1–442); Peter Pan at an anonymous desk job in a corporate cubicle (2/18/94; 2–536); a family pausing at their dinner to notice a band of menacing ghost riders passing through their modest kitchen (8/8/86; 1–600); and Moses by himself, in his bathroom, looking in the mirror, miraculously parting his hair down the middle (1/14/93; 2–456). These cartoons effectively deflated the over-wrought qualities of the original texts by framing them within the banal concerns of day-to-day life. They articulated, in fact, a coherent brand of democratic satire in which sacred cows are questioned, mythic claims are leveled, and idealized heroes are reduced to the status of everyday nerds.

In other parodies Larson used the bracing truths of a naturalistic world-view to undermine repeatedly the pretty myths forwarded by religious texts or children's entertainment. Two vivid examples included the scene from the ark in which Noah says, after observing a pair of white legs with hooves poking up from the deck amidst a group of disturbed-looking animals, "Well, so much for the unicorns . . . But, from now on, all carnivores will be confined to 'C' deck" (12/31/81; 1–177); and the one with two sabertoothed tigers retiring from the scene of a kill, licking their lips, one saying to the other, "I've heard all kinds of sounds from these things, but 'yabba dabba doo' was a new one to me" (9/2/83; 1–326).

Larson also used a naturalist's frame to challenge the cute conventions and comforting ideological messages of Disney films like *Dumbo*, *Pinoc-chio*, *Snow White*, and *Bambi*. This studio's classic films were a deserving

Fig. 2.19. Gary Larson, "Out of order," *The Far Side*, March 17, 1988 (2-149).

and vulnerable target for this type of satiric treatment, since the company was notorious for a number of decades at midcentury for its gentrification (or "Disneyfication") of earlier, more complex folk tales and legends. Familiar myths were effectively cleaned up to make them more palatable (and commercially viable) for a mass audience: old myths that once served as dark, cautionary tales were turned into cheerful allegories of middle-class American exceptionalism; the complexities of real history were often simplified into tidy, romance-filled packages; and real animals in ostensible nature documentaries were anthropomorphized in ways that affirmed an anthropocentric worldview. Larson's parodies of those Disney conventions effectively disassembled the original, tidy packages by reminding readers of some basic realities: life is governed by unforgiving laws like natural selection, history is messier (and more boring) than movies and history books suggest, and in the end, humans are fairly mundane (and sometimes foolish) animals themselves.

Finally, Larson's parodies sometimes achieved a degree of satiric bite by deconstructing the themes, characters, and storytelling mechanisms of the comics page and *The Far Side* itself. This practice of breaking the fourth wall was not new to comedy, of course (think of Shakespeare's actors speaking directly to the audience), but it had become associated by the 1960s and 1970s with a postmodern brand of "metafictive" joking in which the writer deconstructs the tropes of his or her own medium. In the best, most thoroughly self-reflexive examples of this type of comedy, the cartoonist is willing to poke fun at his or her own work as well. In Larson's self-focused parodies he acknowledged his gothic tendencies, made light of default joke patterns, and joshed about the constructedness of his archetypal characters. Key examples included a cartoon subtitled, "Gary Larson, Age 7," in which a group of crudely drawn stick-person children stop their volleyball game to notice, in horror, that they've been playing with a classmate's head ("Aaaaaaa! . . . this isn't the ball!) (7/17/86; 1–593); a cartoon with the caption "At *The Far Side* spy center" that shows Larson's cast of weird humans and animals monitoring surveillance of what's going on in other newspaper comics (10/8/91; 2–354); a street scene containing deflated, unsubstantial-looking *Far Side* types featuring the caption "*Far Side* Lite: Not funny, but better for you" (12/25/90; 2–294); and a panel with an "Out of Order" sign containing a jumbled mass of *Far Side* characters (fig. 2.19).

In conclusion, *The Far Side*'s brands of parody often achieved relatively high degrees of distance and difference from their targets because of the inherently subversive quality of Larson's signature filters: deflation, naturalism, and self-reflexive deconstruction. Moreover, because Larson was so consistent in applying those devices, they gradually contributed to the articulation of a sort of *Far Side* worldview that was irreverent (willing to take on any cultural text, even the Bible), skeptical (wary of the inflated qualities of most mainstream genre entertainment), and democratically modest (keen on subverting ideologies that were unfairly hierarchical or especially self-congratulatory). Core readers—those devoted fans like me who had been eager for the comics page to feature some comedy with edge and originality—received an informal education in critical thinking as they steeped themselves in parodic *Far Side* jokes. In effect, because Larson articulated that skeptical, deflating worldview so consistently, those readers may have essentially worn a figurative set of *Far Side* spectacles, seeing the world in a new way, through a set of absurdly warped (but in this, case decidedly clear and far-sighted) lenses.

Chapter 3

Blandly Drawn, Myopic Pinheads

The Awkwardly Effective Aesthetics of *The Far Side*

As an experiment, I turned to a random *Far Side* cartoon from the latter part of Larson's career (1993) and tried to judge its aesthetic quality through the eyes of a traditional critic. The image in question—a pair of dogs waltzing their way into a human dance studio in order to abduct a cat—does not fare well (at least initially) (fig. 3.1). For starters, Larson's understanding of human anatomy seems a bit shaky; even according to the stylized conventions of mainstream comics, his people are grotesque: bodies are shaped like giant, lumpy pears; backs are hunched, with heads attached directly to the front of chests; feet are connected to legs at strange angles (as if broken or deformed); the structure of the arms is all wrong, with bones bending at odd angles and muscles bulging in unexpected places; and fingers look like broken sausages, dangling from hands in random directions. The anatomy of the animals is equally awkward: stiff legs, joints in odd spots, poorly defined faces and torsos, and little sense of movement or energy on display.

The composition of this cartoon has problems too. For example, the cat—one of the most important figures in the cartoon—is strangely butted up against the far corner of the panel, as if smelling the side of the frame. In addition, there is no apparent hierarchy of importance among all the objects within the panel (whether human, animal, or inanimate), because they are all described with the same, unvaryingly flat line. In sum, it seems a wonder that such an amateurish drawing style was featured in one of the most popular newspaper cartoons of the late twentieth century.

Gary Larson was the first to admit that he was not a stellar artist in the conventional sense of the word. In interviews he was quick to poke fun

As witnesses later recalled,
two small dogs just waltzed into the place,
grabbed the cat, and waltzed out.

Fig. 3.1. Gary Larson, "As witnesses later recalled," *The Far Side*, April
13, 1993 (2-474).

at his clumsy abilities and limited array of character types; he said, "All
my stuff got boiled down to about six faces," "I never drew that well," and
"There are so many cartoonists who can draw circles around me" (Morrissey, "Far Side of Retirement"). Sensitive readers who were offended
by both the themes and the imagery of his strip went much further in
their critiques, complaining about his "ugly and sloppy" drawings full of
"insensitive characters," and charging that his images were devoid of "art,
beauty and intelligence" (Hess 471). Connoisseurs of cartoon art were less
melodramatic in their estimations, but perhaps equally dismissive; they
judged that Larson's drawing ability was either secondary in strength and
importance to his verbal skills or seriously deficient by any standard. One
scholar, for example, suggested that, "If you think too much, Larson's images cannot 'come off.' To understand his art, you must enjoy momentarily
being stupid" (Carrier 21).

In the following pages I happily embrace that stupidity, moving beyond conventional critiques of Larson's art to apply a customized (and more objective) rubric. To elaborate, typical celebrations of great comic strip art tend to apply standards that favor polished "professionals" whose art can be appreciated in an aesthetic vacuum—as great, stand-alone drawings. Styles that receive the most accolades tend to reflect professional training, a mastery of traditional methods, a virtuoso facility with expressive line work, and the construction of "cute" (or at least dynamic) characters who sometimes resemble, in movement and profile, the figures seen in mainstream film animation (rounded heads and bodies full of kinetic energy). Celebrated figures within the established pantheon include Walt Kelly (*Pogo*), Mort Walker (*Beetle Bailey*), Charles Schulz (*Peanuts*), and Bill Watterson (*Calvin and Hobbes*). As illustrated above, those standards automatically dismiss Larson's art as regrettable or forgettable because he was self-taught, influenced by underground or alternative cartoonists, used an awkward and limited visual palette, and favored the grotesque over the cute in character construction.

In contrast, I attempt to judge Larson's aesthetics according to one objective criterion: Did it "work"? Was his art an effective accompaniment to his verbal comedy and satiric intentions—helping him to consistently hit that sweet spot where he paired "the best joke told with the best image" (Doran)? In answering that question, I move from commonsensical judgments to more theoretical frames. First, I illustrate through specific examples how Larson's "bad" art made for funny drawings. Second, I highlight how an understanding of the power and complexity of highly distilled cartoon imagery adds to our appreciation of the effectiveness of Larson's minimalistic style. Third, I frame Larson's art within a history of intentionally "unprofessional," alternative cartooning. Finally, I explore the varied, potential readings of his awkward aesthetics in the cultural context of the 1980s. That last discussion is framed with the help of semiotics, a methodical approach to understanding the construction and resonance of cultural signs; it will aid us in explaining why Larson's grotesque cartooning vocabulary resonated so deeply with core fans while alienating just as sharply the comics readers who found his work offensive or inscrutable.

Awkward Art, Funny Drawings

As a self-taught artist unsteeped in the lore and practices of professional cartooning, Larson's artistic objectives were refreshingly straightforward:

he simply asked himself if an image was funny—and did it communicate its idea effectively? It didn't matter to him if the line work was dynamic and flashy or if the human forms were drawn accurately; as a goofily absurd cartoon, "it just [had] to work" (Morrissey, "The Far Side of Retirement"). The lack of polish and flair in *Far Side* panels did not mean, nevertheless, that Larson was careless and naive in his craft. Out of both pragmatic necessity and larger philosophical objectives, he developed—and even paradoxically refined—his limited cartooning aesthetic in the name of making funnier cartoons and communicating a carnivalesque worldview. As with his comedy, Larson was a perfectionist when it came to distilling and refining his own idiosyncratic style; however, instead of trying to mimic the cute aesthetics of the surrounding comics page, or learning to cartoon in a more polished manner, he worked tirelessly to make his own alternative style both "unambiguous" and "as good as it can be" (Morrissey, "Introduction" xi; Reagan xx). In fact, Larson's jokey assertion that the most essential tool he owned was an eraser had less to do with his limited drawing skills than it did with his devotion to achieving his primary goal of creating funny and provocative cartoons in an economical way—communicating the "most" with the "least" (Larson, "Preface" xvi; Doran). Larson elaborated:

> I used to work harder at some cartoons than probably people would ever expect that I did. But I do have a place I'm going in my mind, and I'll work at it and work at it until I finally get it. It might be just a silly face I'm drawing. Without being that great an artist, in my gut I knew where I wanted to go with something. And I would try to get it there. (Morrissey, "Far Side of Retirement")

With an appreciation of Larson's core objectives in mind, we can look at a couple of *Far Side* cartoons with fresh eyes. Let us reexamine, for example, the cartoon highlighted in the opening pages of this chapter (fig. 3.1). To begin, there is irony, slapstick comedy, and even philosophical import in the depiction of the human dancers as lumpy, ungainly individuals. In an ideal world, social dances like the waltz are meant to highlight youthful grace and romance; in the deflated reality of *The Far Side*, individuals tend to be obese, balding, uncoordinated, and poorly dressed—and Larson's limited drawing ability effectively highlights those imperfections. The characters' obliviousness, moreover, to their own awkwardness heightens the humor; it encourages us to see them as deluded and so absorbed by their inflated, romantic reveries that they fail to notice the incongruous arrival of two waltzing dogs into their midst.

Luposlipaphobia: The fear of being pursued by timber wolves around a kitchen table while wearing socks on a newly waxed floor.

Fig. 3.2. Gary Larson, "Luposlipaphobia," *The Far Side*, October 16, 1985 (1-518).

The animals in this cartoon are also funnier because of Larson's stiff renderings of their forms. The irregular, undetailed outline of the dogs' anatomy, for example, allows the reader to see them as distilled comic archetypes—essentialized mutts focused on one objective: getting that feline, even if it means pretending to be cavorting humans. In addition, the cat's strange placement at the margin of the frame works as an intentionally oafish detail; he is too lost in his own unfathomable thoughts to notice that he is in the middle of a dance floor, poorly placed in the cartoon itself, and completely unaware of his own approaching abduction. Finally, the general lack of dynamism in the cartoon gives both the overall composition a deadpan tone and allows for one or two significant details—like the dogs' anxiously bulging eyes and suspended ears—to take on a great deal of comic importance.

A second example of Larson's funny and effective style of "bad" drawing can be seen in his cartoon about "Luposlipaphobia—the fear of being pursued by timber wolves around a kitchen table while wearing socks on a newly waxed floor" (fig. 3.2). First of all, this is a rare *Far Side* panel in which violent action is on display; if Larson had tried to depict the running of either the wolves, or the boy, with genuine fluidity, however, the realism of the scene might have felt too alarmingly immediate and emotionally charged. Instead, the static quality of the drawing gives it the emotional distance of a frozen stage tableau, a flashback to a weird nightmare, or a slow-motion still from a demented nature documentary. Secondly, the table, the cloth which covers it, and the other inanimate objects in the scene are also drawn with a simple, meandering line, thus emphasizing both the boy's lack of protective cover and the deflated tone of the unfolding tragedy. Third, the wolves are drawn with enough anatomical accuracy to allow us to perceive them as wild canines, but not with the kind of careful detail or energetic dynamism to make them appear truly menacing. In fact, they seem slightly chubby and awkward in their gait, subtly suggesting that they have been forced, perhaps, because of a lack of athletic ability to seek softer, easier prey in suburban homes.

Finally, Larson's untutored rendering of the boy's anatomy amplifies the hilarity and poignancy of this unlikely scene of natural selection. In particular, the lumpy lack of musculature in his torso sweetens the slapstick qualities of his desperate gestures and pokes fun at how a sedentary, nerdy lifestyle does little to prepare a Middle American kid for even mildly taxing physical challenges. There are also connotations of emasculation in the boy's bulging hip and V-shaped crotch, and Larson's careless splaying of the lad's fingers emphasizes the futility of his effort to grasp any support. In addition, the impossible angle of the leg bones in relation to the hot-dog-shaped feet, and the seemingly atrophied, baby-sized proportions of the extended arm underscore the inevitability of his demise. A trained artist would actually have to work really hard—effectively unlearning some of his or her skill—to execute this sort of funny departure from accurate drawing; Larson, unburdened by that knowledge and skill, achieved it organically, refining his "errors" into genuinely funny and suggestively satiric imagery.

The mature version of Larson's graceless but effective style did not arrive overnight, of course; an examination of the evolution of his art reveals that he learned from early missteps and gradually became adept at distilling his images down to what was essential. Early cartoons were sometimes too complicated (full of unnecessary details and busy crosshatching), or too generous in the amount of emotional information they provided (for example, indicating a character's fear with buggy cartoon eyes and agitated motion lines). With time, Larson figured out how to focus a reader's attention by simplifying compositions, eliminating details that did not contribute to the cartoon's overall effect, and refining his characters down to archetypal essences. Perhaps as a result of drawing the same figures so many times over the years, Larson eventually minimalized and standardized his characters' glasses, noses, craniums, and shoulders to such a degree that he began tapping into some of the inherent psychological power of highly distilled cartoon aesthetics.

The Power of Distilled Cartoon Imagery

From a distance, the shallowness of Larson's visual palette (unaffected line work and a limited array of character types) would seem to be a handicap, limiting Larson to simplistic visual gags. A deeper familiarity with Larson's world, however, suggests that these limits did not proscribe complexity and depth. Scott McCloud, in his playfully illustrated book, *Understanding Comics*, gives us some concepts and terminology for supporting that view. Two of his key ideas, in particular, can help us to see the power of Larson's art more clearly: amplification through simplification, and reader identification with iconic cartoon characters.

To begin, a narrow palette does not necessarily exclude comedic variety and satiric depth, because the best cartoonists, like innovative genre film directors, can rearrange a limited set of ingredients in varied and unusual ways. Moreover, the repetitive, distilled quality of key symbols in cartooning can serve dual purposes: providing familiarity on the one hand (resonant archetypes or established motifs), and novelty and innovation on the other (a variety of surprising juxtapositions). That potential to move from familiarity to stimulating variation was especially potent, in fact, within *The Far Side*, because of the absurd logic that ruled Larson's universe. The animal and human worlds were forever overlapping, for instance, and thus the foundational, physical markers he used to describe his characters migrated into strange realms and created hilariously hybrid forms: dinosaurs wearing nerd glasses, cows sporting bouffant hairdos, matronly chickens wearing cat-eye glasses, and so on.

In addition to achieving complexity, distilled cartoon imagery is surprisingly effective at communicating and amplifying abstract ideas or profound emotions. McCloud explains that the practice of boiling an image down to its essential meaning allows a cartoonist to communicate concepts and inner lives in ways that are more incisive and potentially universal in their accessibility than what can be achieved through realistic art (McCloud 30). To be specific, the iconic quality of cartoons makes them potentially more engaging on an imaginative level than more detailed modes of representation, because they are executed in an expressive shorthand that eliminates unnecessary detail and focuses a reader's attention toward underlying meanings. In other words, the cartoonist is communicating essences rather than external particulars. In addition, the open-ended, "unfinished" quality of cartoon symbols invites an active, but almost unconscious, "closure" on the part of the reader. Adept from childhood at decoding the meanings of these abbreviated signs, the reader brings much of his or her own cultural

"So, Professor Jenkins! . . . My old nemesis! . . . We meet
again, but this time the advantage is mine!
Ha! Ha! Ha!"

Fig. 3.3. Gary Larson, "So, Professor Jenkins!" *The Far Side*, July 12, 1983 (1-314).

knowledge and imagination to bear on the completion of meaning in cartoon imagery.

These ideas point to some of the underappreciated complexity in *The Far Side*'s deceptively crude and minimalistic drawing style. As an example, the reductive quality of Larson's drawing of a duck in figure 3.3 heightens the humor of the situation and allows the figure to work as a meaning-packed, archetypal character rather than a descriptive illustration of a waterfowl. To elaborate, in this absurd parody of a spy thriller that features a confrontation in medias res between two longtime adversaries, the duck's minimal size and shape heighten the visual silliness of the encounter, underscoring the incongruity between the scientist's bulk and the seeming physical vulnerability of this small aquatic bird. In addition, with just a single panel in which to suggest an elaborate backstory and set of motivations, Larson intimates a great deal of information in the way he describes the malevolent duck so economically: a bland, static circle devoid of feathers for the body, tiny motionless legs, several parallel lines for the humorless beak, and a flat stroke of the pen for the eyes. That distillation steers one away from the things we might observe and think about in an accurate and detailed drawing of a duck (species-specific anatomy, color, texture, etc.) and instead allows us to dwell on possible backstories and absurd character dynamics. In sum, this minimalist treatment would be blandly meaningless if taken out of context, but within Larson's comedic vignette, it effectively describes a character full of stoic resolve and capable of years of obsessive, narcissistic revenge-plotting.

McCloud elaborates on the distilled potency of iconic comic art by comparing minimalistic cartoon faces to realistic portraits. On the one hand, a detailed drawing of another person's face creates the impression of an "other" who exists in a specific, objective reality beyond ourselves; in contrast, a minimalistic cartoon face—like a pop-cultural version of the distilled imagery of modernist art—can serve as an entry into an expansive realm of emotions, abstract ideas, and universal experiences. Highly iconic character faces, in particular (like Charlie Brown's—a simple, masklike circle with a series of dots and lines for features), are powerful portals that invite identification and vicarious participation in the emotional world of the strip.

When it comes to reader engagement with iconic cartoon faces, Larson pushes and pulls against traditional conventions in the service of his morbid brand of comedy and absurdist satire. To understand his alternative methods, we can compare how a reader might react differently to one of Larson's chubby nerd-kids on the one hand, and a sweet kid like Linus, by Charles Schulz, on the other (fig. 3.4). To begin, there are some narrative differences: in the continuity of the *Peanuts* world, Linus has a rich backstory that we follow over months and years, seeing him deal with various neuroses, a pushy sister, the repeated loss of a comfort blanket, and encounters with mystical figures like the Great Pumpkin. Invested in that narrative richness, we project ourselves sympathetically into his comedic ups and downs and existential crises. That high level of familiarity and character development brings comedic limitations, nevertheless; we are rarely required to speculate about what is going on in his mind (he always tells/shows us), and Schulz can never lead his storyline into absurd

Fig. 3.4. Gary Larson, "Free the Mayonnaise Jar Seven," *The Far Side*, April 12, 1990 (2-245).

or morbid territory without puncturing the realism and emotional consistency of his world.

In contrast, the lack of continuity in *The Far Side* never allowed his characters to reflect the emotional depth of the kids in *Peanuts*. The freedom to go in new directions with each panel however allowed Larson to pursue comedy that was more elaborately absurd and varied in its intellectual tones. In this particular panel, we are blocked from identifying on an emotional level with the juvenile, because we do not know his name or backstory. This suits Larson's purposes within the absurd logic of a stand-alone vignette, nevertheless, since we are asked, in this case, to see him through the eyes of the ants—as an oppressive dictator of sorts. We are given enough homey details in the boy's bedroom and figure, at the same time—his airplane collection, the juvenile freckles—to enjoy the incongruity of the scene. He seems, after all, more like a benign and familiar kid from a typical suburban home than a tyrant.

Turning to aesthetics, Schulz depicts his characters with an emotion-filled, quivering line that gives Linus an endearing, emotional dynamism. Linus's eyes—the most immediate portal through which a reader connects with a character—also invite a high degree of imaginative connection; those simple, bracketed dots are open and worry-filled, prompting us to experience vicariously his hopeful but fragile worldview. In contrast, Larson uses an affectless, unvarying line to describe his nerd-boy and his surroundings, and thus we are not invited to privilege him visually or to connect with him on an immediate and emotional level. Moreover, in terms of movement and dynamism, the bugs appear more alive and interesting than the boy; his static posture connotes thoughtless confusion or complacency. In addition, the kid's lack of pupils—hidden behind opaque glasses—leads us to react to him differently than we do to Linus. On the one hand, that general dearth of emotional information prevents us from connecting with him in a sympathetic way, but it also heightens his potency as a universalized icon of nerdiness. In addition, it invites imaginative closure from the reader, requiring us to speculate on the odd thoughts coursing below the boy's impassive features. In sum, in addition to inviting this higher level of intellectual (rather than emotional) engagement, the affectless and opaque qualities of Larson's cartooning devices in this case effectively short-circuit the comfortingly escapist qualities of cute cartoon aesthetics, forcing us to see (and think about) the world in freshly disturbing ways—such as a non-human perspective, in this case.

The Awkward Art of *The Far Side* in Its Cultural Context

Beyond recognizing the inherently potent qualities of Larson's distilled aesthetics, we can appreciate why the awkwardness of his style was funny and resonant with his fans by looking at his art within the cultural context of the early 1980s. Using that frame, the amateurish qualities of his drawings take on intentional, comedic qualities, and the weaknesses in his style reinforce some of his core, satiric insights about humanity. Core fans, in fact, might have liked Larson's awkward drawings precisely because they were so refreshingly bad and different in that context—like walking through a boring museum of blandly idealized portraits and suddenly encountering a set of vaguely perverse drawings of your immediate family drawn by an unskilled and impertinent third grader. And then, of course, you can imagine why the long-standing patrons of that museum would be equally appalled by the apparent breakdown of the jurying and filtering that had, theretofore, made their visits so pleasant.

To elaborate on how Larson's drawings stood out in that 1980s context—evoking delight and disgust in equal measure—we can borrow some basic ideas about the varied denotative and connotative meanings of cartooning imagery from semiotics, a quasi-science of cultural signs. That theoretical framing allows us to triangulate the larger social meanings that accrued around, and were communicated through, Larson's cartoons. Semiotics was articulated initially in the early twentieth century as a method for linguists to study the constructedness of language systems—the way that denotative meanings are arbitrarily attached to particular words within cultural traditions. Since then, thanks largely to the ideas of Roland Barthes, the field has expanded to encompass studies of how emotional and cultural meanings become attached to words and images; how those associations change over time according to shifting audiences and venues; and the ideological uses of vividly distilled imagery (Storey 95). While the core ideas associated with this theoretical frame are fairly straightforward and commonsensical, the methodical ways they break down the components of visual meaning-making allow one to consider how advertising, films, and cartoons use particular words, iconic images, and stylistic motifs with visceral power, exploiting semiconscious anxieties and desires.

In the case of *The Far Side*, we can use this method to understand how something as seemingly inconsequential as the line quality in Larson's drawings could be read in different ways depending on the reader—either denoting a boring, amateurish style to some, or connoting more hiply "alternative" associations to others. We can also analyze more carefully the multivalence of some of the key symbols in Larson's visual vocabulary: glasses, hairstyles, body shapes, etc. Readers who were thoroughly acquainted and sympathetic with Larson's comedy read those signs as a powerful shorthand vocabulary for a coherent set of satiric ideas and an alternatively ironic worldview; in contrast, uninitiated readers who felt "distant or unfamiliar" with Larson's satirical worldview might have seen these motifs as grotesque or lazily repetitive (Carrier 88).

Line Quality and the "Unprofessional" Style of *The Far Side*

For starters, we can look at the possible cultural connotations communicated by Larson's line work. *The Far Side* was executed in a garage-band version of what comics scholars call a minimalistic, clear-line style, most closely identified with Hergé's *Tintin* (Hatfield 61). In the United States this approach was also associated with underground comix, avant-garde animation, alternative-magazine cartoonists, and a handful of newspaper comics in 1960s and 1970s. In animation, a crop of studios in the 1960s such as Hanna-Barbera and the UPA (United Productions of America) adopted a pared-down aesthetic out of economic necessity and as a way of appearing more culturally current than the baroque style of Disneyesque imagery enjoyed by an older generation of viewers. In the field of underground comix, the reasons for adopting crude line work and unprofessional styles were blatantly antiestablishment; artists like Rory Hayes, Aline Kominsky-Crumb, and Diane Noomin advertised their outsider credentials, mocked genteel art practices, subverted the histrionics of superhero comics, and satirized bourgeois values with scratchy, spare, and grotesque renderings. In panel cartooning, some of Larson's primary influences—S. Gross and B. Kliban (publishing in *The New Yorker* and *Playboy*)—used a similarly stripped-down aesthetic as a way of emphasizing the conceptual constructedness of their ideas and distancing themselves from the squarely "professional" styles in old-fashioned mainstream publications like *Collier's* or *Reader's Digest*.

The traditional comics page was slow to adopt these raw and unaffected styles because of a long-standing resistance to experimental approaches and a favoring of venerable strips that appealed to the aesthetic sensibilities of older generations. Perhaps the closest equivalent to new-wave trends in the 1960s could be seen in the distilled line work of *Peanuts* and *B.C.*—strips whose tones were considered more hip and intellectual at that time than the old standbys that dominated the medium. Schulz and Hart, nevertheless, were still part of a long-standing aesthetic paradigm that celebrated an array of conventional, "professional" tropes: virtuoso pen and brushwork in distilling the human form down to a "realistic" essence, a cute style that anthropomorphized animals and simplified humans into endearingly familiar caricatures, and a professionalism in the general execution of the cartoon's seamless reality so that readers were able to lose themselves effortlessly in the emotional world of the text. As a related aside, pre-1960s Hollywood studio-system films had an equivalent standard of "realism" or

Fig. 3.5. Garry Trudeau, "Say B.D.," *Doonesbury*, October 26, 1970. Doonesbury copyright 1970 G. B. Trudeau. Reprinted with permission of UNIVERSAL PRESS SYNDICATE. All rights reserved.

aesthetic seamlessness that was used to camouflage the constructedness of the filmic text—primarily in the name of facilitating the ideologically untroubling experience of getting swept up in the escapist pleasures of a genre film in a darkened cinema.

Garry Trudeau (*Doonesbury*) was the first newspaper cartoonist, in fact, to challenge the old-fashioned aesthetic practices of the funnies page in a significant way, in 1970. His self-taught amateurism and emotionally neutral line work were key signals of both his outsider status in the profession and the antiestablishment orientation of his worldview (fig. 3.5). His clear-lined style also aligned nicely with the deadpan irony that coursed through his comedic world. The characters in *Doonesbury* were rendered in static poses with heavy-lidded eyes, suggesting that they were fatigued or unfazed by the spectacles of foolishness they had to witness in the worlds of politics and mainstream entertainment.

It was a full decade before Larson would follow in Trudeau's wake, but because so little changed on the ossified comics page during those years, *The Far Side*'s similarly awkward style still had the potential to carry subversive codings for disaffected readers thirsting for something different. Trudeau and Larson, in fact, were both blamed by some observers for introducing "bad art" onto the funnies page—for essentially opening the door for later strips like *Dilbert* (Scott Adams) or *Pearls Before Swine* (Stephan Pastis) that featured minimalistic styles that were considered even more crude. A brief perusal of the indignant charges from disgruntled readers reveals, nevertheless, that frustrations with Larson's art were not only about poor drawing skills invading the comics page. By saying that his style was "ugly and sloppy" and devoid of "art, beauty and intelligence," critics revealed that they were also invested in maintaining the bourgeois respectability that the comics page had achieved—and perhaps unconsciously advocating for a continued privileging of the polished and cute features that encouraged seamless escapism (Hess 471). Awkward art that drew attention to its own constructedness was perhaps linked in their minds with comedy that was "inappropriate" (ideologically subversive, in other words).

In stand-up comedy an affectless delivery is often associated with absurdist joke tellers like Stephen Wright or Demetri Martin; their deadpan delivery served a number of purposes: signaling an alternative or intellectual orientation (in contrast to the overwrought styles of an older generation of mainstream comedians); convincing listeners to suspend disbelief as they presented absurd premises or bizarre logic; and then requiring the audience to essentially close the joke, spotting the incongruity and its twisted implications on their own. That brand of comedy is not universally loved, of course, because of the level of engagement required, as if you're being asked to lean forward in your seat both literally and figuratively, to engage in puzzle-like mental games.

Similar dynamics are at work in how readers reacted to Larson's tamped-down style. Devoted fans liked the challenge of unpacking his deadpan jokes, while more traditional readers—accustomed to the emotive, visual soundtrack created by more polished and affected drawing styles (as if the cartoonist were holding their hand)—felt alienated by the dearth of interpretive clues in *The Far Side*. In effect, Larson's unvarying line quality, combined with the general lack of dynamism and emotion on display in his characters, gave the panel a tone similar to a mock-serious documentary. He was essentially keeping a straight face amidst all of the weirdness of his cartoon world, amplifying the reader's participation and resulting enjoyment of gags that feature bizarre logic, absurd incongruities, or horrific implications. Larson could pull off especially disturbing gags, in fact—like the demented janitor conducting illicit static-electricity experiments in a hospital nursery (fig. 0.3)—without coming across as too wacky or intentionally offensive. It's as if he is asking us, "What's your problem—I'm just reporting what happened."

Finally, Larson's unvarying line can also carry larger philosophical meanings. By treating all objects—human, animal, inanimate—with the same level of simplification and unembellished outline, *The Far Side* emphasized a "democracy of form" in which nothing was privileged and there was a blurring of organic and inorganic shapes (McCloud; Hatfield 61). Consider the cartoon, for example, where a scientist accidentally imprints himself on a mother duck (fig. 3.6). Because every object in the panel is treated with the same unemotional line, it seems strangely plausible that the scientist is governed by the same instinctual laws as waterfowl, and that the man's lab coat and glasses are the human equivalent of protective feathers. In sum,

When imprinting studies go awry

Fig. 3.6. Gary Larson, "When imprinting studies go awry," *The Far Side*, July 11, 1984 (1-404).

the visual leveling of hierarchies effectively reinforces a number of Larson's broader comedic/satiric goals: the blurring of lines between animal and human worlds, the challenging of anthropocentric worldviews with scientific naturalism, and the deconstruction of all things romantic and inflated.

Distilled Cultural Signs

A variety of distilled cultural signs, including spectacles, flat-eyed brows, narrow craniums, and lumpy physiques, carried loaded satiric meanings in *The Far Side*. The cat-eye glasses worn by Larson's iconic female types, for example, were especially significant in communicating some of Larson's alternative tones and intentions. To unpack that potential, we can move from micro to macro meanings.

Cat Eyeglasses

For starters, we can zero in on one of Larson's reductive ink drawings of a pair cat-eye glasses (fig. 3.7a). Due to the abstract minimalism of this isolated image—a set of slanted, ovoid circles with a connecting line—we might not even understand the meaning of this visual signifier without an understanding of its context. As we pull away, the denotative meaning of those marks becomes clear: they are corrective lenses worn by a human female (fig. 3.7b). That initial level of decoding seems fairly straightforward; any reader—even someone from another cultural tradition—could readily understand such a basic meaning. But because this sign communicates a great deal of additional humorous, cultural information beyond "a woman's glasses" within *The Far Side*, things get a little more complex. In the lingo of semiotics, we can move into the realm of secondary, connotative significations where meanings vary according to the cultural formation of the audience—with some readers making humorous, satiric associations, and others simply registering confusion or irritation (Storey 95).

By pulling back further, we identify additional connotative meanings: the glasses are worn by a woman with a sedentary, matronly figure and beehive hairdo (fig. 3.7c). A culturally literate reader thus places her within a set of larger historical and satiric codings: that cat-eye design and elaborately coiffed hairstyle were genuinely popular among American women during the 1950s and early 1960s but gradually became signs used, in alternative texts in the late 1960s and beyond, to connote dogmatism, conformism, and knee-jerk bigotry. And thus, antiestablishment cartoonists, like B. Kliban, Diane Noomin, or Al Jaffey, working in venues like *Playboy*, *Twisted Sisters*, or *MAD*, developed a convention of signaling that a female character was laughably square or obnoxiously conservative by giving her reductive identity markers that were a full decade out of date: an overweight figure, a piled-up hairdo, and the inwardly canted lenses. It makes sense that Larson, as a fan of those cartoonists, and a comedian with a similarly alternative worldview, would adopt that character type into his own fledgling work, with all of its accrued meanings and uses.

At this point we can see how a particular historical moment and venue—the mainstream comics page in the early 1980s—could determine the cultural meanings (or lack of meaning) communicated by this iconic sign. On the one hand, readers familiar with alternative cartooning traditions, and perhaps frustrated by the limited range of comedic voices allowed onto the mainstream comics page, read that sign as an indication that Larson was subversively different; he was a cartoonist intent on challenging

Fig, 3.7a. Gary Larson, "Lunch is ready," *The Far Side*, March 10, 1983 (1-285).

Fig. 3.7b. Gary Larson, "Lunch is ready," *The Far Side*, March 10, 1983 (1-285).

Fig. 3.7c. Gary Larson, "Lunch is ready," *The Far Side*, March 10, 1983 (1-285).

established cartooning practices and mainstream values. At the same time, editors and readers invested in the mainstream comics page as a haven for earnest, family-friendly entertainment (material that was "square," in a positive sense) might have felt irritated or defensive in perceiving the antiestablishment codings in Larson's sign system. And then, of course, there were surely elderly readers who might have been reading the comics page through a literal pair of cat-eye glasses, wondering what was so laughable about the functional corrective lenses they had unselfconsciously worn for decades.

Over time, Larson used those glasses with such consistency and baroque creativity that they eventually became a signature icon within his cartooning brand. This process of comedic sign-building took place over a number of years, of course, and if we survey his cartoons over the first five years of their syndication, it is possible to see a gradual process of refinement. For example, there were instances during Larson's first couple of years when the glasses were too complicated and vaguely formed; he sometimes provided dots for the character's pupils behind the frames or included distracting details—like an extra internal line or decorative flowers on the rims. That degree of visual particularization short-circuited some of the sign's ability to amplify comedic meanings through a distilled form—or to invite intellectual closure.

A year into his career, however, Larson had settled on the distilled representation of those glasses that became associated with this archetypal character: opaque lenses (no pupils), no decorative details, the subtle inward slant, and the minimalistic, unaffected line work. That mature version of the sign began appearing with such regularity, in fact (usually in combination with some of the additional identity markers mentioned above), that readers recognized the emergence of a recurring character with a set of predictable personality traits: complacency, priggishness, dogmatism, narrow-mindedness, and so on. Thus equipped with such a potently distilled icon in his arsenal, Larson could begin to riff upon a variety of comedic and satiric ideas associated with individuals who chose to see the world in narrowly judgmental ways. As an illustration of those dynamics at work, we can pull back even further on our key example and see this woman in her full comedic context: standing on the stairs, berating a husband at lunch time for STILL having the head of a fly (fig. 3.7d).

Within this particular vignette, the woman's glasses communicate a great deal of narrative and satiric information. The subtly slanted angle of the lens makes the wife seem like a person who is perpetually irritated and disapproving, and the omission of the pupil (hiding it behind opaque

"Lunch is ready, Lawrence, and . . . What? You're
STILL a fly?"

Fig. 3.7d. Gary Larson, "Lunch is ready," *The Far Side*, March 10, 1983 (1-285).

lenses) suggests that she is both literally and figuratively myopic. Those at-
tributes of impatience, superiority, and myopia would be merely comical—
even stereotypical in a conventional sense—if the stakes were low or if her
nebbishy husband were stealing a nap on the couch with the newspaper. In
Larson's world, however, genres tend to cross-pollinate, traditional conventions are deconstructed, and stereotypes are bent and often broken—and
connotative meanings were thus more comedically surprising and satirically potent. In this case, her inability to recognize that she has essentially
walked into a horror movie—that Lawrence will probably never be able
to eat a normal, human lunch again—creates a darkly funny incongruity
between her limited perception and his morbid reality.

Fig. 3.8. Gary Larson, "Cover illustration," *In Search of the Far Side*, 1984.

Similar versions of this character make the same mistakes in other cartoons: she belittles her son's creeping sense of horror as he observes a family of monsters casually moving in next door (11/5/85; 1–524); she chides the babysitter witch for going overboard in eating *both* of her children (3/24/82; 1–200); or she sympathizes with a poor shark—"It must have been starving!"—after it devours her husband (12/18/84; 1–441). While each of these cartoons creates a joke out of a basic incongruity—a nearsighted reaction failing to respond properly to either a dire or mundane situation—they also combine to make a larger point about a culture in which insulated, civilized individuals seem incapable of perceiving basic realities or of assigning the proper weight to events on a spectrum from mundane to horrific.

By about the third year of *The Far Side*'s run, a distilled version of this character type also began to feature prominently in promotional materials. Serving almost like a logo or mascot for Larson's universe, she is reduced to her essential identity markers: the hair, the glasses, and a mumu-like dress over a pear-shaped figure. She begins to appear on book collection covers (fig. 3.8), merchandise, and metafictive jokes about Larson's cartoon universe. The glasses, moreover, have become such a potently distilled sign for the array of satiric meanings that have accrued around this character type that they readily transfer those meanings to other figures. During *The Far Side*'s mature years, for example, they appear on dull princesses, schoolmarmish chickens, complacent female cows, angry amoebas, and the brow of a female ape who assumes her husband is having an affair with "that Jane Goodall tramp" (fig. 1.7). In effect, they become independently archetypal, representing in their distilled form some of the key satiric themes of Larson's cartoon world.

Eyes

Moving on, we can explore the cultural connotations for several additional signs related to eyes and vision in *The Far Side*. In keeping with Larson's general aesthetic practice of "less is more," pupils rarely appear in any *Far Side* cartoons. Most often, they are obscured behind thick, circular lenses or hidden within the fold of a flat-eyed brow. Round glasses appear on obese little boys, adult male nerds, occasional grandmas, and bookish academics and scientists. On a satiric level they usually connote bland intellectualism, a sedentary lifestyle, and a narrow range of hyper-focused interests. While the roundness of glasses sometimes indicates a youthful vulnerability and naïveté (especially in cases where the kid is being terrorized by monsters or chased around a kitchen table by rabid wolves [fig. 3.2]), they can also obscure eyes that are intent on conducting mildly sadistic zoology experiments. Moreover, they occasionally appear on blandly amoral scientists like the one who calmly surprises a colleague with a drop of acid on the neck (fig. 3.9); or at other times they can be seen on malicious grandmothers intent on crashing into small children in a bumper car attraction (4/8/81; 1–115). The combination of such questionable activities with this iconic sign of overeducation underscores a classic satiric point made by both Mark Twain and Jonathan Swift: attaining "civilized" knowledge does not necessarily result in wise and moral behavior. The range of motivations hidden behind those lenses, in fact—ranging from the innocent to the malevolent—also highlights the flexibility of meaning in a sign so open-ended, that essentially requires the reader to provide closure based on context, character, and their own imaginations.

Flat-eyed brows in *The Far Side* also ask the reader to fathom the odd corners of a character's internal life. Larson mentions adopting this cartooning device after noticing how the expressions of secondary characters in classic cartoons (the apes in Tarzan comic books, for example) were indicated with such suggestive economy: "The eyes of gorillas were almost never revealed in those early comics; they were only implied by the dark shadow created from an overhanging browridge. I loved that. I stole that" (Larson, "Jungle in My Room" 4). In *Tarzan* and other early comics,

Professor Glickman, the lab practical joker,
deftly places a single drop of hydrochloric acid
on the back of Professor Bingham's neck.

Fig. 3.9. Gary Larson, "Professor Glickman," *The Far Side*, October 18,
1991 (2-356).

this flat-eyed brow usually indicated distant "otherness"—a savage figure
whose motivations were primitive and alien. Never given a close-up, and
often lumped together in a mass of similarly distanced figures, those apes
were meant to remain secondary props with whom we are not meant to
sympathize or identify.

Larson's use of this sign differed significantly. He made little distinc-
tion between central and secondary characters, for example; they are both
drawn with the same distanced economy, and unless a character is unusually alarmed (like the researcher receiving the drop of acid on his neck),
their eyes—whether a cat's, a cowboy's, or the great Creator's—are always
buried deep within that shadowed brow (fig. 3.10). In Larson's world this
convention performs a number of comedic functions: keeping foolish characters at arm's length, sustaining a neutral tone, and drawing the reader

Fig. 3.10. Gary Larson, "Piranha," *The Far Side*, September 14, 1985 (1-510).

into creative speculations. It might also play into one of Larson's larger philosophical intentions: the thorough democratization of peoples and species in Larson's world, effectively lumping together inscrutable ducks, emotionally bland middle-aged men, amoral prepubescent nerds, and dispassionate predators.

Heads

A pinheaded cranium was another sign that carried inherently disturbing and decidedly uncute meanings in Larson's world (fig. 3.11). Thanks to the popularization of pseudoscientific theories like phrenology and eugenics in the first part of the twentieth century, consumers of popular genre entertainment have been conditioned to make unconscious assumptions about

Fig. 3.11. Gary Larson, "Emma . . . the dog ain't goin' for
the new cat," *The Far Side*, January 16, 1987 (2-11).

a character's intelligence and cultural status based on the shape of his head. In science fiction and horror, a bulging prefrontal cortex suggested that that the figure was impressively (and sometimes dangerously) advanced on the evolutionary scale, moving beyond the animal kingdom and everyday humans. In film noir and detective stories, criminals and members of the mafia were often given especially swarthy features and sloping, low brows, connoting inherent deviance.

Less disturbingly, oversized heads featured prominently in the cute kid and animal features that dominated comic strips and children's animation throughout the twentieth century (and still to this day). Animation scholars have conjectured that we have evolved to respond positively, even protectively, toward imagery of children and animals with large, rounded heads. We are apparently naturally attracted to cartoon characters like Mickey Mouse, Garfield, or Hello Kitty that feature a large "cranial bulge with big round eyes atop a small body" (Canemaker 7–8).

In contrast, we never see large heads in Larson's deflated universe; primitive hominids (which appear with regularity in Larson's world) have the sloping brow, of course, but otherwise, all animals, adult humans— and even small children—sport a skull that narrows beyond the brow to a rounded point, like an upside-down pear. On a comedic level, that ubiquitous sign alerted the reader to Larson's intention of undermining, in grotesque fashion, the sweetness that pervaded other cartooning imagery. While the *Peanuts* gang and Dennis the Menace had oversized heads and inviting, innocent eyes, the nerdy kids that populate Larson's world all have narrow skulls accompanied with bad haircuts and thick glasses. One comics scholar, noticing these awkward and intentionally anti-cute drawing strategies, lamented that everyone in Larson's comics—"even the children"—look old, like "they have no future" (Carrier 21). That jaded, premature loss of cuteness even extends to domesticated animals like cats and dogs in *The Far Side*—figures we would expect to be drawn with at least a few inherently endearing visual qualities; instead, they look world-wise and pinched, with tiny heads, flat-eyed brows, and featureless textures.

On a satiric level it seems significant that Larson makes this pinheaded-ness universal among humans. While earlier cartooning traditions built (unconsciously at times) upon the flawed worldview of eugenics—creating visual hierarchies among ethnicities with differing head shapes and body types—Larson democratized humanity in a deflated way. Within his naturalistic and degenerative framing, the entire human race is essentially devolving or squandering its intelligence and education on pointless leisure and wrongheaded scientific pursuits. In addition, the ubiquity of that sign beyond *Homo sapiens*, into the animal kingdom, helped to reinforce Larson's general questioning of human-flattering worldviews; we are essentially no better or different than all of them. The rare exceptions were those cartoons in which a hyperintelligent animal—its shrewdness signaled by a gently bulging brow—is getting the best of its human competitor.

Bodies

Larson's practice of attaching lumpy, rotund bodies to all of these pin-headed skulls might seem like an aesthetic crutch on one level, but it was also an effective comedic and satiric device. For starters, there are inherent comedic advantages to giving all of his characters—even athletes and warriors—physical profiles that are flabby, out of proportion, and poorly constructed. Opportunities to heighten the visual slapstick in each panel emerge, for example, with this motif—as in the vignette where a rotund husband is swinging his wife's ungainly form by an arm and leg around the living room floor (fig. 3.12); the same image would lack comedic heft (ahem) if the figures were svelte and ideally proportioned. According to politically incorrect comedic traditions, violent encounters appear goofy and comical—and romantic rendezvous are playfully deflated—when human bodies are all lumpy and plus-sized.

Given the inherent comedic qualities of ungainly bodies, we still might wonder if there wasn't something cruel or immature in relying so heavily on fat-people jokes. In response, you could argue that obesity was a useful and fair metaphor when it was used to poke fun at characters who represented Middle American culture in general (as opposed to mocking specific weight-challenged individuals). The key characteristics of these endomorphs—rolled shoulders, a spare tire around the midsection, atrophied limbs, poor posture, and a "buffalo hump" at the top of the spine—could be read as symptoms of a variety of contemporary social ills: sedentary lifestyles,

**On the next pass, however, Helen failed to clear
the mountains.**

Fig. 3.12. Gary Larson, "On the next pass," *The Far Side,* April 26, 1984 (1-386).

a detachment from the natural world, subsistence on carbohydrate-rich processed foods, and a general political passivity (fig. 3.13).

The lack of flexibility and dynamism in Larson's human figures set his aesthetics apart from those of the mainstream comics page once again. While many classic strips like *Pogo* and *Calvin and Hobbes* featured figures that were in constant motion, forever crossing new landscapes with youthful energy, Larson's pathetic humans seemed overcome by the forces of aging, inertia, and gravity. That plodding rigidity also connoted other collective, modern ailments: chronic fatigue, laziness, dogmatism, a willful ignorance in the face of new information or change. It seems that few

"Whoa! Mr. Lewis! We don't know what that thing is or where it came from, but after what happened to the dog last week, we advise people not to touch it."

Fig. 3.13. Gary Larson, "Whoa! Mr. Lewis!" *The Far Side*, September 24, 1991 (2-350).

things could compel one of Larson's figures to engage in physical activity: scientists simply stared impassively through thick lenses at boring or absurd data; people at parties stood rigid, bending only an arm to hold a glass; and obese children remained frozen in horror as monsters moved in next door or lurked under their beds. In sum, the universal stasis in Larson's world communicated the vaguely degenerative idea that people cannot really change, that humans are creatures of boring, instinctual habits.

Assuming Larson was also driven by less misanthropic impulses at times, you could say that the chubby formlessness of his characters could occasionally take on vaguely positive or democratic meanings. In the history of stage and film, overweight individuals often served as jovial clowns, energetic buffoons, or gourmands who relished the physical pleasures of life. That energy and joy was rarely on display in Larson's deflated world, but we could still sympathize and identify with nonthreatening, self-indulgent, everyday schmoes. Moreover, from the perspective of carnivalesque theory, there is also something refreshingly subversive about a world where hierarchies of physical perfection do not exist. In premodern, Western culture people encountered in their everyday "first lives" a variety of idealized images of the human form: religious icons, sculptures of accomplished athletes or warriors, or paintings depicting archetypes of romantic or sexual appeal. During seasonal carnival celebrations there was a temporary respite from those elevated ideals, as communal "second-life" celebrations featured democratic inversions and grotesque parodies: images and performances of the human body as flabby, imperfect, and given over to its natural—but often repressed—functions of eating, dancing, laughing, passing gas, and so on. If we update this analogy for late twentieth-century society, we could say that *The Far Side* acted as a deflated carnivalesque mirror, inverting all of the idealized imagery of human bodies that people encountered in fashion magazines, cute cartoons, advertisements, and genre films. In Larson's world there are no Olympic athletes, svelte models, sweetly proportioned toddlers, or fit twenty-something hipster friends hanging out in coffee shops; instead, we encounter a cavalcade of puffy nerds bumbling their way through an imperfect world.

The general sameness of Larson's human figures also ran counter to conventions of ethnic typing in earlier twentieth-century cartoons. In Larson's world, facial features, skin color, and body types, for example, are largely constant across cultural borders and historical periods. The almost complete absence of darker skin types in Larson's figures could be attributed in part to the difficulties of describing coherent gradations of value in a black-and-white medium—especially for a self-taught artist unaccustomed to using Ben-Day dots or subtle cross-hatching. It might also be a reflection of Larson's upbringing in a largely white, suburban neighborhood, as well as a default strategy (for good and ill) of avoiding ethnic humor altogether. On the positive side, the omission of ethnic markers is rightly democratic and even scientifically accurate, emphasizing the reality of genotypic sameness in the human family—as opposed to old-fashioned conventions of ranking "races" based on exaggerated phenotypic differences. Less generously, you could say that there's a bit of timidity in featuring, by default, a bland, white, Middle American type in most of his panels and missing out on the rich comedy that could emerge from pushing and pulling against a history of visual ethnic tropes in the medium.

"Are they gaining, Huxley?"

Fig. 3.14. Gary Larson, "Are they gaining, Huxley?" *The Far Side*, April 26, 1982 (1-208).

We can see the latent potential for that kind of deconstructive, self-aware treatment of ethnic issues in the one significant exception to Larson's use of the white, pear-shaped body: his renderings of indigenous peoples. In most cases their facial features conformed to Larson's tamped-down, homogenized template, but their bodies were usually straight-backed and physically fit (fig. 3.14). By contrasting that kind of healthy figure against the pear-shaped explorers from the developed world, Larson implies that the physical distinctions are cultural rather than genetic; the poor posture and obesity of the white interlopers is an outgrowth of contemporary lifestyles in an entertainment-addled, technology-driven Western world. Significantly, the indigenous people were also drawn with the flat-eyed brows that traditionally connoted alien otherness in golden age comic books. In this case the sign seems to suggest that these people are folkwise and can see with greater no-nonsense clarity than the overeducated and myopic explorers.

Turning to sign systems for gender, we can observe that most midcentury male cartoonists in the magazine and newspaper fields relied on a set of reductive female body types deeply embedded in the cultural imagination: the hourglass-shaped, dim-witted object of desire; the sharply angled, streetwise vamp or man-killer; and the oversized, lumpy, battle-axe spouse. There were exceptions to this rule, of course—in particular, innovative strips like *Krazy Kat* that made gender identities ambiguous, and a plethora of kid and girl strips (often drawn by women) that departed from sexist conventions. The most popular strips on the funnies page at midcentury, nevertheless, seemed to mirror popular genre films of the time in emphasizing male and female physical differences to a hyperbolic degree (e.g., *Li'l Abner, Beetle Bailey*, and *B.C.*).

One might expect the countercultural comix movement of the 1960s to be a medium where less offensive visual signs for femaleness might have emerged, but for the most part that was not the case. There were progressive-minded female cartoonists like Trina Robbins, Diane Noomin, and Aline Kominsky-Crumb, who introduced feministic rebuttals to mainstream conventions, but the dominant male figures in the field like R. Crumb and Gilbert Shelton tended to objectify and fetishize the female form in unhinged ways. Even alternative panel cartoonists like B. Kliban had persistent blind spots in this area, satirizing patriarchal culture at times, but often portraying sexualized female bodies in gratuitous ways.

Finally, in the 1970s, a new generation of panel and comic-strip artists like S. Gross, Garry Trudeau, and Lynn Johnston introduced drawing styles that tamped down exaggerated physical typing. With a few caveats, Larson generally belonged to that emerging trend. Idealized, young female bodies never appeared in *The Far Side*, and men and women generally had the same flabby, middle-aged forms no matter their age or background. That sameness of male and female bodies not only leveled gender hierarchies in *The Far Side* but also effectively deromanticized or de-eroticized (but without desexualizing, in a scientific sense) courtship vignettes. Romantic encounters were always comically deflated, never titillating a male or a female gaze; and mating practices were depicted as mundane and clinical, like a comic parody of a bland nature documentary (fig. 3.15).

You could argue, perhaps, that the iconic, heavyset woman who appeared so often in *The Far Side* was one blind spot in Larson's generally

When ornithologists are mutually attracted

Fig. 3.15. Gary Larson, "When ornithologists are mutually attracted," *The Far Side*, Feb. 4, 1988 (2-136).

progressive treatment of the female form. She seems like a reductive female type, after all—a close cousin to the tired image of the heavyweight, asexual housewife who continually berated her poor "little man" in midcentury panel cartoons. In Larson's version of the dynamic, however, both the wife and husband had similarly closed facial features (the opaque glasses or eye slit below the brow) and equally large and ill-defined torsos; as a result, the traditional gender hierarchy/dynamic of those old, vaguely sexist jokes were generally short-circuited. Neither figure in the couple was privileged over the other in terms of sympathetic visual treatment or potential reader identification.

In closing, it is significant, too, that Larson's practice of leveling visual hierarchies of identity extended beyond the human species as well.

The same awkward body types, narrow skulls, opaque glasses, and eyeless brows appear across carnivores, herbivores, amphibians, dinosaurs, etc. Domesticated animals in particular—cows, ducks, chickens, cats, dogs, etc.—tend to look very similar to the heavyset, middle-class nerds with whom they interacted in absurd but mundane encounters. This transspecies visual sameness could suggest a variety of satiric points: humans tend to impose arbitrary hierarchies of value on other species; all animals, including humans, are driven by instinctual needs; and *Homo sapiens*, in their softened and sedentary forms, had perhaps become a brand of vulnerable, domesticated animals themselves. In sum, it is difficult to feel too uppity about your gender, ethnicity, or species after immersing yourself in a world where all animals—including *Homo sapiens*—are part of the same pathetically flabby and nearsighted clan.

Chapter 4

The Accidental Cartooning Auteur

The Business Side of Gary Larson's Career

My favorite *Far Side* book cover, on the first *Gallery* collection published in 1984, depicts Larson's signature cast of weirdos pouring forth from a jar like a clandestine science experiment gone wrong (fig. 4.1). Beyond working as a supremely simple and funny image, it posits an accurate metaphor: Larson's comic was like a mutant virus that under normal lab conditions would never have been exposed to the world of mainstream funnies. It took an extraordinary amount of luck, serendipity, and even bumbling naïveté for Larson to overcome (or simply bypass) the obstacles that would have tripped up an average cartoonist on his or her path to national syndication. And then once established in its new host, *The Far Side* strain exhibited a freakish resistance to the kinds of antibodies—commercial pressures, editorial meddling, indignant readers—that normally prevented cartoonists with alternative sensibilities or unusual aesthetics from thriving on the mainstream comics page. Finally, within just a half dozen years, Larson's creation—which had started as a pesky niche infection—became so widely loved and deeply embedded in the funnies page that it essentially qualified as a legitimate—albeit, still vaguely mutant—species that would dominate its ecosystem for another ten years.

The details of how this happened—how Larson maintained the health of his creation in a largely unsuitable environment at the various stages of his career—are worth exploring. In the following pages we do just that, looking at the behind-the-scenes aspects of Larson's work: the negotiations and business practices that undergirded the long-term quality and integrity of *The Far Side*. From a distance, this topic—which includes discussions of contracts, merchandising, artists' rights, and sabbaticals—may not sound

Fig. 4.1 Gary Larson, "*Far Side* characters," cover art for *The Far Side Gallery*, 1984.

as interesting as Larson's comedy and art; but upon closer inspection, it has fascinating dimensions and mildly comic and dramatic episodes. They include tricky interactions with editors, appalled letters from disgruntled readers, and significant breakthroughs born out of Larson's stubborn and quiet resolve to follow his own slightly perverse muse (the one with the old-fashioned glasses and outsized hairdo). A bit of theoretical framing, moreover, will help us to understand how *The Far Side*'s especially original art and comedy was inextricably linked to how Larson and his collaborators dealt with a variety of institutional and commercial pressures. In particular, qualified notions of auteurship and sateurship will help us to explore the particular decisions and events that allowed such an unlikely cartoonist to create one of the most popular and genuinely counterdiscursive works of popular satire in the late twentieth century.

The Daunting Field of Professional, Syndicated Cartooning

To begin, we can review the challenges faced by aspiring syndicated cartoonists at the start of the 1980s. During that era there were only two or three spots that opened up for a new comic, from year to year, on the mainstream funnies; the likelihood of a young, aspiring cartoonist garnering one of those openings was ridiculously difficult. Consider the competition: each of the five major syndicates received, on average, two to three thousand submissions each year. Of that number, only four cartoonists were given development deals per syndicate, and then perhaps only two out of those four would actually win a chance to be marketed nationally (Staake 234). In sum, we have a half dozen syndicates winnowing several thousand submissions down to perhaps ten strips, total, vying for two or three available spots.

The challenges did not dissipate, of course, once an artist was successfully promoted to fill one of those coveted openings. Despite gaining an initial foothold in a few dozen papers, the chances were minimal that a newly syndicated cartoon would last more than one or two years. Fickle readers and jumpy editors (who were continually bombarded with the next great feature) made those entry points notoriously unstable. Given the combined odds, it would have been easier in 1980 to become a successful actor in the Hollywood film industry than a superstar cartoonist on the syndicated comics page. One of Larson's former editors described it this way: "Imagine that the only bookstore in town has a selection of just two dozen titles, some of them 70 years old, and you have a fairly accurate idea of what cartoon syndication is like: it's a very competitive business. The odds are stacked against you" (Morrissey, "Introduction" xi).

In addition to the problem of limited real estate, the funnies page was plagued by a conservative inertia among readers and editors. Eager to please the largest swath of subscribers (and to offend no one), editors often relied on unscientific popularity polls to manage their limited lineup of cartoons. The most vocal participants in those polls tended be sensitive, older readers who both cherished the familiarity of venerable strips that had been around for decades (sometimes long after the original cartoonist had passed on), and resented the arrival of any comics that challenged the tame, family-friendly orientation of the page. It was clear in their responses to polls—and in their indignant letters of complaint about particular strips that broke the rules (like *The Far Side* or *Doonesbury*)—that they felt protective of *their* comics page. As an example, consider this letter in opposition to Larson's work, written when he was first promoted on a national level:

> I am writing at this time to tell you that I feel that it was very bad judgment, or worse than that, to incorporate the comic *The Far Side* into your paper. For an area of the country that prides itself in its clean, wholesome, country, family-oriented atmosphere, an item such as this which is so totally morally and religiously degrading should not, and cannot, be tolerated. I do hope that this item will soon be eliminated from our paper, and thank you for your consideration in this matter. (Hoogendoorn 471)

In light of such indignant pushback, it is understandable that many harried editors were loath to adopt new strips like *The Far Side* that could be seen as "difficult," or to make any changes at all to their regular lineup of safe comics from year to year.

That wariness rippled back along the production line. Syndicate strategists, observing the conservative mind-set of newspaper editors, tended to be, in their turn, highly cautious about the kinds of cartoons they chose to develop and promote each year. Because it could cost several hundred thousand dollars to develop a single cartoon for syndication (and in many cases the bulk of that money might be lost as the strip petered out into relative obscurity over the course of several years), they wanted to invest in sure bets. In fact, syndicates were most eager to discover and nurture the rare blockbuster strip that would gain a long-term hold on the comics page, generate large syndication fees for decades, and make millions of dollars in profit through merchandising. Of course, that sounds very similar to what *The Far Side* achieved for Larson and his forward-thinking editors in the long run, but because most syndicates in the field tended to be averse to both financial risk and controversy, they usually placed their chips on cute and inoffensive mediocrity rather than high-quality weirdness. Stuart Rees, a legal scholar who observed firsthand the internal workings of syndicates, confirmed this institutional timidity, noting that many challenging, "high quality strips that the syndicate executives believe[d] would be popular with the public [were] never signed because the syndicates [felt] that the newspaper editors [would] not buy risky or different material" (Rees 21).

These harsh business realities were passed down the line to cartoonists through trade publications and how-to guides. "Experts" emphatically advised aspiring artists to avoid any humor or subject matter that might offend the most sensitive readers and newspaper editors (Hurd, "What Happens," 8–10; Hurd, "Trip"). And thus, savvy cartoonists who had studied the intense pressures and competitive odds in the field were inclined to self-censor even before submitting their work, essentially attempting to predict the kind of safe characters and cute comedy that a syndicate would feel good about promoting.

Once in the door of most syndicates, pre-vetted strips would face additional layers of grooming in the name of maximizing their breadth of appeal. This meant, on one level, diminishing those elements of the work that were still unpolished or potentially offensive (untutored art, topical satire, risky subject matter, etc.); on another level, it meant amplifying those qualities that seemed most likely to lead to blockbuster success (cute aesthetics, gentle comedy, endearing characters, and so on). Standing as a stark anomaly to the end result of that traditional production line, *The Far Side* did not fulfill any of the expectations of a safe and profitable newspaper comic: the aesthetics were awkward and untutored, the characters were grotesque rather than cute, there was no continuity of narrative or character development that would build long-term reader identification and devotion, the comedy was rife with morbid and irreverent material that would offend traditional readers of the comics page, and the satiric ideas at its core were unsettling.

So beyond the miracle of breaking into the exclusive field of national syndication, an observer might wonder how Larson managed to protect the weirdness of his art and comedy from traditional mediations and then continued to excel in the field against enormous odds once he made his big break. In order to give a complete explanation of how Larson bent or bypassed his profession's rules, we can first pull our focus back a bit and provide some theory and context. In particular, it will be helpful to compare Larson and the obstacles he faced to those confronted at mid-twentieth century by film directors like Preston Sturges and Alfred Hitchcock (who were also fairly weird by the mainstream standards of their eras, and who somehow broke into, and excelled within, a similarly restrictive medium).

A Qualified Notion of the Auteur Theory

To begin, we can compare the institutional and commercial practices of the newspaper comics industry in the 1980s to those of the studio system in Hollywood before the 1960s. Comic strips, like cinema, had started out at the opening of the twentieth century as a rowdy, widely accessible art form that had the potential to speak to, and for, working-class and immigrant audiences (a "disordering medium appealing to disordered and disoriented classes," according to the comics scholar David Kunzle) (Kunzle xix). Business people in these two emerging industries were primarily interested in making their mediums stable and profitable, however, and thus syndicates and studios methodically tried to gentrify or "clean up" their respective art forms for an imagined national audience. In practice, this amounted to catering to the most desirable (or feared) demographic: middle and upper-middle-class, white, Anglo-Protestant patrons. In cinema the gentrification process included the construction of movie palaces that were more "respectable" than storefront nickelodeons; the enforcement of predictable and comfortingly bourgeois and familiar storytelling patterns (continuity scripts and strict genre categories/conventions); the adoption of censorship codes; and the use of restrictive contracts to rein in the experimental impulses of actors and artists. Studio bosses, in fact, were so eager to protect the familiar and noncontroversial quality of their product that they greatly limited the artistic license of directors; in the term of French film critics, they were simply asked to be *metteurs en scène*—scene setters who followed a script and familiar genre pattern with a high level of technical proficiency.

The gentrification of newspaper comics followed a similar pattern from the 1920s through the 1960s: a regularization of formats and gradual shrinking of sizes, the promotion of distinct and predictable genres (kid, girl, animal, action-adventure strips, etc.), unofficial but strict censorship codes, and contracts weighted in favor of syndicates. Those contracts in particular have been blamed by many observers of the field for restricting the freedoms of cartoonists and limiting the creativity and variety of tones that could be featured in the newspaper funnies. Clauses weighted against the creators included giving up ownership of their work; missing out on vacations, sabbaticals, or retirement on their own terms; ceding control of merchandising decisions; and relinquishing final approval of content to syndicate editors. If cartoonists were slow to deliver work, or unpliable in responding to editorial input, the syndicate could simply fire them and assign the feature to a new artist (an ugly practice that happened with regularity during the field's early years). In addition, when a cartoonist's advanced age or death got in the way of the cartoon's daily production, the strip could be passed on to a different artist. In sum, syndicated cartoonists, in a majority of cases, were treated like *metteurs en scène*—highly proficient (but replaceable) writers/artists expected to deliver a reliable and uncontroversial product on a daily basis for decades.

Interestingly, Hollywood's lack of flexibility in adjusting to emerging pressures at midcentury (competition from new media like television, and changing tastes in the rising youth culture) led to the general collapse of the centralized studio system and its oppressive contracts and rigid filtering mechanisms. To survive these challenges beyond the late 1950s, the industry was forced to pare back and decentralize its production methods. Moving into the 1960s and early 1970s, that slackening of direct control changed the form and content of films in dramatic ways: genres cross-pollinated and narrative conventions loosened, allowing for dark, tragicomic tones and hybrid character types to emerge; New Wave directors introduced self-consciously experimental filmic devices into the medium; and some creators felt emboldened to explore material with antiestablishment (but not fully countercultural) tones (as in satiric movies like Billy Wilder's *The Apartment*, Stanley Kubrick's *Dr. Strangelove*, or Mike Nichols' *The Graduate*). Later, at the start of the 1980s, the economic pressures of blockbuster filmmaking effectively reinstated some of the gentrifying mechanisms of the earlier, studio era, but the industry was still forever changed by the fecund creativity of that decade and half when the strictest rules of the industry were slackened. While discerning audiences still had to endure a lot of formulaic, committee-driven fare coming out of Hollywood in subsequent years, there was at least greater space for independent voices and alternative aesthetics to thrive going forward.

In contrast, newspaper comics remained a conservative holdout during that period of pop-cultural liberalization from the 1960s into the mid-1970s. Devoted newspaper readers tended to come from older demographics, and thus the pressures faced by editors to adjust course were not especially intense. Looking back, there were signs that the newspaper industry would endure a long and dramatic collapse in the latter decades of the twentieth century as younger readers (and a culturally and ethnically diverse readership) found better entertainment in more flexible and dynamic media like television and the Internet. At the time, however, editors were uninterested in changing a set of business and editorial practices that seemed timelessly profitable. The pace of that doomed trajectory was further quickened by practices that limited the size, number, and variety of voices that could be featured on the comics page—all in the name of maintaining a reliable and theretofore lucrative status quo.

The Auteur Concept

Despite the general accuracy of this account of how film and newspaper comics were heavily gentrified by commercial pressures and institutional controls, there were some significant wrinkles that should be included in the narrative. First of all, even during the most restrictive periods in these mediums' histories there were always a handful of creators who found ways to resist or bypass the worst strictures of their industries. French critics and filmmakers in the 1960s noticed, for example, that some popular film directors found ways to evade the most oppressive mediations of the "industrialized" Hollywood studio system, creating, as a result, a body of work that reflected their peculiar aesthetic visions or vaguely antiestablishment worldviews. Key examples included Orson Welles, John Ford (working in Westerns), Alfred Hitchcock (psychological thrillers), Preston Sturges, and Billy Wilder (both in romantic comedies). To differentiate these iconoclastic directors from more run-of-the-mill *metteurs en scène*, the French critics dubbed them "auteurs"—the genuine authors or artists of their texts.

In subsequent decades the concept of the auteur was justifiably questioned and qualified. There were significant problems, for example, with the notion that one individual (usually male) could be assigned authorship for a text that emerged from such a highly collaborative process involving so many contributors (the "cult of the director" fallacy). Closer inspection of a typical A-list film's construction revealed that significant shaping was also performed by producers, writers, cinematographers, actors, editors, composers, and so on. In comics, the lone cartoonist more readily embodies the notion of a sole author, but it is also critical to acknowledge the way that syndicate editors and other collaborators (such as a spouse, an adult child, or assistants) contribute to the cartoon text as well. And then the notion that a film or comic is a wholly original, stand-alone artistic text in a traditional Romantic era or Modernist sense is complicated by the fact that these popular creations have such hybrid and intertextual qualities. A successful film or comic strip is shaped by a number of forces and influences beyond a sole creator's complete control, emerging at the intersection of deep genre patterns, influential mentors or predecessors, reader feedback, currents in the zeitgeist, and various institutional expectations.

With those caveats and limitations in mind, a qualified notion of auteurship is still useful in framing the career of a free spirit like Gary Larson who occupied a middle ground between challenging avant-gardism and the conventional entertainment created by compliant cartooning *metteurs en scène*. For example, unlike the avant-garde experimentalist, a popular auteur chooses to work in, and through, popular media and follows the foundational institutional rules and artistic conventions that come with that territory. They also ultimately wanted to please and connect with a broad audience over a sustained period of time, and thus they were not likely to alienate fans with incoherent experimentation or radically countercultural ideas. At the same time, cartooning auteurs differed from their more traditional peers by choosing to challenge many of the institutional mediations or commercial pressures that they considered too restrictive—that had the potential to flatten the spikey contours of their unique art and comedy. As examples, we can see how legitimate auteurs like Garry Trudeau (*Doonesbury*), Walt Kelly (*Pogo*), Lynn Johnston (*For Better or Worse*), Bill Watterson (*Calvin and Hobbes*), Berke Breathed (*Bloom County*), and Aaron MacGruder (*Boondocks*) were often the most vocal critics of unfair artist contracts, excessive merchandising practices, unnecessary outsourcing of writing and drawing to assistants, or intrusive meddling and censorship from newspapers editors. As a result of these attitudes and practices, their cartoons tended to be especially vivid reflections of their peculiar worldviews. In addition, it is perhaps no coincidence that their work also tended to feature aesthetic and narrative conventions that could be considered counterdiscursive—or comedy that was explicitly satiric. In fact, because these cartoonists conducted their battles over artist rights and negative industry practices in the name of creating especially challenging comedy, they deserve the more specific designation of *sateur*—auteurs who used their hard-won freedom and clout to create cartoons that included some brand of topical or cosmic satire.

The unusual level of independence exercised by an auteur is often achieved early in a career by negotiating a contract that gives the director or cartoonist an unusual level of creative freedom and control over his or her work. This was true in Walt Kelly's case: in his second contract he secured not only the copyright ownership of his strip but also the final say on ancillary endeavors. As an example in the film industry, Preston Sturges leveraged his early success as a screenwriter to win later contracts that allowed him to write *and* direct his films. And then the popular success achieved by each of these creators in the subsequent years effectively protected them from the draconian filtering endured by their peers at midcentury. In Kelly's case, he was able to use the broadly appealing aesthetics and comedy of his cartoon, *Pogo*, to create satire that challenged the reactionary politics of the McCarthy era (fig. 4.2). Sturges also capitalized on his popularity to push against many Hollywood conventions: infusing his romantic comedies with pointed social commentary, subverting genre

Fig. 4.2. Walt Kelly, "Poisoning is too good ..." *Pogo*, June 2, 1953. "Copyright Okefenokee Glee & Perloo, Inc. Used by permission. Contact permissions@pogocomics.com."

conventions, and sometimes creatively working his way around the strict Hay's censorship codes with playful innuendo and coded treatments of unusually serious subject matter (see *The Miracle of Morgan's Creek*). The iconoclasm of these artists irritated some cultural guardians, editors, and studio bosses, of course, but they were protected by both the grassroots support they enjoyed from fans and the undeniable success of their creations.

While studio bosses and syndicate editors may have grudgingly honored the idiosyncratic methods of these sateurs, their respective industries ultimately benefited from both the innovations and controversies that followed in the wake of their distinctive comedy. In theory, the tamest, most gentrified texts should be the most reliably lucrative; in practice, however, the bland products created according to entertainment industries' most rigid rules or formulas often inspire only lukewarm (albeit sometimes stable) fan devotion. In contrast, cultural products of high quality and originality that innovate from familiar starting points—and reflect the quirky worldview of a particular artist—inspire, over the long run, the most lasting and enthusiastic followings (think of Hitchcock's enduringly resonant body of films or the richness of Trudeau's decades-long chronicle of baby boomer culture.)

In those earlier eras, mainstream popularity for nonconforming artists was rarely achieved immediately; because auteurs tended to bend the conventions and break the rules of their mediums it often took time for audiences to develop a degree of familiarity with their unusual methods. Popularity was often garnered, in fact, through word-of-mouth recommendations or other grassroots mechanisms.

Once established, avid fan bases created a number of benefits, opportunities and productive challenges for auteurs. On the plus side, devoted followers understood intuitively that the unique qualities of a comic strip (or body of films) was an outgrowth of a particular creator's independent worldview or aesthetic. This often led to curiosity about the artist—wanting to know more about his or her biography, worldview, and methods. In turn, that degree of interest could lead fans to merge in their minds the persona of the artist with his or her body of work (it was *Walt Kelly's Pogo* or *Alfred Hitchcock's Vertigo*). With comic strips, public awareness of the creator behind the text helped to protect the cartoonist's work from being canceled; fans would rush to the defense of a beloved artist like Kelly or Trudeau, sensing that the cartoonist's independence was contingent on grassroots support. In addition, as this grudging tribute from a newspaper editor (below) suggests, the conflation of comic strip and creator in fans' minds created other important protections:

> In the field of cartooning . . . in the old days of syndicate ownership of properties, the market didn't respond negatively if artist A was replaced with artist Y. Today, a number of features are so closely identified with their creators that it's very difficult to envision anyone else doing them. I can't imagine anyone else doing a *Doonesbury* or a *Cathy* or a *For Better or For Worse* or a *Calvin and Hobbes*. So when an artist or a writer says, "I can't do this," you have to deal with it. (Heintjes)

A highly engaged readership could also create an interesting set of challenges for an auteur-like cartoonist. On an extreme end, avid identification with a creator sometimes led fan(atic)s to engage in inappropriate, stalkerish behavior or to criticize any deviations from what they desired the cartoon to be. On a less psychotic level, die-hard fans might simply feel invested in, and protective about, their beloved product, expecting a high level of consistency, quality, and creator–fan interaction. The neediness and intensity of that level of engagement could be oppressive at times; this led some famous cartoonists, such as Trudeau and Watterson, to create protections against overly eager followers. Even Walt Kelly, who was famous for inciting and engaging with the "Pogomaniacs" following his work, would sometimes bemoan the fickle and unrealistic demands of his hordes of college-age fans (Crouch 112). Intense fan devotion was ultimately beneficial on the whole, nevertheless, sometimes amounting to a productive, media-age call-and-response relationship. In effect, the cartoonist's awareness of fans could inspire him or her to create a consistently original body of work that satisfied ideal readers' intellectual interests and psychological needs.

Larson as an Accidental Auteur

Turning our attention to the particulars of Larson's case, we can chart
the peculiar ways he followed the auteur's trajectory in the early stages
of his career: achieving clout and relative independence through naïveté
and stubborn resolve (and the help of key collaborators); exercising that
power in the protection of his work, and the advancement of his career;
exerting pragmatic modesty as he relied on the help of principled editors
and a tough-minded spouse; and then maintaining massive success in
spite of—and ironically thanks to—the oppressive filtering practices and
moribund state of his field in the 1980s and 1990s. And then we can see
how he ultimately used his clout to achieve the profile of a sateur—quietly
resisting and sometimes critiquing industry practices, and articulating in
the sum of his comedic themes a bracing brand of cosmic satire.

To begin, it was significant that Larson was relatively uninterested in,
and unfamiliar with, the mainstream newspaper comics page when he
entered the field. As a young adult, he "didn't really have too much of a
notion about newspapers and newspaper comics" (Morrissey, "Far Side of
Retirement"). His artistic and comedic sensibilities had been shaped by alternative cartoonists like B. Kliban who had been working within the looser
strictures of the magazine and book industries. This meant that Larson
had neither groomed his cartoon to fit the profile of a typical mainstream
cartoon nor prepared himself to deal with the commercial pressures and
institutional rules of newspaper syndication. Untutored and thus relatively
unintimidated, he wandered into one of the more progressive syndicates
(Chronicle Features) in the industry—a firm that was so small, in fact,
that the editors there felt they had "total freedom to try new features"
(Astor, "Universal" 44). Larson thus bypassed, through ignorance and good
fortune, a gamut of obstacles that would have initially tripped up most
nontraditional cartoonists.

In typical industry fashion, nevertheless, his first contract favored the
interests of the syndicate over his rights as a popular artist; eager to make
an initial break in this highly competitive field, he agreed to an assigned
name for his panel, ceded copyright ownership and editorial control of
his work, and committed to a grueling schedule that made no allowances
for significant vacations, down weeks, or sabbaticals. Nevertheless, as an
early sign that Larson would eventually assert his rights in effective (if
often indirect) ways, he was able to resist the *Chronicle* editor's suggestion
that he reshape his panel as a continuity-driven strip with familiar (and
potentially merchandisable) characters.

During the gestation phase of *The Far Side*—as it was being prepared for syndication—Larson actually benefited from the kind of editorial input that in other scenarios might have been obtrusive or flattening. In particular, Larson appreciated Stan Arnold's objective and respectful methods of feedback. Without trying to change the essential qualities of Larson's work, Arnold pushed him to be more consistent in his aesthetics, to clarify jokes that were obtuse, and to think twice about gratuitously bizarre or morbid ideas that might have confused or put off even open-minded fans of alternative comedy. Sensitized through this editing process to the concessions he needed to make in order to achieve greater consistency, quality, and clarity in his work, he kicked off his national syndication in 1980 with a feature that was still rough but largely coherent. This more polished version of *The Far Side* was still marked, thankfully, by the alternative ingredients and tones that would eventually allow it to stand apart as something weird and special on the bland comics page: awkward but genuinely funny drawings, refreshingly irreverent humor, clever and original daily gags, and an absurdist worldview.

As Larson continued to refine his cartoon during the first several years of national syndication, he was fortunate that his *Chronicle* editors remained generally tolerant of his weirdness; he reported that they would only "occasionally" censor his jokes, "deleting scatological references or asking him to soften a caption" (Kelly 86). They were also patient, continuing to promote him through two years of gradual gains in popularity and syndication numbers. The rate at which he added papers during that time, in fact, was probably slower than most syndicates would have tolerated in an era when blockbuster-creating priorities condemned most niche strips into rapid obscurity and cancellation (Larson was published in under 300 papers by year three—well below the thousand-plus mark that signals a cartoon's mass popularity). That unusual degree of patience allowed *The Far Side* to build an audience in lasting, grassroots fashion, with fans doing much of the legwork: posting clipped cartoons on office doors, lending book collections, perhaps even converting friends who were normally disinclined to read the comics page.

Larson and his *Chronicle* editors began to see, in fact, an encouraging pattern: if they could get a toehold in a paper, and if *The Far Side* could just "[hang] in there for a while, it would find an audience or a readership and . . . would make it through" the early, precarious months when a new cartoon usually fails. The real "problem" or hardest obstacle "to break down" in terms of an initial chance, was the "resistance of newspaper editors" (Morrissey, "*The Far Side* of Retirement"). Hesitation from these gatekeepers was not a result of their excessive piety or a provincialism, as you might imagine; for the most part they were indeed capable of "getting" and personally appreciating Larson's humor. Instead, they displayed a blanket resistance to comics that were either flash-in-the-pan novelties or catalysts for headache-inducing controversy. Stuart Dodds, one of Larson's early syndicate sales reps, describes the type: "newspaper editors [are] . . . cautious and diplomatic people—judicious in their praise, given rarely to hyperbole or boundless laughter at the slightest occasion—above all, as having an immunity to outrage (a languor in the face of eccentricity) that borders on world-weariness! (Dodds 55).

The challenge for *Far Side* sales reps was to convince such jaded types that the benefits of running Larson's cartoon (which they argued had the potential to generate interest among younger demographics and nontraditional comics page readers) would outweigh the deficits (the inevitable controversies and indignant letters and calls of complaint from older, traditional readers). A typical, initial rejection went something like, "We'd get too much flak. I'd like to watch it for a while" (Dodds 55). In light of that general level of caution among editors, each new paper that joined the syndication list must have seemed like a major victory. Larson, in fact, felt a deep sense of gratitude to editors who were willing to give his fledgling work a chance (Larson, "Acknowledgments" xviii).

The headaches these editors dealt with once they welcomed Larson on board were certainly real and fairly regular. Perhaps only *Doonesbury* came close to *The Far Side* in the number of disgusted and indignant letters of complaint it elicited in the 1980s. A sampling gives a vivid (and strangely entertaining) picture of the consistent grumbling and requests for cancellation that these editors had to endure:

> I was so upset after seeing the enclosed comic page! It [a *Far Side* cartoon about torturers in a castle dungeon] was the ugliest, (most) obnoxious and sadistic cartoon I have ever seen in a family paper. The so-called artist, Gary Larson, must be sick. I hope you agree. I believe that you, being in touch with the various branches of your editorial staff, have more "clout" than I could have and would see that never again such a vile cartoon would be printed. It certainly is not fit for exposure to children. (Keefe 15)

> I have never written to a newspaper before to complain but I feel compelled. The *"Far Side"* cartoon [about an alligator being shooed out of a hospital nursery (4/1/85; 1–471)] is anything but a cartoon and is

purely "sick" in its presentation. Never in any paper have I seen such poor taste. I would suggest you discontinue same. We have enjoyed the paper since we moved here eight years ago. The contents are informative and entertaining—that is why I was somewhat surprised that you would degenerate same with the "Far Side." (Sedlar 471)

Why has the *Journal Tribune* discarded excellent art-work, all the interesting and family-oriented people, delightful humor and the impish *Dennis the Menace*? Is it possible that the ugly and sloppy drawing, the insensitive characters, and the pseudo-sophisticated "humor" of *The Far Side* are now your standards for your readers? Is *The Far Side* just another prime example of far from art, beauty and intelligence—and do we need it? (Hess 471)

The *Times-Union* is a better newspaper than to be associated with Gary Larson and his *Far Side* smut! I've had enough! This is a letter of protest! I read the *Times-Union* every morning and ignore *The Far Side* because I find it very distasteful and unedifying. However, on Feb. 12, it caught my eye and it totally disgusted me [a cartoon about a baby preserved in a mantelpiece bottle, like a miniature sailing ship (2/12/88;2–137)] . . . How utterly revolting! Larson's expressions of himself are dehumanizing, demoralizing and insulting. I am offended, not only for myself and my children, but for all the other decent folks out there who patronize the *Times-Union* and don't have the time to let the newspaper know how they feel. Unfortunately, there are too many sick minds in this world. None of us are perfect for we all fall short of the glory of God. But Larson is showing us all the inside of his mind by communicating to the world his *Far Side* material. If Larson must earn a living by selling his material, I suggest that he peddle it elsewhere. There are plenty of junk publications that his material would appeal to. Does the *Times-Union* really need it? It is a quality publication. I hope it is kept that way for everyone's sake. (Harnisch 137)

The Minneapolis Tribune should drop *The Far Side* until Gary Larson completes psychotherapy to overcome his problem. *The Far Side* does not represent humor. It represents illness. Please send Gary Larson a copy of this letter. He needs to know that a whole lot of people don't think he's funny. (Enger 171)

I cannot understand the cleverness of this Gary Larson. Do these come from inmates of prisons & are sold to him which he in turn sells (them) to you? What lies behind these warped cartoons? I wish someone would clear their meaning (of them) to me. To me they are a waste of space and are an insult to an *L.A. Times* reader who can find no reason for them in your newspaper. (Lewis 203)

This cartoon does not belong in the "funny papers" because it isn't funny. This type of humor belongs in an adult magazine—not something in a local paper that is (and should be) read by a child. The other mothers I have spoken to feel the same way. If necessary, to be rid of this, I can start a petition of concerned parents or if you can see your way clear, for you, the press, to ask your readers if they want it or not. (Martin 582)

Why don't you get rid of that garbage? We don't need it on the family funny page, and I want to keep my subscription. Whatever happened to *Annie?* (Jorgenson 582)

I am April Marie Armani. And I'm 8 years old. And I like to read the funnies on Sunday. On Sunday, June 8, I was very disgusted with the comic called *The Far Side* [about dogs in hell, forever scooping up their poop, fig. 4.3]. I thought that to me, as a Christian, it was very unnecessary. (Armani 582)

A minority of editors were cowed enough by these kinds of complaints to attempt canceling the strip. Larson and his syndicates were continually impressed, nevertheless, by how many newspaper editors were willing to defend *The Far Side*. A select few, in fact—like the following, insightful editor—were willing to challenge readers' entrenched assumptions about the heightened sanctity of the comics page and the fragility of children's impressionable minds. In response to a particularly vehement request that his newspaper cancel *The Far Side*, one editor responded,

Gary Larson's strip is one of my favorites. . . . So I am not a good candidate to carry your message of disenchantment. But I will say this: Don't worry about the children. They don't get it. And when they do, they will not be as much affected, or infected, as they are now, daily, by the offerings of television or the hypocrisy of fundamentalists. Satire is an ancient tradition. . . . To a few of us, satire is what makes it possible to deal with the outrages of daily life. (Keefe 14)

Dog Hell

Fig. 4.3. Gary Larson, *The Far Side*, June 6, 1986 (1-582).

Savvy local editors probably sensed that popular momentum was on Larson's side too, and thus they were better off siding with the growing legions of *Far Side* fans than in affiliating with out-of-touch detractors. Indeed, once *The Far Side* established itself in a paper, it was rarely dropped—and if it was canceled, it was always quickly reinstated as a result of pushback from ardent supporters. Many fans were aggressively protective of the feature, in fact, actively campaigning for the strip when it was canceled, and writing letters of support, saying things like "*The Far Side* is more than a cartoon . . . it is a lifestyle," this cartoon is "for friends of real deep humor," and "Thank you for making our mornings a real pleasure. Your cartoons are weird, but delicious" (Hicks; Dinerman 320). In sum, the achievement of genuine, grassroots popularity (the kind that provokes readers to protect the artist and his or her text) was one clear sign that Larson was beginning to embody a cartooning auteur by the mid-1980s.

Larson's Move from Chronicle Features to Universal Press Syndicate

Despite the growing success of his strip under the guidance of Chronicle Features, Larson still worried near the end of his first contract in 1985 that his success would be of the flash-in-the-pan variety. Wanting to capitalize on the momentum he had achieved in those years—and perhaps emboldened by the relative security he had garnered with the help of editors and fans, he began searching for a more artist-friendly, freedom-enabling contract. He was encouraged in this endeavor by an agent—Arnold Schwartzman—who was famous (or notorious if you were an old-school syndicate boss) for championing artist rights in the industry. Interestingly, Schwartzman later left the field after getting in trouble for ethical violations such as forging cartoonists' signatures and making false promises to some of his clients; nevertheless, at the time, he was seen by many people in the industry as a righteous crusader who was helping to level the playing field for creators (Astor, "Review").

To achieve that higher level of clout and freedom, Larson switched in 1985 to a different syndicate, Universal Press, that also had a progressive reputation in the industry for several reasons. First, they were at the forefront of a small group of syndicates willing to give creators ownership of copyright under certain conditions. While not completely thrilled with the emerging rhetoric about "creators' rights," key editors at Universal, like Lee Salem, acknowledged in a pragmatic way that contracts had to change with the times; as a result, they were willing to engage in give-and-take negotiations with established cartoonists like Larson, effectively nibbling "around the edges of the contract to accomplish" mutual goals (Heintjes). In Larson's case, they were "less concerned with copyright ownership than with ancillary rights" (Heintjes). To translate, this meant that it did not really matter to them who owned the copyright as long as Larson was willing to collaborate with them in lucrative merchandising activities and book publishing. That caveat helps to explain why another cartooning auteur, Bill Watterson, had such a bitter and contentious relationship with Universal. They were less flexible with him when it came to copyright ownership because he was so categorically opposed to any of the ancillary endeavors (other than book publishing) that provide a syndicate with its greatest profits. In contrast, Larson was generally willing (with just a few limitations) to collaborate with Universal in selling his cartoons on posters, T-shirts, and calendars; he had also developed a friendly and profitable relationship with the syndicate's book publishing division, Andrews, McMeel & Parker, during his time at Chronicle.

While we do not know the precise details of Larson's contract with Universal, it is clear from reading interviews with Salem that the syndicate was initially worried about whether they could "cover the numbers" as they emerged from their negotiations—indicating that in addition to ceding copyright ownership, they also had to grant Larson an unusually generous percentage of syndication and merchandising profits (Astor, "Meet the

New Prez"). After a brief back-and-forth among the top executives, they decided it was worth the gamble in light of the blockbuster potential of Larson's work. Both sides essentially won in these negotiations in the end. On Larson's side, his chutzpah garnered him ownership of his work and a greater share of the financial rewards; on Universal's side, they hitched themselves to a highly merchandisable cultural text that continued its exponential rise in popularity. Salem later effused, in fact, "We ended up exceeding the numbers much earlier than we expected" (Astor, "Meet the New Prez").

Universal was also forward-thinking in its practices when it came to granting vacations, tolerating sabbaticals, and generally nurturing and respecting cartoonists with "visions" that were "personal and challenging" (Heintjes). Sensing that their cartoonists could stand out against the traditional strips that dominated the funnies page, they actively sought out artists like Trudeau, Larson, and Johnston who were opening "doors for new subject matter and new approaches to the art form" (Heintjes). They were savvy enough to recognize, moreover, that not all cartoons had to cater to an imagined family-friendly demographic that preferred safely cute fare; there was room, in their view, for hard-edged cartoons that could appeal to niche audiences through satire and alternative aesthetics. Salem, in fact, had strong opinions about the short-sighted practices that had dominated the field for so long, saying, "I think every comic strip trying to appeal to every member of every family would be the death of the art form" (Heintjes).

This detailed account of Larson's productive relationship with his second syndicate helps to give a more sympathetic view of progressive-minded syndicate editors and the competing pressures they face. From a distance it is easy to caricature businesspeople in the industry with broad strokes, lumping in all executives with the stereotypical movie bosses who were content to see innovative art flattened under the wheels of commerce. Forward-thinking figures like Salem complicate that simplistic portrait and even prod us to think of the auteur model in more expansive ways, considering how creators could neither achieve their popular success nor construct the more resonant and accessible qualities of their work without those collaborators' help. The executives at Universal held this more generous opinion of themselves, of course, and claimed even greater levels of importance as contributors to the craft; in slightly overwrought public relations materials they asserted that they gave voice to some of the great "storytellers of our age" and "discovered, nurtured and promoted many of the bards of our time" ("Andrews McMeel").

Larson's potential as an unlikely bard of the morbid and absurd was definitely amplified in his subsequent years under the guidance of Universal's editors. His relationship with Jake Morrissey, his principal editor, was especially productive: Each Monday morning Morrissey would receive a week's worth of rough drafts in the mail; he and Larson "would then discuss each cartoon . . . editing language or modifying art when [they] agreed it was necessary" (Morrissey, "Introduction" ix). Larson was aware that his humor could be obtuse at times and thus relied heavily on Morrissey to spot weaknesses, disconnects, or overly obscure references. Anticipating those potential problems, Larson often attached notes to his drafts—"last minute comments" about ways to improve captions or clarify drawings. Sometimes he would even reveal a bit of insecurity about whether his humor translated beyond his own head; in those cases he would ask Morrissey if a "cartoon was funny at all," or prod him with joshing questions about whether he "got it" immediately (Morrissey, "Introduction" viii).

Morrissey earned Larson's trust and confidence in several ways: first, he was good at identifying the strength of a nascent idea and helping Larson maximize its potential. About this talent, Larson effused that Morrissey always knew "where the true humor was in each panel" and would sometimes write mock-angry thank-you notes like " . . . your version was the best of all. (Damn it!)" (Morrissey, "Introduction" ix). Second, Morrissey set himself apart from other mediators in being especially nurturing and protective of the peculiarities in Larson's humor and worldview. Whereas another editor might have tried to smooth out Larson's quirkiness (insisting, perhaps, that he eliminate all potentially offensive jokes or create more endearing characters), Morrissey understood that he should not try to improve the humor of a creator with a worldview as idiosyncratic as Larson's (Morrissey, "Introduction" ix). To illustrate how that attitude worked in practice, Morrissey always opted for gags that were weirdly hilarious (but potentially offensive or obscure) over those that were safely humorous (Morrissey, "Introduction" x).

Beyond Morrissey, perhaps the most significant contributor to the ongoing excellence of Larson's work from mid-career and beyond was his spouse and eventual business partner, Toni Carmichael. Like his best editors, she was adept at helping him refine jokes without trying to adjust his personal vision. Additionally, she gradually began managing the business side of his career, helping him with merchandising decisions, copyright issues, and other tasks that he felt "he was entirely unfit for." He added, "She's my pit bull, but a nice one" (Weise).

With the proper clout of an auteur and the help of collaborators like Morrissey and Carmichael who knew how to amplify the essential strengths of *The Far Side*, Larson was set up nicely in the last decade of his career to create funny and provocative cartoons. There were still significant pitfalls to avoid, of course, given the highly commercialized nature of his medium and the complications that come with superstar popularity. In particular, Larson had to deal with heightened attention from fans and detractors, the danger of overmerchandising his cartoon, and the burnout that can result from producing so many original cartoons day after day, year after year.

Larson's Relationship with Readers

In the latter part of his career Larson had little to fear from critics who objected to the irreverent or morbid aspects of his work. There was no risk of him losing syndication numbers, and the zeitgeist of the early 1990s dovetailed nicely with the alternative tone of his work. The momentum was so much in his favor, in fact, that he could simply ignore hate mail (adding it to the pile filling up an entire room in his home) or co-opt the funnier complaints for promotional materials. In a strategy shared by Garry Trudeau, Larson began to include especially pious or clueless attacks from readers as blurbs in his book collections. The hysterical silliness of the attacks undermined their credibility, of course, and the fans who purchased his books could feel a sense of communal superiority in reading them—a notion that they belonged to a crowd of hip, engaged readers who could appreciate and understand Larson's weird humor better than square detractors.

When it came to avid fans, Larson felt appreciative and indebted to those who had come to his defense whenever campaigns emerged to cancel his cartoon; looking back, he said,

> I must thank you. I found myself so often in hot water when my work crossed some invisible line, I intermittently thought, "Well, that was fun while it lasted." The Humor Police, it seems, are always hovering around; I just didn't know you were out there as well. Boy, did you guys save my butt on more than one occasion. My gratitude knows no bounds. (Larson, "Acknowledgments" xviii)

It is tempting to exaggerate Larson's rebellious impulses—imagining him not only gleefully flouting the rules of his field but also not caring about the impact of his comedic land mines after they left his desk. The reality was quite different. In addition to feeling gratitude toward protective fans, he was genuinely worried about meeting their expectations; he explained,

> "I don't mean to sound corny about it, but I was very respectful of readers. Whoever was following my work I was going to try to treat well. I thought of every day as a little curtain going up and it's show time, and you better know how to dance" (Morrissey, "Far Side of Retirement").

That kind of productive anxiety helped to ensure the ongoing quality of *The Far Side* from year to year and might have even played a role in Larson's decision to retire his strip "early" (or at least earlier than most blockbuster strips). He did not want to linger on for years, cashing in on his work's fading popularity while gradually alienating longtime fans with rehashed jokes. His tolerance for dealing with the pressures of fame was also especially low, given his fundamentally shy and self-effacing nature. As much as he appreciated devoted readers—and benefited from their high expectations—he largely avoided engaging with them directly once his career was fully established. In addition to being rattled by stalkers and the pie-in-the-face incident at the book signing, Larson grew tired of requests for advice from aspiring cartoonists and unsolicited suggestions for cartoon ideas. The sheer volume of curious letters, hate mail, and interview requests eventually compelled him to retreat almost completely from the public eye.

While remaining invested in satisfying his core fans, Larson was content during the latter half of career to meet their expectations from a professional distance. For his own safety and sanity, there was wisdom in avoiding the fanatics and exhibitionists, and Larson had discovered that he did his best work in relatively stress-free isolation. His core creative method, in fact—plumbing the depths of his own psyche for absurd juxtapositions—required long periods of uninterrupted time in the studio and peaceful engagement with the flora and fauna surrounding his home (fig. 4.4). As a result of these needs and anxieties, Larson began to follow a mild version of the Thomas Pynchon model of celebrity: eschewing public appearances, begging off participation in professional meetings, refusing interviews, and generally avoiding book signings (Piraro). In retirement he remains private, hidden behind layers of syndicate reps, agents, and employees, emerging only occasionally to give an interview about conservation issues.

Fig. 4.4. Gary Larson in his home studio, circa 1985.

Larson and the Internet

While we can sympathize with Larson's retreat from the public eye in general, it is harder to understand why he refuses to interact with fan communities online or to allow his work to migrate in official or unofficial ways onto the Internet. Other intensely private cartoonists, like Garry Trudeau and Berke Breathed (*Bloom County*), embraced social media as a safe way of connecting with fans or expanding their roles as public satirists; Larson has only a defunct website that advertises out-of-stock DVD copies of his TV special and provides an email address that leads curious fans back to Universal's generic site.

Larson is also especially protective of his copyright in the online realm, aggressively policing unauthorized uses of his cartoons. In an open letter to readers, he explained,

> I'm walking a fine line here. . . . On the one hand, I confess to finding it quite flattering that some of my fans have created web sites displaying and/or distributing my work on the Internet. And, on the other, I'm struggling to find the words that convincingly but sensitively persuade these *Far Side* enthusiasts to "cease and desist" before they

have to read these words from some lawyer. . . . My effort here is to try and speak to the intangible impact, the emotional cost to me, personally, of seeing my work collected, digitized, and offered up in cyberspace beyond my control. . . . It's like having someone else write in your diary. . . . [my cartoons] come from an intensely personal, and therefore original perspective. To attempt to be "funny" is a very scary, risk-laden proposition. . . . These cartoons are my "children," of sorts, and like a parent, I'm concerned about where they go at night without telling me. And, seeing them at someone's web site is like getting the call at 2:00 A.M. that goes, "Uh, Dad, you're not going to like this much, but guess where I am." . . . Please send my "kids" home. I'll be eternally grateful. Most respectfully, Gary Larson

Fan reactions to Larson's protective strategies have been mixed. Some respect his stance, asserting, "Making quality art is hard work (Yes, *The Far Side* is quality art and it IS hard work), and an artist's copyright is the only thing he or she has to guarantee income from that hard work." Others feel a bit indignant, complaining that his rigid policy is "sad" or "such a shame," since tribute sites are essentially "free advertising, and fanmail." On an extreme end, a handful of readers claim that they completely stopped reading Larson's comics after learning about his policy on Internet reproductions of his work.

From a theoretical perspective, Larson's strategies place him, for good and ill, within an older, modernist paradigm of art production and ownership where the meanings and uses of a text are tied closely to a particular creator's intentions and control. As a sateur with a critical vision of human society and behavior, it mattered that each cartoon within Larson's oeuvre could be traced back to his pen and mind. In addition, his control and protection of the copyright of his work allowed him to benefit financially from the uses of his work and to protect his capacity to create original and counterdiscursive comedy in the face of commercial pressures and institutional filters. Finally, the democratic cheapness of the newspaper medium—its mechanical reproducibility—allowed him to maximize the distribution and social reach of his work in ways that he and his syndicate could control (Benjamin 225).

In a postmodern internet age, this model of artistic production has become complicated by the extreme ease with which comic texts are reproduced, sampled, repurposed, or parodied. On the downside, some artists are bemoaning a loss of control and profits as their work is widely pirated and sometimes misused in creative mashups. In Larson's case, there was already a long history of businesspeople and academics using his cartoons in presentations and lectures without permission, but much of that borrowing could probably be justified according to fair-use clauses in the copyright laws, and Larson was famous enough that the present-ers were usually eager to acknowledge that it was his work. As one scans the current, unauthorized uses of *The Far Side* on the Internet, however, it becomes clear that in addition to well-meaning tributes, there are also opportunistic commercial sites that simply borrow cartoons and jokes from all over, do not bother with attributions, and sometimes misiden-tify cartoonists, or mash up jokes in meme-like ways, sometimes even adding egregiously profane gags. For anyone interested in promoting or celebrating the power of popular, socially responsible satire, these kinds of developments are troubling.

Nevertheless, a complete avoidance of all Internet iterations of his work—either unofficially recycled, or officially sanctioned—seems ulti-mately to be a shortsighted practice. To begin, the free sharing of *Far Side* cartoons in analog form (clippings passed around, mailed to friends, or posted on doors) was a key facet of Larson's early grassroots success. And thus by making a categorical ban on all kinds of digital sharing and post-ing of his work, Larson's company has significantly hobbled the long-term potential for *The Far Side* to reach new fans. The FarWorks company would be wise, in fact, to follow the lead of a cartoonist like Scott Adams, who has developed effective ways to both control and amplify his online reach. An industry expert describes his simple solutions:

> just like Larson and *The Far Side*, Adams has to deal with a publisher/
> syndication company that wants to sell his books. And, yet the *Dilbert*
> website has a full archive of all *Dilbert* comics for free, with a nice
> search engine. It also makes it easy for anyone to share and embed
> the strips on their website if they want to do that (for free). On top
> of that, not so long ago, they created a nice feature that makes it
> ridiculously easy to license any *Dilbert* strip for all sorts of uses, with
> a couple of clicks and a simple price. And it doesn't sound like any of
> this has "harmed" *Dilbert*'s ability to earn money. In fact, it has done
> quite the opposite. (Masnick)

Larson's rigid approach might also be out of synch with positive facets of digital culture that enable a type of postmodern comedy-making that is highly participatory. Henry Jenkins describes the recent emergence of a "convergence culture" in which fans and creators use new media to participate in elaborate world-building exercises, collaborative authorship, and transmedia storytelling (Storey, 235–237). At times these practices are simply new opportunities for entertainment companies to maximize the profits of franchises through multiple media platforms; in other cases there are genuinely creative and democratic aspects to how fans create their own text-inspired fictions, transformative art, parodic memes, and syncretic mashups. Applying this model to *The Far Side*, if Larson could allow for a select number of his cartoon images to be made publicly usable—like building blocks in an open source code—then perhaps his cartoon universe could morph into a dynamic, perpetually vital franchise that converts new generations of fans. It is fun to speculate about the strange things that could occur in online venues where readers are creating and sharing their own *Far Side* cartoons, using elements or templates drawn from Larson's storehouse of images, types, and themes. Or what would it be like to explore a three-dimensional, comedically dystopian *Far Side* world in a video game format that also poked fun at anthropocentric worldviews or promoted conservation causes? While some of the satiric stability or clarity at the core of Larson's work might be lost, a rich, participatory experience in comic absurdity and bracing satire could be gained.

Larson's Book Collections

Beyond the printed cartoon itself, the twenty-three book collections (selling over 45 million copies) were the most critical element in how Larson achieved success in a grassroots fashion. While reading a single *Far Side* panel on the regular comics page might have been confusing to many readers (like confronting a randomly generated funnies-page glitch), encountering a larger, thematically similar collection of Larson's jokes and images added coherence to the reading experience. In effect, by seeing the repetition of recurring jokes, visual motifs, and satiric ideas across a hundred pages, readers could develop a fluency with the interpretive cues needed to appreciate fully Larson's world. The books also served as proselytizing tools, allowing readers to share Larson's idiosyncratic work with friends and family. It seems likely, in fact, that the books helped to convert certain demographics—like academics or scientists—who may not have been avid comics readers otherwise.

In terms of packaging and marketing strategies, the earliest books were compact, featured a representative cartoon on the cover, highlighted two cartoons per page, and did little more than corral a certain period's run of installments. As Larson's brand became more popular, and his character types and themes more thoroughly established, the packaging of books became more elaborate. The larger anthologies, for example—which were all *New York Times* bestsellers—included the following additional elements: a specially drawn cover that highlighted archetypal themes and characters, blurbs and endorsements, introductory essays by famous figures such as Stephen King or Jane Goodall, and quirky photos of Larson. All of these additions helped fans to feel like they were part of an extended *Far Side* community.

Perhaps the only misstep among these book collections was the decision to cap off the sum of his career-long work in 2003 with a lavishly packaged, double-volume collection of every one of his 4,300 cartoons. On the positive side, these volumes bring all of Larson's cartoons together in an organized, chronological fashion (an essential help for this study); they also work as an impressive tribute to Larson's legacy—a "death" book, as the cartoonist labeled it (Stein). He also described them as labor of love, devoting three years to overseeing the production, making sure that every panel was re-printed with clarity. The books include never-before-collected cartoons, vivid personal essays, and fascinating letters to the editor and notes from collaborators. On seeing the end product, Larson joked, "I just like to feel the weight. It's a 20-pounder, Mom! It can alternate as a murder weapon" (Stein).

On the downside, these massive hardbound collections are perhaps too expensive for average fans (setting the record for the most expensive book to make the *New York Times* bestseller list, at $135), and ultimately not that user-friendly. For example, on a practical level they are simply too hard and heavy to be enjoyed as a reading experience; while the paperback anthologies could be slipped into a backpack, read in bed, or easily passed to a friend, these unwieldy tomes can only serve as coffee table browsers. In addition, on a theoretical level, they have little of the exhibition/use value associated with cheaply reproducible, democratic art; instead, the whole package con-notes (albeit in a self-aware way) the exclusivity and prohibitive expense of highbrow art or literature.

Moreover, perhaps in an effort to convince longtime anthology collectors that there was added value in this expensive collection, the editors made the mistake of colorizing a large number of Larson's original black-and-white images. In a handful of cases, the full-color images are a slight improve-ment (night scenes, for example, which benefit from a spookier set of dark values), but in most instances, they feel like fussy embellishments, drawing too much attention to insignificant details or obscuring the core point of the gag. After perusing a string of these elaborately watercolored versions, you long for the black-and-white clarity and comedic potency of Larson's original cartoons.

To be completely fair, Larson and his editors were aware of the pretentiousness signals sent through this endeavor and played up the highbrow elements of the packaging in self-mocking ways. The scripts on the covers are especially stuffy, and Larson includes versions of his iconic cow and domineering matron dressed as Renaissance era aristocrats. While you can appreciate those self-deconstructive gestures on an abstract level, they do not remedy the practical deficiencies of the volumes. Thankfully, Larson and Universal published a cheaper and more user-friendly paperback version of the collection in 2014.

The Far Side **TV Specials**

The only significant elaboration of *The Far Side* world beyond the newspaper cartoon itself was a set of television specials created in 1994 and 1997: *Tales from the Far Side I* and *Tales from the Far Side II*. The first one aired in the US on CBS in 1994 as a Halloween special; the second one was aired only in the UK and shown at animation festivals. An assessment of the quality and cultural impact of these films leads to some mixed conclusions. To begin, Larson cannot be accused of selling out his alternative credentials in the pursuit of these films. Although the first special was shown on a mainstream network, CBS, the executives of that company had no influence over its production. In fact, Larson exercised his auteur-like independence to an extreme degree in its construction, writing the script without editorial input and producing the animation with the help of a non-Hollywood animation studio in Canada—Vancouver's International Rocketship. The result was a text that remained radically true to the spirit of *The Far Side*: a series of morbid and absurd vignettes that were designed, according to Larson, to provoke offense, confusion, and laughter (the "big three" reactions, according to him, upon which his career was built) (Holguin, "Gary Larson's Farewell" 5H). The opening sequence of the first film, for instance, features a man parachuting into a kennel of rabid dogs, a parrot echoing a man's last words ("Is this thing loaded?"), and a group of anthropomorphized farm animals slouched against a farmhouse, chain-smoking cigarettes.

As animated texts, the specials are especially clever in their use of filmic devices and genre tropes that appropriately amplify the darker tones in Larson's work. Horror movie conventions play a big role in the dissonant soundtrack, and there are echoes of Hitchcock's films in the use of canted angles, extreme high- and low-angle perspectives, and slow pans of the action that have a creeping, voyeuristic quality. The films are not perfectly constructed comedic texts, nevertheless. Their length, for example—though only thirty minutes—feels a bit long. The plodding quality of the action highlights, perhaps, the difficulty in translating isolated panel cartoons to a format better suited for narrative storytelling. Moreover, the flow of vignettes feels disjointed, with the lack of continuity and character development contributing to a detached viewing experience. One can dip into and out of the action with little gained or lost in terms of coherence or emotional engagement.

In interviews Larson had a sense that he and his collaborators had perhaps erred on the side of too much alternative integrity. He admitted at the time that "it's fairly experimental"—and then elaborating, warned,

> The good news is that we didn't have a network looking over our shoulder telling us what to do. The bad news is that we didn't have a network looking over our shoulders telling us what to do. . . . We were all like a bunch of mad scientists running around doing this thing and, as a result, I think it's going to be a real mixed bag of strange things. (Holguin, "Gary Larson's Farewell" 5H)

Larson's semi-sheepish admission about the obtuse quality of the films seems to highlight his own awareness that the independence of a comedic auteur benefits from some limiting parameters or editorial input. One can imagine, for example, how a savvy producer might have compelled Larson to create a better set of scripts in which a loose, central thread tied the vignettes together; showcased interconnected self-referential jokes; poked fun at animated cartoon conventions in metafictive ways; and allowed for funny character development (perhaps following that old-school matron or an everyman/fool cow through a rambling set of adventures). That kind of narrative structuring or building of themes might have allowed the films to articulate some of *The Far Side*'s core philosophical ideas in newly profound ways.

Larson's Approach to Merchandising

Merchandising is another facet of Larson's career that requires a thoughtful and fair analysis. From a distance, the sheer magnitude of these commercial endeavors seems to undermine Larson's alternative credentials; indeed, it is hard to resist the notion that he "sold out" to some degree when we observe that *The Far Side* became the center of a $500 million industry in the 1990s that included ubiquitous T-shirts, posters, coffee mugs, daily calendars, and so on. A closer examination of the details related to how these products were produced and used, however, allows us to come to a more nuanced conclusion—one that suggests that Larson largely protected the integrity of his cartoon from the worst aspects of thoughtless merchandising. A bit of history, moreover, of how other cartoonists have dealt with the pressures and decisions related to merchandising, allows for some productive comparisons.

To begin, from the days of *Buster Brown* in the 1910s, a cute cartoon aesthetic (preferably featuring children or animals) was traditionally seen by syndicates and cartoonists as the most reliable vehicle for lucrative merchandising; that kind of imagery is inoffensive and universally accessible. Vaguely scientific conjectures about the unconscious, emotional appeal of cute cartoon figures supports the business logic of that practice. John Canemaker, a scholar of animation, asserts that we have evolved to respond positively—even protectively—toward "creatures with soft, rounded forms" and babies with "a large head with big, low-set eyes and a small nose and mouth; a little, rounded body; chubby limbs with tiny hands and feet." The rounded, interlocking shapes within those cute cartoons carry inherently sensual, pleasurable connotations in some cultures, symbolizing "infinity and eternity," and denoting "wholeness and continuity—survival." Given that array of soothing qualities, it is no wonder that the most popular and widely merchandised cartoon icons of the twentieth century—the Yellow Kid, Buster Brown, Felix the Cat, Mickey Mouse, Snoopy, Garfield, Hello Kitty—were constructed out of interlocking circles and resembled cherubic toddlers featuring a "cranial bulge with big round eyes atop a small body" (Canemaker 7–8).

Most middle-class consumers also gravitate toward imagery that has the familiarity and cultural capital of an established brand name. Thus, widely promoted animated films and nationally syndicated, continuity-oriented comic strips provide the ingredients for establishing that kind of almost universal appeal: familiarity, cute aesthetics, gentle comedy, and endearing characters. With time, those elements can converge in supporting merchandising empires like Schulz's *Peanuts*, in which the imagery can be applied to dolls, children's clothing, stationery, pillows, backpacks, bathroom decor, insurance ads, and so on.

While there is nothing inherently wrong with people consuming and enjoying cartoon characters in this way, it can have a negative impact on the meanings and uses of the original cartoon if done indiscriminately or to an excessive degree. Overly aggressive commodification, in effect, can deflate the quality of the original comics texts through oversaturation and a gradual transformation of characters from rich comedic types into largely decorative motifs of generic cuteness or nostalgia. In the case of *Peanuts*, for example, observers like Art Spiegelman lamented, "The strip radiated integrity, but why did everydog [Snoopy] have to flog everything from boxer shorts to insurance?" (Spiegelman 63). Spiegelman felt disgruntled in part because the cute aesthetics of the strip itself had long belied (or cleverly camouflaged) a complex narrative that was deeply melancholic and even bracingly existential at times. But that richness seemed to diminish in the strip's final decade and after Schulz's death, when his syndicate and estate used *Peanuts* imagery in atomized and undiscriminating ways across so many products. In effect, the cute merchandise warped the original complexity of the characters and their environment, supplanting to a large degree Schulz's richer and darker worldview with a gloss of sentimentality.

Other cartooning auteurs like Bill Watterson and Garry Trudeau witnessed the way that indiscriminate merchandising practices could damage the integrity of a cartoon text and thus tried to limit ancillary treatments of their work. In Trudeau's case, he sanctioned merchandise on two occasions but insisted that it be done in ironic, self-aware ways and for the benefit of charities. Watterson was even more resistant to any kind of merchandising beyond book collections; as indicated earlier, he fought with Universal over this issue for years, asserting that cute byproducts would dilute the quality of the strip itself. He felt quite bitter, in fact, about the way his editors pressured him on this issue, elaborating about the conflict in surprisingly candid detail in his *Tenth Anniversary* book collection:

> I had signed a contract giving my syndicate all exploitation rights to *Calvin and Hobbes* into the next century. . . . Universal would not sell my strip to newspapers unless I gave the syndicate the right to merchandise the strip in other media. . . . For years, Universal pressured me to compromise on a "limited" licensing program. The syndicate would agree to rule out the most offensive products if I would agree to go along with the rest. . . . My contract was so one-sided that quitting would have allowed Universal to replace me with hired writers and artists and license my creation anyway, but at this point, the syndicate agreed to renegotiate my contract. The exploitation rights were returned to me, and I will not license *Calvin and Hobbes*. (Watterson 11, 12)

Interestingly, Watterson's categorical ban on any use of his images beyond the books led some unscrupulous entrepreneurs to create contraband products featuring Calvin's image—most famously the back window truck sticker where Calvin is urinating mischievously on a variety of interchangeable symbols. When Watterson and his syndicate tried to put an end to those infringements, they were stymied for two reasons: the fly-by-night nature of the small companies that produced the images made it difficult to find anyone to sue, and also, ironically, because Calvin had never been licensed in other ways. Simply put, if a character is tied to other licensed merchandise in the public realm, it is easier to make a legal case that the infringements have hurt the earnings of the copyright owner.

Despite the crudeness of the contraband Calvin decals, they affirmed Watterson's core argument about the fragility of a cartoon's integrity in unexpected ways. In effect, Watterson's extreme efforts to keep his cheeky protagonist from being cute-ified on decorative products ultimately protected—and also amplified—the potency of Calvin's subversive meanings and uses. And thus, since Calvin was completely absent as a cute spokesman in the culture at large, he was enabled to serve as a potent symbol of youthful disrespect for truck owners looking to thumb their nose at genteel culture or political correctness.

Larson's practices fell somewhere between the puritanical stridency of Watterson and the unbridled permissiveness of Schulz. To assess his particular attitudes and practices, we can first look to his relationship with his syndicate during his prime merchandising years. While Universal was known for finding and fostering alternative talent, it is understandable that they were also unapologetic about maximizing the ancillary profits of a blockbuster entity like *The Far Side*. Their earnings from the basic syndication of the cartoon, after all, were fairly insignificant: $5 to $100 a week per paper, depending on the size of the newspaper—resulting in a "low to middle five figures" that they split evenly with Larson (Meisler). And given the artist-friendly nature of their contract with Larson, it was critical that the book collections and other merchandise sold well in order to "cover the numbers"; those profits would justify the freedoms, copyright ownership and favorable percentages they'd offered to Larson (Astor, "Meet the New Prez").

Universal was also well situated to expand the cultural reach and profitability of a grassroots hit like *The Far Side*. In addition to syndication, the company had developed an Andrews McMeel Publishing wing in the 1980s—the avenue through which Larson first encountered their editors—and they had opened a corporate division called "Oz" that specialized in the packaging and marketing of gift items, greeting cards, and calendars. Larson's work became the center of Oz's line, which by the end of the 1980s included ninety-nine greeting cards, ninety-six postcards, twenty different coffee mugs, and yearly cartoon-a-day calendars ("Andrews McMeel").

Given that Larson experienced relative poverty as a young adult, barely making enough to cover his monthly rent while toiling as a record store employee, you can imagine that it was a massive relief to earn enough money by the middle of his cartooning career that he would never have to endure financial worries again. A hefty income also enabled him to travel extensively to places like Africa and the Galapagos Islands, pursue his passion for jazz guitar, and devote a great deal of his resources to charitable causes like conservation efforts. He was always ambivalent, nevertheless, about his work's blockbuster success, and like Watterson, he sensed that excessive merchandising could dilute the potency of the cartoon itself or cause fans to question the integrity of his creative motivations. On a number of occasions throughout his career, he expressed trepidation that "the merchandising monster" would "destroy the very special rapport he's got with his readers" (Sherr):

> I wouldn't want the readers who are really following me to suddenly get this sense that it's becoming real mainstream, that, you know, it's all for the dollar. I think it's getting to be these days almost where the comic pages are becoming mostly little advertising vehicles for other things that are where the real money is. And I think it sucks. I think it should be humor. (Sherr)

> I don't want to let it become something that I've seen happen in some other cartoons, where they simply become little industries and the reason for having done it in the first place seems to have been buried somewhere. (Holguin, "Voice from the Far Side")

In terms of surface appearances, Larson's alternative credibility was indeed complicated by the massive amount of merchandise that he and his syndicate produced from the mid-1980s onward. The perception of The Far Side becoming overly commodified—even corporatized—was perhaps further reinforced when he set up his private company, FarWorks, "on the sixth floor of a chrome-and-marble-decked office building in the heart of downtown Seattle," to manage merchandising efforts and deal with misuses of his work (Gumbel). A reporter from a British paper who visited the site in 1999 described a friendly staff who were "attired in no-nonsense business suits," and an office space decorated with *Far Side* paraphernalia that seemed more like the "accumulation of corporate trophies" than markers of "an easy-going artistic environment" (Gumbel). Perhaps sensing the disconnect between his unpretentious persona and this sterile, corporate setting, Larson sheepishly suggested to the reporter,

> I come in here about once a week and stay for an hour. . . . This isn't my environment at all. . . . The need for an office sort of crept up on me. My wife, Toni, took over as my business manager, then we realized we needed to hire an assistant, then two, then three. Luckily I have a short enough attention span that I don't think about it too much. (Gumbel)

Despite the corporate aura of these endeavors, a less strident view on what qualifies as "selling out" allows us to look past surface appearances and do a more nuanced appraisal of Larson's commercial endeavors. The FarWorks company and corporate offices, for example, could be seen as necessary protections for an artist who had successfully wrested control of his work away from syndicates in both legal and literal senses. Being able to monitor copyrights and regulate merchandise close to home, with his own employees, was much better than allowing it to take place in less careful ways in the offices of a large syndicate on the other side of the country. And if we are concerned with a satirist like Larson being able to protect his time and maximize his own creative efforts, what better way to do that than to delegate the day-to-day business side of his work to close allies, like his spouse and collaborator, Toni, and some hand-picked employees.

Looking closely at the actual *Far Side* merchandise Larson produced also helps one to come to a more nuanced assessment. We can see, first of all, that Larson was careful in protecting the deeper, genuinely alternative qualities of his work by resisting any ancillary uses that might have "cuteified" his aesthetics or subdued the morbid tone of his cartoon world. For instance, he sanctioned neither ironic treatments of his characters in advertising nor atomized uses of the characters' faces and bodies beyond the cartoons themselves. In fact, Larson limited his merchandise to products that were essentially reiterations of the cartoons on a different surface or medium: calendars, T-shirts, posters, mugs, greeting cards. As a result, he was able to protect to a significant degree the counterdiscursive qualities of his art and his comedy.

Second, the products he approved generally served as amplifying ambassadors of Larson's awkward aesthetics and carnivalesque brand of satire, allowing his irreverent cartoons to find their way into buses, office spaces, and college dorms. To elaborate, Larson's awkward and grotesque aesthetics were naturally resistant to—and a poor match for—decorative paraphernalia of any sort. The pinched, passive, and flat-eyed animals in Larson's world stood in stark contrast, for example, to the dominant Disney model of anthropomorphized animals with dynamic forms and big-eyed, sympathetic faces. In addition, Larson's human figures do not send the kinds of comforting psychological signals that would make them an easy match for bedsheets, baby clothes, or beach towels. They are constructed with lots of round forms, for sure, but those shapes are in the wrong places: fat jowls, rotund bellies, and thick, eye-obscuring glasses. The *Far Side*'s pear-shaped, pinheaded children, in particular, are complete antipodes to the classic model of a cartoon kid with oversized round eyes and a large, oval head atop a diminutive body. Thus, instead of signaling the cherubic innocence of childhood, Larson's youngsters denote obesity, poor eyesight, and bad haircuts—and perhaps connote our devolution into a lifestyle filled with narrow sedentary pursuits.

Speculations on the way that fans might have used his products can also affirm a more favorable assessment of Larson's merchandising practices. We can rule out the possibility, for instance, that fans wore/displayed a *Far Side* product as a traditional fashion statement that connoted a generalized aura of cuteness or nostalgia; the sheer ugliness of the drawings and the intact specificity of the morbid jokes on each product short-circuited those kinds of detached uses. Other motivations for buying and displaying Larson's products, as a result, were at work: the desire to alarm friends and strangers with aggressively anti-cute weirdness or morbidity, or the impulse to advertise the buyer's unique sense of humor and membership in a hiply narrow cartoon club that detested the lame entertainment and cute imagery that dominated mainstream media. Displaying a Larson product was like wearing the T-shirt of an alternative band or owning paraphernalia from your favorite fantasy franchise—a way of letting your nerd flag fly. If it confused or offended a family member or stranger who didn't understand its uncute, insider qualities, all the better—it reinforced the owner's sense of being part of a special comedy club.

To further underscore the integrity of Larson's merchandising choices, we can highlight his most popular product—the cartoon-a-day calendars— as the best example of merchandise that reinforced the core meanings and uses of *The Far Side*. It is hard to imagine, for starters, a more accessible and potent package of Larson's worldview than a small square of stacked cartoons that sits prominently on a person's desk or countertop. We could even argue that because of a calendar's focused location within a reader's quotidian habits, and the fact that they allowed access to just one joke a day, they were even more effective than the book collections at allowing a reader to imbibe the essence of *The Far Side*. The book collections, after all, were often used with great intensity initially and then shuffled away into a bookcase or loaned out—essentially forgotten for long periods of time. Moreover, the kind of isolated binge reading associated with the books might have led, for some readers, to a state of addled exhaustion from spending too much time immersed in Larson's consistently morbid and absurdist tone. In contrast, with the daily calendars the reader could easily get a single potent and digestible dose of Larson's weirdness per day.

Given the concentrated potency of that reading experience, it is no wonder that these calendars were Larson's most popular product over the years—even outselling other calendars in bookstores five to one (Weise). They continued to sell at high numbers, in fact, for seven years beyond the retirement of the cartoon itself. Feeling like he was outstaying his welcome with fans, Larson ended their production in 2002, reviving them only once, in 2006, as a way of earning money for animal habitat conservation efforts. In closing, it is interesting to note that the rise of the calendar's popularity in the mid-1990s—and continuing on into the turn of the millennium—coincided with the dramatic collapse of the newspaper industry and the radical changes in the way that comics fans turned to book collections, calendars, and the Internet—rather than the traditional funnies page—to follow their favorite cartoonists. Given these disruptive trends, future discussions of what constitutes the "original" cartoon text—in contrast to ancillary, merchandising iterations—will become even more complicated.

Sabbaticals and Retirement

A final facet of Larson's auteur-like clout was his unusual control over his work schedule and the decision of when he could and should retire. From a distance, it was easy to deride highly successful cartoonists working in the 1980s for needing vacations and sabbaticals; it seemed they were living a dream, after all, that few artists could achieve. Other aspiring creators, in fact, tended to be less than sympathetic toward superstars who asked for these allowances; typically, they wondered why these professionals could not simply push through the fatigue and be grateful for their success. Comics readers of that era were also generally intolerant of any cessation or break in the publication of favorite strips; they tended to think of the comics page as a public utility that was reliably delivered to their doorstep day after day, year after year, without disruption. And if readers became especially attached to a particular strip or panel, they expected it to be published in perpetuity—a timeless, familiar text that would forever greet them as they had their coffee each morning.

Syndicates were responsible for creating these unrealistic expectations surrounding the uninterrupted publication and longevity of particular strips. For example, their standard contracts did not factor in the need for vacations and sabbaticals—requiring the artist to work overtime, amassing several weeks of upcoming installments, if they wanted time off. Moreover, retirement on the artist's own terms or timetable was out of the question; because the syndicate owned the work and considered it a long-term investment that should pay dividends for decades to come, they were prepared to simply transfer responsibility for the strip to a new artist if age or fatigue prevented the original artist from continuing its production.

Up until the 1970s, artists working in the field were generally unwilling or unable to challenge these norms. In fact, many midcentury comics superstars saw themselves as working-class Joes/Janes who had come from humble roots and the ranks of newspaper bullpens; as a result, they tended to worry that any effort on their part to challenge industry norms—especially ones that had to do with how long or how hard a cartoonist had to work—would be perceived by syndicates, editors, and their peers as entitlement, laziness, or ingratitude. The National Cartoonists Society, in fact—the official, professional organization for comic strip artists—tended to discourage any kind of agitation for artist rights or more progressive contracts well into the 1960s. The older, superstar cartoonists in charge did not want their organization to become a site for unionizing efforts or other progressive endeavors; they were loath to rock the industry boat, and were content to use the Society as a convivial supper club for those who had achieved elite success (Kelly, "NCS Newsletter 1953" 2).

Given the ossified state of those industry attitudes and practices, successful cartoonists working between the 1930s and 1970s tended to deal with the overwhelming pressures of the craft by hiring assistants, using ghostwriters, and relying on formulaic gags or story templates in which they essentially repeated the same jokes in different guises. Cartoonists were generally reluctant to admit to the public that they needed this kind of help, however, and thus everyone involved maintained the illusion that the superstars in the field were prolific, joke-producing geniuses who could casually crank out their text day after day without breaking a sweat. As you can imagine, the effort to obscure the reality of cartoonists needing and using elaborate help led to assistants being underpaid, treated poorly, and rarely given proper credit.

In the 1970s Garry Trudeau finally challenged these industry practices with the support of Universal Press Syndicate. With his auteur-like clout he negotiated a sabbatical for himself in 1975 to recharge his creative batteries; and given the conservative nature of his profession, it is unsurprising that the reaction from newspaper editors and the old guard in the field was fairly harsh. He was charged with being ungrateful, for acting like a prima donna; Charles Schulz even grumbled that his agitation for sabbaticals and additional artist rights was "unprofessional" (Marschall and Groth 13). Other artists benefited, nevertheless, from Trudeau's chutzpah, and Universal and a few other forward-thinking syndicates made it common practice to give artists a one-month break from the production schedule each year starting in the mid-1980s.

Larson took advantage of those yearly vacations when he joined Universal in 1985, and because of his own achievement of auteurdom, he was able to negotiate a full fourteen-month sabbatical in 1988 and a special arrangement in which he would create only five—rather than seven—original panels each week when he resumed work. A small number of editors and readers were disgruntled by these lapses in *The Far Side*'s production, and a few colleagues griped about the privileged nature of these kinds of allowances. Nevertheless, thanks to Trudeau's path breaking—and perhaps because readers were generally aware that Larson had a special, even delicate, kind of genius—the backlash was fairly muted. In terms of impact on his syndication numbers, he lost eleven papers, but then gained another twenty when he returned.

Although Larson's popular clout gave him the freedom to insist on a variety of artist rights, it was his impulse to be a sateur that helps to justify why he and Trudeau sought and deserved what seem like unusually flexible working schedules. As a comedian who created highly original and often satiric panels day after day, Larson was working at least twice as hard as a typical syndicated cartoonist. While a traditional peer leaned on formulaic gags, repetitive jokes, and fluffy filler materials that might sometimes play out in continuity-based strips, Larson challenged himself to do a completely unique and highly absurd panel each time he sat down at his drafting table. The quirky, do-it-yourself nature of his art, moreover, ruled out the possibility of him using assistants. It is hard to imagine a professionally trained helper, after all, intentionally mimicking the crude and often anatomically inaccurate drawings of *The Far Side*. Larson's satiric vision, moreover—his continual inversions of conventional platitudes and anthropocentric conceits—was so unique to his persona and worldview that it is difficult to fathom how a ghostwriter could echo it in an authentic way. Finally, the iconoclasm of Larson's art and comedy was tied inextricably to his cachet of being a quietly stubborn industry rebel. Any artist who was willing to break almost all of the rules related to subject matter, tone, and aesthetics would naturally feel little compunction about flouting his industry's labor conventions as well.

Larson's status as an iconoclast was fully cemented when he chose to retire early in 1995. He explained that he was suffering from the "simple fatigue" and "torture" that came with fifteen years of relentless deadlines (Weise). He was also determined to conclude *The Far Side*'s run when its quality was still high and its cultural relevance still intact; he did not want to drift, in other words, into what he called the "Graveyard of Mediocre Cartoons" or the ranks of the "The Drawing Dead" (Weise; Astor "Widely"). Larson also felt compelled to bring things to a close because of his perfectionistic streak. He could not bear the thought of becoming detached or thoughtless in his craft. He explained, "You have to retain a little dose of fear with it [speaking of the creative process], to keep your edge, to feel like every day is show time. . . . You can just start coasting a little bit. I didn't want that to happen. I wanted to bring it to an elegant conclusion" (Cook). He was alarmed, in fact, that during his final year he had "finally started to lose that fear" of repeating himself or sending in mediocre installments— "things that, in the past, [he] wouldn't have sent in." The creeping sense of complacency he was experiencing "was a red flag to [him] that maybe [he] was sitting on [his] laurels a little bit" (Holguin, "Voice from the *Far Side*").

Fans responded with confusion and dismay to his retirement announcement; perhaps because *The Far Side* had become such an important part of readers' daily routines—and in some cases, such an integral facet of some diehard fans' comedic identities or sensibilities—they seemed to feel especially possessive about the text, as if it belonged to them as much as it did to Larson. The degree of shock expressed was also an illustration of how rarely superstar cartoonists retired in the field. Because blockbuster cartoons could serve as a reliable engine for immense syndication and merchandising earnings for decades, syndicates placed immense pressure on a creator to continue the strip as long as his or her health would allow. In Larson's case, it was his ownership of the copyright to his work that made this retirement a possibility in the first place. Universal was understandably frustrated by his decision, but there was little they could do to stop him.

Interestingly, Bill Watterson had a much tougher time in his retirement negotiations with Universal during the same year. His approach to the issue was complicated by the facts that he did not own the copyright to his work and that he refused to allow Universal to do any merchandising beyond the book collections once he concluded his strip's run. He thus had neither the legal clout nor the flexible approach in dealing with commercial and institutional pressures that marked Larson's exit. With the departure of *The Far Side*, Universal was perhaps more inclined to relent pressure in negotiations because they were assured a steady stream of ancillary earnings in the following years; thus, even in a postcareer context, Larson was able to both protect the quality of text and amplify his legacy by charting the middle course of a pragmatic auteur between the demands of original art/comedy and the pressures of commerce.

With Watterson, Universal could have ultimately behaved like an old-school syndicate and tried to assign *Calvin and Hobbes* to a new artist; to their credit, they resisted the temptation and let Watterson close shop on his own terms. And even though that kind of draconian move was never a possibility in Universal's dealings with Larson, the idea of him voluntarily letting someone else take over *The Far Side* was floated by some observers and readers. A journalist, for example, said, "We do not expect him to be totally indefatigable. We do not expect him to be a one-man show. It may be time for Larson to accept an executive position in his own organization while training and challenging other creative talents to follow his path" (Lynch 10A). While this notion of assistants keeping the cartoon going was not foreign to the craft of syndicated cartooning (and might have pleased less discriminating fans), it was ultimately unworkable in Larson's case. *The Far Side* was so distinctive in its awkward aesthetics and comedic worldview that the most-devoted fans had come to see Larson and his text as a single package. In sum, it was largely due to Larson's fifteen-year-long success in producing a genuinely original and distinctly counterdiscursive text, through a stubborn and sometimes naive insistence on exerting the rights of an auteur, that his cartoon would always be known in the public eye as Gary Larson's *The Far Side*.

Chapter 5

Absurdly Naturalistic

The Cultural Significance of *The Far Side*

Decades from now *The Far Side* will most likely live on in a radically atomized state: individual cartoons scattered across the far corners of the Internet like fading, faintly radioactive particles of some long-forgotten, comedic big bang. Upon encountering one of those potent droplets (perhaps the
classic panel "The real reason dinosaurs became extinct" [fig. 5.1]), a future
reader might be momentarily intrigued by Larson's clever gag and distilled
aesthetics. A fleeting chuckle, however, will likely be all that comes from
that brief encounter as the reader moves on to the next unrelated cartoon
or humorous meme. This prospect of *The Far Side* eventually decaying in
our collective memory, with individual cartoons losing some of their larger
meanings or resonance, is strange for readers who grew up with Larson's
work, cutting out favorites, collecting book anthologies, and using the daily
calendars. For these avid fans, a similar encounter in the future with an
isolated Larson cartoon might remain a powerful experience, triggering a
cavalcade of memories of other favorite *Far Side* panels.

In the name of preserving the gravitational pull of *The Far Side* as a whole
on its fragmented parts for future readers, I explore in this final chapter
the possible ways that Larson's distilled visual-verbal jokes were read and
used at the height of their popularity as a set of mutually reinforcing texts
that included newspaper comics, clippings, book collections, calendars,
and merchandise. These speculations about the cultural power of cartoons
in earlier decades will help to lay a foundation for identifying the larger
satiric and philosophical meanings that accrued around individual *Far
Side* panels over the years—in particular, ideas about deep time, naturalism, anthropocentric foolishness, and the virtues of skepticism. While

The real reason dinosaurs became extinct

Fig. 5.1. Gary Larson, "The real reason dinosaurs became extinct," *The Far Side*, Dec. 15, 1982 (1-264).

this discussion might help those meanings to emerge most brightly for readers who actually experienced the unlikely emergence and radioactive growth of *The Far Side* in real time, it can also intensify their lingering glow, perhaps, for readers of any generation who are invested in understanding the interconnected themes embedded in Larson's 4,300 cartoons spanning fifteen years.

At first glance it might seem like a stretch—a type of semiotic aggrandizement—to imagine a single newspaper comic like the dinosaur installment serving as a portal into a world of significant satiric or philosophical meaning. Some educated observers, for example, might be skeptical because of an unconscious bias against cartoon mediums that seem to lack cultural weight or authority, and that appear, from a distance, to be ephemeral and shallow in their meanings (Schudson 56). Influenced by formalistic and highbrow traditions, that brand of critic might automatically grant deep cultural significance and inherent complexity to literary or didactic texts that are word-based, long in narrative form, and sober in tone; *The Far Side*, in contrast, would have several strikes against it: the panels are seemingly simple in form and content, image-heavy, hybrid in their visual-verbal construction, and fun to read in their irreverent silliness.

We can challenge these assumptions about the shallowness of Larson's work by highlighting both the practical and theoretical ways that those seeming deficits might have paradoxically amplified *The Far Side*'s larger cultural meanings and potent fan uses during the height of its popularity. To begin, not all cartoons, of course, are created with the same level of intentional meaning or satiric intent. On the least significant level, we can point to highly slick and generic images that capitalize on the power of distilled cartoon imagery without having much to say. Decorative comics like *Hello Kitty*, for example, serve primarily as an exercise in achieving maximal cuteness and iconic distillation in the service of a $5 billion-a-year mass merchandising industry. This franchise was created in 1974, in fact, primarily as vehicle for selling products and only later graduated into web comics and television shows for children. Moreover, because the distilled *Hello Kitty* images are so slickly produced—as if by an unfailing machine or bullpen of anonymous graphic designers—their meanings are polysemic in a sterile way, maximizing their flexibility as merchandising icons without indicating any specific message beyond "I am cute." The fact that these cartoons are rarely accompanied by any clarifying text heightens those purely decorative, open-ended qualities; they cannot be tied to a particular artist/writer with even a generic joke to share.

The conventions of the traditional funnies page add semiotic weight to distilled cartoon imagery. For starters, strips and panels are tied to a particular artist with an identifiable sense of humor and way of seeing/ thinking about things—and thus we expect each installment to work as a stand-alone joke as well as an expression of a larger worldview. In addition, newspaper comics are an inherently hybrid medium in which words and images exist in a symbiotic relationship, building and limiting (in a productive way) each other's possible meanings. These mechanisms for grounding and specifying meanings have not always resulted in cartoons with something profound or original to say, of course; despite the comedic potential of the medium, panels like *Marmaduke* or *Ziggy*, for example, tended to rehash familiar gags about difficult pets or sweet platitudes concerning the ups and downs of daily life. In addition, if a newspaper comic was merchandised too aggressively—and in ways that emphasized the superficially decorative qualities of the cartoon imagery, divorced from context and a specific, verbal joke—the grounded qualities of the medium could erode to a degree, as we suggested in the discussion in chapter 4 about Schulz's *Peanuts*.

In the case of Larson's dinosaur cartoon, his clever drawing of pre-historic creatures incongruously behaving in humanlike ways, is clarified and moved from vaguely funny imagery to structured joke with a rich set of satiric points and references when tied to the words "The real reason dinosaurs became extinct." That interdependence of words and images in a newspaper comic may seem like an obvious point, but it is a significant aspect of the medium's (and *The Far Side's*) comparatively strong semiotic nature. And the fact that the linkage between those visual and verbal elements remained intact as Larson's most popular cartoons were used in ancillary products like calendars, T-shirts and coffee mugs is a critical point; despite being aggressively merchandised, each panel always remained a coherent reflection of Larson's verbal-visual satire and naturalistic worldview.

Dwelling a bit more on aesthetics, we could say that newspaper comics, like twentieth-century hieroglyphics, developed over the decades a distilled visual vocabulary that had the potential to communicate specific and relatively stable comedic/satiric meanings. If that sign system was harnessed to shallow purposes (as suggested in the *Hello Kitty* example above) or executed in ways that felt too slickly professional, it could come across as shallow, square, or generic in its connotative meanings. Thankfully, though, there were quirky iconoclasts in every era of the medium's history—figures such as George Herriman (*Krazy Kat*), E. C. Segar (*Popeye*), Cathy Guisewite (*Cathy*), Nicole Hollander (*Sylvia*), Scott Adams (*Dilbert*), and Stephen Pastis (*Pearls Before Swine*) —who created individualized, and sometimes even acutely antiprofessional aesthetics that had the potential to articulate satiric meanings peculiar to that cartoonist's worldview.

Larson's customized cartooning aesthetics shaped and supported his satiric intentions in a variety of ways. For starters, his self-taught, clear-lined style connoted in a general fashion his garage-band irreverence and authenticity. Second, the distilled signs he gradually developed for eyes, glasses, bodies, craniums, and so on served as visual metaphors for a number of cultural ills: intellectual myopia, complacent dogmatism, lazy devolution. Finally, his intentionally grotesque (or anti-cute) treatments of human and animal forms signaled his carnivalesque purposes: creating an aesthetic that inverted the typical conventions of the gentrified funnies page.

Applying these ideas to the dinosaur cartoon, we can see that the figures were anthropomorphized in a distilled and efficient manner—denoting their essential dinosaurness and connoting the hunched postures of human juvenile delinquents. The drawing style was also void of the dynamic line work and cute flourishes that might invite emotional identification from the reader. Instead, the deadpan approach encouraged a more cerebral approach to the panel, reading it as a satiric, visual-verbal puzzle created by an alternative cartoonist. While perhaps alienating readers accustomed to cute, comedically unchallenging cartoon texts, it would have been readily deciphered by fans familiar with the tone and meanings of Larson's customized hieroglyphics: it was a satiric parody of a public service announcement.

Moving from aesthetics to a broader view of Larson's panel as a hybrid, verbal-visual whole, perhaps we can test the semiotic weight of his collective cartoons through a comparison to an officially anointed carrier of weighty meaning, such as a classic novel in an academic setting. First, we are naturally inclined to see novels as superior in their ability to articulate complex meanings because of their narrative richness and capacity to invest us in characters' inner, psychological lives. A book, after all, can develop those characters and themes in a poetically consistent way across a great number of pages and chapters. In contrast, we usually think of newspaper cartoons as single, isolated gags. If we reframe our understanding of *The Far Side* text as a multicartoon, interconnected whole, however, the comparison becomes more interesting.

For starters, a large collection of Larson's panels have none of the poetically structured elegance of a novel, but in terms of developing overarching themes or philosophical ideas, there is perhaps different, but comparable, richness. When you read a large number of *Far Side* cartoons in one sitting, for example, you appreciate how Larson revisited and distilled character types and themes over the years, harnessing them repeatedly to similar satiric ideas. In other words, in reading them as a collection (as most fans did who purchased the books and calendars), rather than as isolated gags, the connective threads between cartoons thicken into solid, thematic cords, and a satiric narrative emerges that is coherent and begins to feel almost epic in its multiyear, hundred-plus-cartoons sweep. Readers, moreover, who read Larson's work in this connected and expansive way developed such a familiarity with key tropes and ideas that the reading of a single panel could amount to more than the appreciation of an isolated gag; like reentering Larson's world through the tip of an iceberg, it amounted to a

Dirk brings his family tree to class.

Fig. 5.2. Gary Larson, "Dirk brings his family tree to class," *The Far Side*, Sept. 4, 1986 (1-609).

rereading—or reinforcement—of remembered, related cartoons and the worldview articulated by *The Far Side* as a collective whole.

Applying this idea to the dinosaur cartoon, we can establish that Larson consistently reinforced themes of naturalism, evolution, and interspecies relations over the years, returning repeatedly to vignettes about dinosaurs, early hominids, and Neolithic megafauna. Vivid examples include the panel in which a proud, early-human boy brings his family tree to class, gesturing toward ancestors that include monkeys, dinosaurs, and a pair of amoebas named Hilda and Ned (fig. 5.2); the cartoon in which an early hominid is disappointed to learn that he won't be moving on the next grade in elementary school with his more evolved, Cro-Magnon classmates (1–461);

"The picture's pretty bleak, gentlemen. ... The world's climates are changing, the mammals are taking over, and we all have a brain about the size of a walnut."

Fig. 5.3. Gary Larson, "The picture's pretty bleak," *The Far Side*, Nov. 7, 1985 (1-524).

and another installment where a dinosaur at a lectern tells his fellow sauropods, "The picture's pretty bleak, gentlemen . . . the world's climates are changing, the mammals are taking over, and we all have a brain about the size of a walnut" (fig. 5.3).

Within a flow of consistent images and ideas about evolution, Larson's cartoon about smoking dinosaurs begins to stand out as a small but significant chapter in a sort of years-long comedic text about deep time. And for core readers who avidly followed the development of that thematic comedy through Larson's sprawling body of cartoons over the years, the accretion of all those related jokes articulated a set of coherent philosophical ideas in a jokey but powerful way: that our human history is a small slice of the planet's epic development, that we are just one species among many existing within complex and fragile ecosystems, and that we are evolved animals uniquely capable of foolishness on a species-ending scale. It is also worth pointing out that the mere assertion in comic—but emphatic and repetitive—form that our world can best be explained through the naturalistic laws of evolution is no small accomplishment in a mainstream culture that was (and continues to be) surprisingly resistant to acknowledging the reality of those scientific truths.

Although difficult to quantify, it is also useful to consider the emotional and intellectual potency of *The Far Side* by considering the different ways readers engaged with favorite panels like this dinosaur cartoon in the 1980s and early 1990s: as an isolated gag in a daily newspaper on inexpensive newsprint; as a clipping that was adhered to refrigerators and office doors for months; as a slide in business presentations and academic lectures; as a featured installment among similarly themed *Far Side* cartoons in several book collections (colorized and enlarged in one anthology to fill an entire page); as an early Internet meme; and as a wearable or portable summation (in both T-shirt and coffee mug form) of the entire *Far Side* comedic/ satiric worldview. On a theoretical level these different iterations of this iconic panel emphasize the ways that mechanically reproduced, widely distributed comics texts exhibited a great deal of democratic use-value in the twentieth century (as opposed to the concentrated but limited cult value of a work of high art isolated in a museum) (Benjamin 225). A vast number of people, in other words, could "use" and reuse Larson's work in accessible and psychologically powerful ways (reading, sharing, collecting, posting, displaying, wearing, etc.).

Building on these issues of reception and uses, and returning to the comparison with the classic novel, we can borrow a bit of framing from meme theory. Canonized cultural texts, like *The Great Gatsby* or *Heart of Darkness,* that have been celebrated by critics and assigned perennially in high school and college syllabi have a massive head start in getting their core ideas into cultural circulation. Mark Twain pointed out long ago, however, that in an American cultural context, those educational endorsements might actually be counterproductive, condemning a classic to become "something that everybody wants to have read and nobody wants to read." Moreover, in academic settings, where these books are required reading, young people are notoriously creative at finding shortcuts or replacements to a full-fledged engagement with the text: plagiarized notes, online summaries, cursory viewings of the movie adaptations, and so on. And thus despite the effort involved in assigning individuals to not only read these texts, but also to use them actively in discussions, and written assignments, the authors' complex philosophical ideas often remain latent in the face of so much inattentive, uninvested, and resisting reception. In some cases that kind of superficial engagement leads to readers (using the term generously) misunderstanding and misusing the text in ironic ways. Consider, for example, the contemporary popularity of *Great Gatsby*–themed parties or weddings that celebrate the very cultural practices that the original novel satirized.

As a grassroots source of philosophical memes, *The Far Side* did not have the help (or curse?) of highbrow advocates, but it did have the ease of distribution that comes with syndication, cheap newsprint, and inexpensive books and merchandise. With that democratic accessibility as a starting point, *The Far Side*'s key themes and ideas found a genuinely receptive readership; people effectively "voted" for the significance or resonance of key cartoons with their eyes, scissors, overhead projectors, computers, and pocketbooks, seeking out opportunities to reproduce and spread Larson's comedy and satiric ideas. In effect, Larson's most iconic cartoons went viral and stayed culturally resonant in pre-Internet fashion. In sum, the high level of eagerness among fans not only to dwell upon key installments through several forms, but to make the proactive effort to share them with others, suggests a high degree of emotional and intellectual investment—one that easily surpasses in enthusiasm and focus the amount of attention invested in understanding official, culturally sanctioned big-idea (or meme) carriers like classic novels in an academic setting.

The Far Side as a Carnivalesque Anti-Sermon

Another way we can think about the weight of meaning or degree of resonance emerging from an encounter with an irreverent, popular text like *The Far Side* is to contrast it with how people might receive and think about a traditional Sunday sermon. At first glance, this sort of juxtaposition may feel a bit contrived and unfair—like I'm targeting the stuffiest, most boring strawman in the room. Perhaps it can be justified, nevertheless, in a few different ways. First, the earliest critics of newspaper comics (in the decades that straddled the start of the twentieth century) worried publicly that the reading of Sunday comics supplements was displacing and undermining traditional Sabbath day activities, like attending church. Second, a noted critic of popular culture studies used the Sunday sermon as an example of a cultural text that carries more cultural weight and meaning than bits of ephemeral entertainment like comics (Schudson 57). Finally, ideas about the power of carnivalesque cultural texts allow us to make a vivid contrast between the "first-life" sober-seriousness of a Christian sermon against the rowdy, "second-life" silly-seriousness of a text like *The Far Side*.

In theory, a sermon should exert a high level of cultural meaning or clout because of its inherent seriousness, its sanctioned status as a carrier of moral verities and scriptural truth, and its showcased delivery to an assembled, focused audience in a church. In observing the reception of that text in a typical, real-life setting, however, some of that communicative ability and semiotic significance might rapidly vanish. For example, those of us who actively attend Christian congregations in contemporary culture are familiar with the creative way that large swaths of the people in attendance (young people, ambivalent agnostics, genuine doubters, etc.) often tune out—or even actively resist—the messages of authoritative, lecturing talks.

Turning to newspaper comics, from a distance it might seem like the medium was also generally read in inattentive or fleeting ways—the meanings of different panels and strips barely parsed, as readers casually scanned the crowded funnies page. Since especially popular cartoons attracted invested fans, however, it is more accurate to say that readers approached the comics page with shifting degrees of interest and attention, radically alternating the time and effort each panel or strip received. For an especially beloved comic like *The Far Side*, the level of imaginative attention that invested readers devoted to unpacking, and then deeply imbibing, the meaning of the text easily surpasses the intensity of attention typical churchgoers might give to listening to a talk or lesson. When the beloved cartoon text is satiric, moreover—when it requires the decoding of topical references, coded allegories, layered parodies, or philosophical allusions—the reader is perhaps investing a level of voluntary (instead of religiously or academically compulsory) critical thinking that is especially meaningful. It could amount to such a satisfying form of emotional and intellectual communion, in fact, that readers feel compelled to share it with others—proselytizing the beloved text and its larger meanings, in a sense, through the exchange of clipped cartoons or dog-eared book collections.

It is significant too that highly compelling, irreverent cartoons were associated through much of the twentieth century with large, vividly colored Sunday supplements. When most households subscribed to newspapers, those installments of favorite comics were read with more avidity by subscribers of all ages and demographics than any other part of the paper. Numerous memoirs recall the delicious pleasure of spreading the pages across

Fig. 5.4. Gary Larson, "And just to make it interesting,"
The Far Side, July 22, 1994 (2-562).

a living room floor, relishing the crazy adventures and jokes of their favorite characters on a lazy Sunday morning. Early, turn-of-the-century critics of the emerging medium had been justifiably worried, in fact, that the reading of this new medium on Sabbath mornings would become a more important family tradition than attending church to listen to a sermon. It was as if newspaper comics, in their early, multivoiced, rowdy richness, functioned as a sort of populist anti-sermon, rebutting pious "first-life" dogma with a cavalcade of irreverent, folk-wise jokes (Bakhtin 7, 10).

That irreverence was tamed over the decades to a degree, as the industry reduced sizes, imposed unofficial censorship codes, professionalized the aesthetics, and put limits on the range of ideas and voices that could appear on the page. And so when we get to the early 1980s, (Larson's era), a majority of the jokes on the funnies page were perhaps fairly compatible with the homilies one might hear in a typical Sunday sermon. Within that relatively tame context, Larson's grotesque aesthetics, morbid irreverence, and emphasis on naturalistic themes would have stood out as a revival of the genuinely carnivalesque qualities of the medium from its earliest days, updating the rowdy anti-sermons one might have encountered in comics like *Mutt and Jeff*, *The Katzenjammer Kids*, or *Popeye* (or *Thimble Theatre*).

In fact, beyond the generally subversive tone and aesthetics, *The Far Side* also featured content that explicitly countered the comforting verities that listeners might hear in a traditional Christian church. Instead of biblical lessons about faith and the potential for divine intervention in our lives, readers encountered in Larson's work humorously packaged truths about the violent naturalism of the animal world, the reality of deep evolutionary time, and the constructedness of comforting religious myths. Some of my favorites in this vein included the panel with Noah deciding to put carnivores on a lower deck after discovering two dead unicorns on board the ark (12/31/81; 1–177); the image of God muttering, "Uh-oh," from the heavens after a bottle marked "humans" accidentally falls to the Earth and breaks open, releasing its obnoxious contents onto an innocent world (9/18/82; 1–243); the panel in which God is at His computer, poised to press a "SMITE" key that will drop a suspended piano on a poor fool's head (9/17/91; 2–347); and the classic installment that shows a white-bearded God in a chef's hat thinking to himself, "And just to make it interesting . . . ," while sprinkling some JERKS onto the planet (fig. 5.4). While not designed to promote morality and cleanse sin in the Christian sense of those words, an everyday communion with skeptical jokes like this did perhaps encourage a brand of critical, ethical thinking, inviting engaged readers to recognize and playfully deconstruct (without necessarily wholly rejecting) a variety of comforting social and religious beliefs.

Larson's Influence on Late Twentieth-Century Comedy and Culture

Having investigated the case for *The Far Side*'s significance as a carrier of meme-like jokes with philosophical weight and lasting resonance for devoted fans, we can conclude by assessing the ways that Larson's comedy impacted the cultural imagination of late twentieth-century American society. These reflections from invested followers of *The Far Side* can be divided into two groups: everyday readers, and professional comic writers and artists who admired, and were influenced by, Larson's work. To begin, the huge volume of letters Larson received—both positive and negative—over the course of his career from newspaper readers suggests that *The Far Side* was touching upon sensitive cultural nerves, shaping (and sometimes challenging) worldviews, and influencing individual and collective psyches in small but significant ways. In book collections, over the years, Larson was willing to share the content of the most hyperbolic hate mail he received, but perhaps because of his private and self-effacing nature, we know little about the contents of fan letters. With no access to that raw data, we are forced to locate a contemporary equivalent within online sites where longtime readers share thoughtful reflections on why they love *The Far Side*, how it first captured their attention, and ways that they continue to share favorite installments and collections with a new generation of readers.

The idea that *The Far Side* gave many of its original readers their first exposure to alternative worldviews—and introduced many young people to the mechanisms of satire for the first time—is supported in online reviews. Gen X readers, for example, repeatedly recall thinking that Larson was "ahead of his time" in the 1980s, introducing morbid humor to a mainstream audience, creating "a completely bizarre alternate universe," and pointing out "how profoundly strange and unsettling the real world was" (Hahn-Branson, "The Far Side Gallery"). A few recollections get more specific, suggesting that Larson altered readers' worldviews by prodding them to see the world in fresh (and less complacent) ways through the "eyes of a mischievous child, an alien, an insect, a snake, an amoeba . . ." (Gary, *The Far Side Gallery* 3").

Other fans recall a similar progression of initially being confused, then mesmerized by Larson's work, gradually growing to understand his dense references and parodic jokes, and laughing explosively at some of the most outrageous installments. They also remember the effort required to decode a typical *Far Side* cartoon—and the resultant payoffs once they "got it"—as critical parts of their long-lasting affinity for Larson's work. His panel differed for them, in effect, from other comics that evoked a passing chuckle; in contrast, it made them "think, laugh and then ponder in quick succession. Sort of like a party in the brain . . ." (De Silva, "*The Far Side Gallery* 3").

That high level of enjoyment and intellectual engagement was amplified, too, when readers imbibed larger doses of *The Far Side* world in book collections, as reported by this fan:

> When viewed side by side, for any extended length of time, the effect [of hilarity] multiplies not just cumulatively, but *exponentially*. I have almost had to be hospitalized a number of times due to *Far Side* induced seizures. The first time I read this collection I needed an asthma inhaler by the time I got to the cartoon in which Dorothy and friends encounter the marathon runners on the yellow brick road, and I don't even have asthma! I'm lucky to be alive. (Rich, "*The Far Side Gallery*")

Many of the accounts of how readers first discovered *The Far Side* are especially effusive, reading almost like nostalgic conversion stories. Fans recall being introduced to it by an especially permissive parent, an older sibling, or a likeminded friend. In a pre-Internet era, those first contacts came through a clipping in the mail, from borrowing a much-used book collection from a friend, or by seeing key panels posted on a refrigerator or office door (Davis, "*The Far Side Gallery*"). In turn, these new converts felt compelled to tell other friends about their special find, and for many of them the passing of the years has done little to dim that evangelical enthusiasm. The following fan, for example, was still keen on introducing new generations to Larson's world:

> I grew up reading *The Far Side*. I cut them out of the newspaper and posted them on my bulletin boards. When I got older and had an office of my own, I bought the desk calendars and gleefully tore off yesterday's page to reveal another day full of *The Far Side*. When I started running my own libraries, I bought desk calendars for my front counters so my customers could enjoy them as much as I always have. (Angela, "*The Complete Far Side*")

In a few cases, readers' experiences echo my own encounters with Larson's panels to a large degree; they elaborate on how *The Far Side* played a role in helping them to develop an identity or a sensibility—usually in contrast to that of their parents. Consider this reader's memories:

> I was a kid looking for my own identity. Whatever it was, it was going to be different than my parents' button-down worldview. I wasn't a hellion, so I didn't feel I needed to go overboard. What better mentor than Gary Larson's slightly askew humor?! Larson's work was subversive, maybe not in a poignantly political way, but more in a silly way, which is perfect when you are a young teen looking for something more edgy than *Family Circus* and *Garfield*. . . . Back when Larson's work was current and I was a mildly rebellious teen, I wasn't looking to necessarily "stick it" to the 'rents, more like, thumb my nose at them. For example, Dad was big into outdoor sports, so Larson hit the target . . . with his numerous strips centered upon the man vs. beast struggle. Anything that poked fun at what they held so precious was gold to me. (Koivu, "*The Far Side Gallery 3*")

Aging fans have also noticed that the comedy landscape has caught up with Larson in the intervening decades, and thus his work no longer seems to have the subversive kick it could deliver in the 1980s—nor does it have the potential to operate as a rebel text to annoy stuffy parents:

> Nowadays, it seems like most people—or most entertainers, at least—have just accepted that the world really is as odd as Larson always said it was, so some of his stuff now reads as the first iteration of a type of joke that has been made hundreds of times since: Rapunzel has an afro! Mathematicians cheer each other on like champion athletes! Here are some boomerangs having a domestic dispute! (Hahn-Branson, "*The Far Side Gallery*")

Interestingly, as the subversive qualities of *The Far Side* have become comparatively muted, and as its original fans have become parents and grandparents, it has transitioned from being a controversial text that cultural guardians and protective fathers and mothers denounced, to a relatively benign—and even intellectually beneficial—reading choice for young people. For example, in one review a mother described how the gift of a *Far Side* book collection felt like a godsend to a son who was restricted in his comedy intake to "clean" humor (Larson's work, in other words, passed that test) (Liv, "*The Far Side Gallery*"). Another parent praises *The Far Side*'s potential to teach critical thinking skills: It is "great for helping kids learn to think outside of the box. If your six year old can get *The Far Side*, he or she has developed the higher cognitive skill of inference. When my son burst out laughing at 'I'm afraid you have cows, Mr. Farnsworth,' I knew he was going to be ok in this world" (Thomas, "*The Far Side Gallery*"). A few readers go even further in celebrating the safe or comforting qualities of *The Far Side*, highlighting its almost quaintly focused and contemplative nature in a frenetic digital age. In particular, they promote its capacity to relieve stress, appease anxious patients in waiting rooms, comfort individuals dealing with terminal illnesses, or bond family members across generations. Implied in those suggestions is the idea that our culture has come to embrace the therapeutic merits of engaging with morbid humor in packaged doses or in decoding absurdist, puzzle-like satire.

Tributes from Colleagues and Comedy Professionals

Larson received generally positive reviews over the years from his colleagues, with an occasional mixed reaction. Sometimes he irritated old-timers in the newspaper field with his self-taught drawing style and his tendency to poke fun at mainstream strips like *Garfield* or *Peanuts*. Other contemporaries were put off by his aloofness from professional meetings and what they perceived as a privileged resistance to normal industry practices (his insistence on sabbaticals and an early retirement, for example) (Kaltenbach; Astor, "Larson Fans"). In the end, nevertheless, there was always a grudging respect for his chutzpah in forging his own path and for the originality of his comedy and art. His peers recognized, moreover, that he was making an enormous impact on the medium and the culture at large. Bill Watterson, for example, described him as "one of the most inventive guys in comics," and Garry Trudeau admired his energy, inventiveness, and professionalism in creating wholly original, absurdist cartoons on a daily basis (Christie 31; Plotz).

In the sincerest form of flattery, a number of cartoonists in the 1990s tried, with varying degrees of success, to copy Larson's style or to match the absurdist tone of his work. In most cases their jokes were too self-consciously wacky or broad—or their art too careless or studied in its awkwardness—to compare favorably to *The Far Side*. The mere fact, nevertheless, that syndicates were willing to promote offbeat cartoonists in the wake of *The Far Side's* blockbuster success attests to how Larson impacted his own medium, expanding the palette of comedy that could be featured in the funnies. The best of those edgy panel cartoons were distinct enough in their aesthetics and worldview to read ultimately as progeny of (or distantly related cousins to) *The Far Side*, rather than as opportunistic knockoffs. Dan Piraro's *Bizarro*, for example, was actually introduced as a "replacement" to *The Far Side* by Chronicle Features when Larson left for Universal, and despite the overly obvious title, it flourished on its own terms with a densely elegant drawing style and arch brand of humor. John McPherson's *Close to Home*—which was picked up by Larson's syndicate Universal, in 1992—also featured, like *The Far Side,* a world of awkwardly drawn nerds; but it felt largely original, in its scratchy aesthetic, scenes of everyday humiliation, and absurdist twists on conventional sports and pastimes.

More recently, the excellent panel comic *The Argyle Sweater*, by Scott Hilburn, revisits some of the same territory covered by *The Far Side*: clever wordplay, morbid themes imposed on daily life, inversions of familiar fairytale tropes, and so on. Hilburn, refreshingly, is not defensive about the similarities between his work and Larson's, openly admitting that he was heavily influenced by the earlier comic; he relates,

> I was a huge *Far Side* fan growing up . . . I think Larson's tone heavily influenced my own style of humor. What I loved about his work was that he had this ability to capture a moment just before or after some funny event had happened. He didn't always draw the funny moment—he drew the event leading up to it or the aftermath—and then let the reader fill in the blanks. That a-ha moment made the joke even better and made me feel like I was in on the joke . . . I've tried to incorporate that element in my comic as well. (Hart, "Scott Hilburn Interview")

As a current professional in the field who is syndicated by Chronicle Features, Hilburn is also able to offer an objective view of Larson's legacy within the medium and beyond:

> To my mind, he's the most brilliant one-panel cartoonist ever. He set the bar for offbeat humor and has clearly influenced, to varying degrees, every syndicated single panelist since then—and lots of strip cartoonists too. The amazing thing is that it's been over 20 years since he retired and he's still the standard bearer. I see his work still referenced on sitcoms, movies—even in answers to *Jeopardy* questions. I see influences of his work in TV commercials, routines of popular comedians and even online in memes. (Hart, "Scott Hilburn Interview")

Comedians working in related fields recall the formative influence Larson had on them when they were young or just beginning their careers. Peter Kuper, an avant-garde cartoonist and illustrator, for example, remembers being "amazed" that Larson was able to carry the "darker sensibility" of alternative panel cartoons "to the staid newspaper format every day." In fact, seeing how Larson "upped the intelligence level he assumed in his readers compared with most newspaper strips," Kuper felt justified in pursuing his own quirky muse and challenging aesthetic style (Hart, "Peter Kuper Interview").

Peter Mehlman, one of the key writers behind *Seinfeld*, admired and emulated Larson's work for several reasons. First, he remembers being blown away by Larson's "ability to be relevant and utterly surreal at the same time," effectively introducing absurd and "supernatural circumstances" in affectless ways that were "totally relatable." Second, he marveled at Larson's brevity—his ability to communicate "so much in so few words," and to excise anything superfluous to the essence of the joke. Mehlman, in turn, consciously tried to emulate that "rare dynamic" in his "own peculiar view of the world" as a comedy writer; and he remembers that Jerry Seinfeld and his staff of writers pursued a similar strategy of distillation in their construction of each episode, always living by the maxim "In comedy, if it doesn't add, it subtracts" (Hart, "Mehlman Interview").

Jon Vitti, a prolific comedy writer for *The Simpsons*, *King of the Hill*, and *The Office*, recalls that many of the best writers on *The Simpsons*, such as John Swartzwelder and George Meyer, were big fans of *The Far Side*; they admired and tried to emulate Larson's straight-faced delivery of absurdist material. He goes on to cite a number of specific ways that Larson may have influenced his own comedic sensibility:

> There was never anybody better [than Larson] at offhanded, casual depictions of crazy stuff. The fact that everyone accepts what's going on in Gary Larson's strange scenes makes it all seem stranger. That's absolutely something we tried to achieve when *The Simpsons* got really weird. Was that from reading *The Far Side*? Honestly I don't know. When someone does a landmark piece of work like *The Far Side* you never look at comedy exactly the same way again. So everything you do might be different after that. (Hart, "Jon Vitti Interview")

He continues, taking a shot at assessing (with the inevitable caveats) Larson's impact on popular comedy in general over the last several decades:

> My favorite standup comedians have always been the conceptual comedians like Stephen Wright and Mitch Hedberg. Strange sci-fi comedy has come into its own in the twenty-first century. Are those descended from *The Far Side* or just done by kindred spirits? You'd have to ask the people involved, but every comedy professional accepts that special honor goes to the person who did it first. And nobody ever did it better than Gary Larson. (Hart, "Jon Vitti Interview")

Conclusion

Perhaps the most fascinating aspect of Larson's immense success and his long-lasting influence on comedy and the worldviews of so many devoted fans and professionals is that he did it all with so little forethought and calculation. Untutored in the craft of cartooning and naive about the workings of the newspaper industry, he essentially wandered into the profession of syndicated cartooning. Once in the door, his numerous shortcomings, oddly, became significant strengths. First, the nerdy narrowness of his interests (science, animals, guitars, fringe humor), and a reclusive personality, allowed him to create an original brand of morbid and absurdist comedy in relative isolation. Second, his social anxieties and general shyness allowed him to remain consistent for years in following that weird muse; he effectively tuned out the noise that comes with immense fame and listened only to the feedback of his own brain and a small set of collaborators and core fans interested in protecting his originality. Third, his lack of professional drawing ability helped him to create an awkward but powerfully distilled aesthetic that was genuinely funny; the do-it-yourself quality of his cartooning also signaled to core fans his rebel credentials within a popular field of art that had become blandly gentrified over time. Fifth, Larson's stubborn naïveté, when it came to business matters, helped him to become an accidental auteur in his industry—an iconoclast who leveraged his popularity into achieving and exerting artist rights that protected the original and subversive quality of his comedy. Finally, his neurotic perfectionism allowed him to distill the comedy and art in his cartoons down to gemlike essences; over time that peculiar obsessiveness wore him down and led to an earlier retirement than readers would have preferred, but it resulted in a staggering accomplishment: the creation of an original and genuinely funny cartoon almost every day, for fifteen years.

Depending on one's perspective, you could also say that Larson's melancholic (and at times even misanthropic) temperament was a poor starting point for a person tasked with making people laugh on a daily basis. In practice, the relatively perverse and bleak comedy that emerged from Larson's pen did not please everyone; as we've seen in vivid detail, his cartoons were actively abhorred by a large swath of the reading public who preferred humor that was lighthearted and optimistic. The consistently degenerative flavor of his comedy, nevertheless, did not leave his invested readers with an acrid, nihilistic aftertaste, as you might imagine. After a reader invested a serious level of time and thought in enjoying *The Far Side*, he or she could decipher an inspiring set of satiric ideas beneath the dark exterior: that we should overcome a species-centric hubris that leads to a great number of foolish beliefs and shortsighted (and sometimes cruel) behaviors; that we benefit from regular doses of philosophical naturalism—in particular, using a view of deep time as an antidote to the side effects of buying into many of

"Thank God, Sylvia! We're alive!"

Fig. 5.5. Gary Larson, "Thank God, Sylvia! We're alive!" *The Far Side*, December 8, 1981 (1-172).

society's misleading platitudes and myths; that it is wise to approach other cultural texts with a skeptical, scientific (even organically deconstructive) mind-set; and that the injustices and humiliations of everyday life—both large and small—can be best endured with an absurdist sense of humor or worldview. On the one hand, the haphazard articulation of those ideas across similarly themed cartoons over many years makes it difficult to see *The Far Side* as a coherent, reformative work of satire—a text that takes down specific targets and offers hopeful remedies. On the other hand, the open-ended qualities of *The Far Side* as a years-spanning text allow the sum of Larson's work to function as a work of humanely cosmic satire—a sprawling tragicomic drama that models and nurtures a kind of humorous and skeptical intelligence that might steer individuals and society away from the most chronic brands of human foolishness.

In light of the satiric strength of Larson's collected body of cartoons, we could fault him for being too possessive and protective of his work during his retirement years; it seems, at first look, that he has hobbled *The Far Side's* potential to reach new audiences. Indeed, when it comes to imagining Larson's legacy in future decades, it is tempting to conclude that the satiric brightness of individual cartoons will fade dramatically as his body of work fails to find a new life in the digital world. I wonder, however, if Larson's reticence to change with the times will be largely justified. As the work of an auteur (and sometimes sateur) with such a peculiar aesthetic, sense of humor, and philosophical worldview, *The Far Side* may be appropriately seen as a finite, interconnected series of cartoons from a particular era and a unique mind. And perhaps this study's effort to appreciate the significance of Larson's creation within its original context, and in light of the sad decline of the traditional funnies page, will help in a small way to direct future fans back to Larson's work in its most semiotically concentrated form: collected together in the dog-eared pages of portable, shareable, comfortingly tactile book collections. And if some of the darkest vignettes that Larson imagines for a future of extreme environmental degradation and self-destruction come true, then subsequent generations—like the poor descendants of Sylvia and her daftly cheerful husband in their underground bunkers (fig. 5.5)—will appreciate the analog durability of those anthologies; like anyone who comes across one of these books in the future, they will find lasting comfort and distracting hilarity in the darkly prescient humor found within. Here's to hoping we learn a lesson or two from Larson's absurdist satire, and it doesn't come to that.

Works Cited

"Andrews McMeel Universal." *Reference for Business*. 2001. Web. 11 Sept. 2016.

Angela. "The Complete Far Side." Goodreads Reviews, Oct. 25, 2014.

Armani, April Marie. "Far Side Is Disgusting." *Times Advocate*, 19 Jan. 1986. *The Complete Far Side*, Vol. I. Kansas City: Andrews McMeel, 2003. 582.

Astor, David. "'Far Side' Cartoonist Gary Larson Signs with UPS." *Editor & Publisher*, 28 July 1984: 37.

———. "The Far Side to Return with More Clients." *Editor & Publisher*, 30 Dec. 1989: 34.

———. "Gary Larson and Life beyond the Far Side." *Editor & Publisher*, 21 Mar. 1998: 34–35.

———. "Larson Explores the Far Side of Life." *Editor & Publisher*, 2 July 1983: 31–32.

———. "Larson Fans Praise His Departing Panel." *Editor & Publisher*, 15 Oct. 1995: 36.

———. "Larson's Web Warning Worked." *Editor & Publisher*, 21 Mar. 1998: 35.

———. "Meet the New Prez, a Syndication Veteran like the Old Prez." *Editor & Publisher*, 22 May 2006. Web. 9 July 2016.

———. "Retired Cartoonist Receives a Reuben." *Editor & Publisher*, 21 Mar. 1998: 35.

———. "Reuben Award for 'The Far Side' Creator." *Editor & Publisher*, 25 May 1991: 52.

———. "A Review of the Syndicate World in 1990." *Editor & Publisher*, 5 Jan. 1991: 75.

———. "Universal Is Buying Chronicle Features," *Editor & Publisher*, 27 Sept. 1197: 44.

———. "The Widely Syndicated 'Far Side' Is Being Discontinued by Larson." *Editor & Publisher*, 8 Oct. 1994: 45.

Bakhtin, Mikhail. *Rabelais and His World*. Bloomington: Indiana UP, 1984.

Barry, John. "*Far Side* Fans Honor Cartoonist Gary Larson." *Greensboro News Record*, 10 Dec. 1994: D5.

Baumgartner, Jody C., and Jonathan S. Morris. "One 'Nation' under Stephen? The Effects of *The Colbert Report* on America's Youth." *Journal of Broadcasting and Electronic Media* 52.4 (2008): 622–643.

Benjamin, Walter. *Illuminations*. New York: Schocken Books, 1968.

Bernstein, Fred. "Loony 'Toonist Gary Larson Takes Millions for a Daily Walk on the Far Side." *People*, 4 Feb. 1985: 103–105.

Bhabha, Homi K. *The Location of Culture*. New York: Routledge, 1994.

Canemaker, John. Felix: The Twisted Tale of the World's Most Famous Cat. New York: Da Capo Press, 1991.

Carrier, David. The Aesthetics of Comics. University Park: Pennsylvania State UP, 2000.

Christie, Andrew. "An Interview with Bill Watterson." Honk!, no. 2, 1986: 28–32.

Cook, Rebecca. "Gary Larson Revisits 'The Far Side' in New Book." Online Athens. AthensBanner Herald, 2 Dec. 2003. Web. 9 July 2106.

Crouch, Bill. "Milton Caniff Talks about Walt Kelly." Phi Beta Pogo. Ed. Selby Kelly and Bill Crouch Jr. New York: Simon and Schuster, 1989. 106–112.

Daigneault, Henry W. "Letter to Gary Larson." The Complete Far Side. Vol. I. Kansas City, Andrews McMeel, 200. 296.

Dale, Alan. Comedy Is a Man in Trouble. Minneapolis: U of Minnesota P, 2000.

Davis. "The Far Side Gallery." Goodreads Reviews, 22 Mar. 2013.

De Silva. "The Far Side Gallery 3." Goodreads Reviews, 25 Aug. 2014.

Dinerman, Janet A. "Letter to Gary Larson." The Complete Far Side, Vol. I. Kansas City: Andrews McMeel, 2003. 320.

Dodds, Stuart. "Memo from Stuart Dodds to Stan Arnold." The Complete Far Side. Vol. I. Kansas City: Andrews McMeel, 2003. 55.

Doran, Tom. "Less Is Moo: The Genius of Gary Larson." Daily Beast, 22 Mar. 2013. Web. 16 Sept. 2016.

Engel, Sue. "Offensive 'Far Side.'" Arizona Daily Star, 1 Sept. 1987. Reprinted in The Complete Far Side. Vol. II. Kansas City: Andrews McMeel, 2003. 80.

Enger, R. E. "Letter to the Editor of the Minneapolis Tribune." The Complete Far Side. Vol. I. Kansas City: Andrews McMeel, 2003. 171.

Evanier, Mark. Mad Art. New York: Watson Guptill, 2002.

Ferguson, Kelly. "A Walk on the Far Side: The Life and Times of Gary Larson." Mental Floss, 12 Nov. 2007. Web. 9 July 2016.

Freud, Sigmund. Jokes and Their Relation to the Unconscious. New York: W. W. Norton, 1905. Republished 1990.

Gary. "The Far Side Gallery 3." Goodreads Reviews, 17 Jan. 2009.

"Getting Sarcastic with Kids." Science Daily. 9 Aug. 2007. Web. 22 Aug. 2016.

Goodall, Jane. "Foreword." The Far Side Gallery 5. Kansas City: Andrews McMeel, 1994. 5–9.

Gordon, Ian. Comic Strips and Consumer Culture: 1890–1945. Washington, DC: Smithsonian Institution Press, 1998.

Gould, Stephen Jay. "Foreword." The Far Side Gallery 3. Kansas City: Andrews McMeel, 1994. 9–12.

Gumbel, Andrew. "The Far Side of Gary Larson: An Audience with the World's Most Successful Cartoonist." Independent, 17 Nov. 1999. Web. 9 July 2016.

Hahn-Branson. "The Far Side Gallery." Goodreads Reviews, 8 Jan. 2012.

Hanson, Victor H. II. "Letter to the Editor." Birmingham News, Aug. 23, 1994. Reprinted in The Complete Far Side. Vol. II. Kansas City: Andrews McMeel, 2003. 367.

Harnisch, Dennis. "Gary Larson's Far Side Goes Too Far This Time." Florida Times-Union, 21 Feb. 1988. The Complete Far Side. Vol. II. Kansas City: Andrews McMeel, 2003. 137.

Hart, Anne. Jon Vitti interview. Unpublished, 31 July 2016.

———. Peter Kuper interview. Unpublished, 20 Aug. 2016.

———. Peter Mehlman interview. Unpublished, 19 Aug. 2016.

———. Scott Hilburn interview. Unpublished, 28 July 2016.

Hatfield, Charles. *Alternative Comics: An Emerging Literature.* Jackson: UP of Mississippi, 2005.

Heintjes, Tom. "Universal Soldier: The Lee Salem Interview." *Hogan's Alley: The Magazine of the Cartoon Arts*, 8 Nov. 2103. Web. 9 July 2016.

Hess, Pauline Whitcomb. "Misses the 'Menace.'" *Journal Tribune* [Biddeford, Maine], 17 Nov. 1986. *The Complete Far Side*. Vol. I. Kansas City: Andrews McMeel, 2003. 471.

Hicks, Stephanie. "Gary Larson's *Far Side* Cartoons." *Hubpages*, 13 Aug. 2014. Web. 16 Sept. 2016.

Holguin, Robert Saiz. "Gary Larson's Farewell Is Also a Hello to Animated TV." *Baltimore Sun*, 23 Oct. 1994: 5H.

———. "Voice from the 'Far Side': Gary Larson Opens Up about Retiring." *Seattle Times*, 14 Oct. 1994. Web. 9 July 2016.

Holt, Kevin M. "Letter to Gary Larson." *The Complete Far Side*. Vol. I. Kansas City: Andrews McMeel, 2003. 431.

Hoogendoorn, Pete. "'Far Side' Not Welcome Here." *Argus Leader. The Complete Far Side*. Vol. I. Kansas City: Andrews McMeel, 2003. 431.

Hurd, Jud. "A Trip with a Syndicate Salesman!" *Cartoonist Profiles* 82 (June 1989): 10–11.

———. "What Happens to Your Strip?" *Cartoonist Profiles* 66 (June 1985): 8–10.

Hurst, Beth. "Dear Mr. Larson." *The Complete Far Side*. Vol. II. Kansas City: Andrews McMeel, 2003. 102.

Hutcheon, Linda. *A Theory of Parody*. Chicago: U of Illinois P, 1985.

Jorgenson, Jerry. "'Far Side' Is Garbage." *Times Advocate*, 19 Jan. 1986. *The Complete Far Side*, Vol. I. Kansas City: Andrews McMeel, 2003. 582.

Kaltenbach, Chris. "Aargh—No More Peanuts." *Baltimore Sun*, 15 Dec. 1999. Web. 19 Aug. 2016.

Keefe, Nancy Q. "Beyond the Bounds of Decency? Or Simply Humor Out of This World?" *Herald Statesman*, 19 Feb. 1987. *The Complete Far Side*. Vol. II. Kansas City: Andrews McMeel, 2003. 14.

Kelly, James. "All Creatures Weird and Funny." *Time*, 1 Dec. 1986: 86.

Kelly, Walt. "NCS Newsletter 1953." 1953 newsletter found in "NCS Dossier" of The Walt Kelly Collection, Ohio State Library Cartoon Collection.

Kliban, B. "Free Rubber Chickens Regardless of a Person's Beliefs." *Jumping Up and Down on the Roof, Throwing Bags of Water on People*. Ed. Mark Jacobs. New York: Dolphin Books, 1980. 49–75.

Koivu. "*The Far Side Gallery 3*." *Goodreads Reviews*, 29 Dec. 2014.

Kunzle, David. *The History of the Comic Strip: The Nineteenth Century*. Berkeley: U of California P, 1990.

Larson, Gary. "Acknowledgments." *The Complete Far Side*. Vol. I. Kansas City: Andrews McMeel, 2003. xviii–xx.

———. "A Bad Day in Cartoon Land." *The Complete Far Side*. Vol. I. Kansas City: Andrews McMeel, 2003. 356–357.

———. "Big Ungulates, Little Bipeds." *The Complete Far Side*. Vol. I. Kansas City: Andrews McMeel, 2003. 446–448.

———. "Commencement Address to Graduating Class at Washington State University, 1990." May 1990. Washington State University Library Archives.

———. "Creative Process." *The Prehistory of the Far Side: A 10th Anniversary Exhibit*. Kansas City: Andrews McMeel, 1989. 42–105.

———. "The Eye and I." *The Complete Far Side*. Vol. I. Kansas City: Andrews McMeel, 2003. 540–541.

———. "Final Thoughts." *The Complete Far Side*. Vol. II. Kansas City: Andrews McMeel, 2003. 524–525.

———. "The Fossil Record." *The Prehistory of the Far Side: A 10th Anniversary Exhibit*. Kansas City: Andrews McMeel, 1989. 13–38.

———. "The Good Wetch." *The Complete Far Side*. Vol. II. Kansas City: Andrews McMeel, 2003. 122–123.

———. "I Remember." *The Complete Far Side*. Vol. II. Kansas City: Andrews McMeel, 2003, 450-451.

———. "The Jungle in My Room." *The Complete Far Side*. Vol. II. Kansas City: Andrews McMeel, 2003. 4–5.

———. "The Minefields of Mirth." *The Complete Far Side*. Vol. II. Kansas City: Andrews McMeel, 2003. 374–375.

———. "On Dorothy Parker, Gorilla Masks, and a Very Close Call." *The Complete Far Side*. Vol. I. Kansas City: Andrews McMeel, 2003. 4-7.

———. "On Monsters." *The Complete Far Side*. Vol. I. Kansas City: Andrews McMeel, 2003. 268.

———. "Preface." *The Complete Far Side*. Vol. I. Kansas City: Andrews McMeel, 2003. xvi–xvii.

———. "The Second-Most Asked Question." *The Complete Far Side*. Vol. II. Kansas City: Andrews McMeel, 2003. 222–223.

———. "Sorry for the Confusion." *The Complete Far Side*. Vol. II. Kansas City: Andrews McMeel, 2003. 298–299.

———. "The Syndrome." *The Complete Far Side*. Vol. I. Kansas City: Andrews McMeel, 2003. 180–181.

———. "This Is My Brother's Fault." *The Far Side Gallery*. Kansas City: Andrews McMeel & Parker, 1984. 1.

———. "To Whom It May Concern." *The Complete Far Side*. Vol. II. Kansas City: Andrews McMeel, 2003. 11.

———. "A Tribute to Stephen Jay Gould." *Natural History*, Nov. 1999: 48–57.

Lewis, R. E. "Letter to the Editor of the *Los Angeles Times*." *The Complete Far Side,* Vol. I. Kansas City: Andrews McMeel, 2003. 203.

Liv. "*The Far Side Gallery*." *Amazon Reviews*, 8 March 2014.

Lynch, Bill. "Far Side Fan Begs Gary Larson to Say It Isn't So." *Sun Sentinel*, 18 Oct. 1994: 10A.

Marschall, Richard, and Gary Groth. "Charles Schulz interview." *Nemo*, Jan. 1992: 9–14.

Martin, Joy. "Cartoon Not Funny." *Herald Statesman*, 16 July 1986. *The Complete Far Side*. Vol. I. Kansas City: Andrews McMeel, 2003. 582.

Masnick, Mike. "Dear Gary Larson: Your Kids Go Out at Night; Let Them Be." *TechDirt*, 4 Jan. 2011. Web. 9 Sept. 2016.

McCarthy, Susan. "Gary Larson." *Salon*, 21 Dec. 1999. Web. 9 July 2016.

McCloud, Scott. *Understanding Comics: The Invisible Art*. New York: Harper Collins, 1994.

Meisler, Andy. "The Media Business; A Job Crisis for a Comic Menagerie." *New York Times*, 17 Oct. 1994.

Miller, Thomas. "The Far Side of Science." *Natural History*, May 1989: 78–79.

Morrissey, Jake. "Dear Mrs. Hurst and Class." *The Complete Far Side*. Vol. II. Kansas City: Andrews McMeel, 2003. 102.

Morrissey, Jake. "The Far Side of Retirement." *Los Angeles Times*. 7 Oct. 1996. Web. 9 July 2016.

Morrissey, Jake. "Introduction." *The Complete Far Side*. Vol. I. Kansas City: Andrews McMeel, 2003. viii–xiii.

Piraro, Dan. "Piraro Meets Larson." *Bizarro*, 31 Mar. 2010. Web. 18 Aug. 2016.

Plotz, David. "An Interview with Garry Trudeau." *Slate*, 25 Oct. 2010. Web. 18 Aug. 2016.

Reagan, Michael. "Production Note." *The Complete Far Side*. Vol. I. Kansas City: Andrews McMeel, 2003. xx.

Rees, Stuart. *Thesis on Syndicate Contracts*. Thesis. Harvard Law School, 1997.

Rich. "The Far Side Gallery." *Goodreads Reviews*, 22 May 2008.

Sammond, Nicholas. *Birth of an Industry: Blackface Minstrelsy and the Rise of American Animation*. Durham: Duke UP, 2015.

Schudson, Michael. "The New Validation of Popular Culture." *Cultural Theory and Popular Culture: A Reader*. Ed. John Storey. New York: Pearson, Prentice Hall, 2006. 528–536.

Sedlar, Mervin. "He's Definitely Not a Fan of 'The Far Side.'" *Journal Tribune*, 17 Nov. 1986. *The Complete Far Side*. Vol. I. Kansas City: Andrews McMeel, 2003. 471.

Sherr, Lynn. "Interview with Gary Larson." *20/20*, ABC, 8 Jan. 1986. Television.

Spiegelman, Art. "Abstract Thought Is a Warm Puppy." *The New Yorker*, 14 Feb. 2000: 61–65.

Staake, Bob. *Humor and Cartoon Markets*. Cincinnati: Writer's Digest Books, 1991.

Stein, Joel. "Life beyond the Far Side." *Time*, 29 Sept. 2003. Web. 9 July 2016.

Storey, John. *Cultural Theory and Popular Culture: An Introduction*. Athens: U of Georgia P, 2006.

Swift, Jonathan. "Verses on the Death of Dr. Swift, D.S.P.D." *Jonathan Swift: A Critical Edition of the Major Works*. New York: Oxford UP, 1989. 514–530.

Thomas. "The Far Side Gallery." *Amazon Reviews*, 25 June 2015.

Watterson, Bill. *The Calvin and Hobbes Tenth Anniversary Book*. New York: Andrews McMeel, 1995.

Weise, Elizabeth. "Larson Is Drawn to the Wild Side." *USA Today*, 22 Dec. 2006. Web. 9 July 2016.

Index

absurdist theatre, 100–101
Adams, Scott, 122, 167, 186
Addams, Charles, 12, 43
Adult Swim (Cartoon Network), 6
aesthetics: alternative qualities/styles, 111, 112, 120–25; amateurish qualities, 25, 109, 119–20, 137, 147, 180–81; amplification through simplification, 15, 115–17; animation, influences from, 111, 172; anti-cute qualities, 4, 10, 11, 35, 97, 111, 119, 132–33, 137, 147, 176–77, 186–87; awkward quality of, 7, 11, 15, 109–10, 119–20, 176–77; carnivalesque qualities, 112, 186–87; cartoon aesthetics, complexity of, 115–19; closure, 115–16, 119, 128, 130; in context, 119–25; critiques of, 14, 109–10, 122–23, 157; cute styles, 111, 119, 121, 172, 185; democracy of form/democratic qualities of, 123, 133, 136–37, 140–41; Disneyesque, 121; distilled quality of, 47, 59, 66, 112, 114, 119, 124, 183, 201; ethnic identity, depictions of, 133, 137–38; film aesthetics, connections to, 121–22; gender, representations of, 138–41; grotesque qualities/imagery, 109, 132, 137, 147, 157, 176–77; as hieroglyphics, 186–87; ideological dimensions, 120; line work, clear-lined style, 121–24, 186–87; line work, deadpan or

affectless, 15, 32, 59, 66, 109, 113–14, 119, 121–24, 187; minimalistic quality of, 7, 11, 15, 32, 66, 111, 114, 116–17, 130; modernist art, comparison to, 117; professional styles, 111, 121, 185, 186; reader identification, 15, 115, 117–19, 131, 140, 187; satiric qualities, 111, 120; self-taught, nature of, 15, 111–12, 114, 137, 180–81, 186–87, 201; semiotics, 15, 111, 120–41, 177; static qualities, 66, 81, 113, 117, 119, 122; universal qualities, 115; unprofessional/antiprofessional qualities, 111–12, 121–24, 180–81, 186; visual vocabulary of, 186–87; weaknesses, early on, 32, 114, 127
Algonquin Round Table, 19
Alley Oop, 22
Amnesty International, 39
Andrews, McMeel & Parker, 160, 174
animation, 15, 97, 111, 121, 133, 170, 172
antiestablishment comedy, 47
Argyle Sweater, The, 198
Arnold, Stan, 29, 30–31, 47, 155
auteur theory, 15, 144, 147–53, 161

Bakhtin, Mikhail, 72–73, 191–94
Bambi, 106
Barthes, Roland, 120
B.C., 77–78, 100, 121, 139
Beattie, Bruce, 54

Made in the USA
Middletown, DE
14 December 2022

18547862R00137